An Introduction to
the Complete Dead Sea Scrolls

An Introduction to the Complete Dead Sea Scrolls

Geza Vermes

FORTRESS PRESS

AN INTRODUCTION TO THE COMPLETE DEAD
SEA SCROLLS

Cover design: Scott Moszer
Cover photo: 1QIsa from *Scrolls from Qumrân Cave 1*,
Copyright © 1974 John C. Trever.

ISBN 0–8006–3229–X

Library of Congress catalogued the earlier edition of this work as
follows:

Vermes, Geza, 1924–

The Dead Sea Scrolls

Bibliography: p.
Includes index.
1. Qumran community.   2. Dead Sea Scrolls—Criticism,
interpretation, etc.   I. Vermes, Pamela, joint author.   II. Title.
BM175.Q6V47   1981   296.8'15   80–2382
ISBN 0–8006–1435–6

AF 1–3229

04   03   02   01   2   3   4   5   6   7   8   9

Contents

Preface

The 'Qumran era' has completed its half-century and this introduction to the Scrolls, first published in 1977 and revised in 1994, has once more become out of date. The Hungarian edition of the book, published in 1998, has offered me a fresh opportunity to supplement the work in the light of the considerable progress in knowledge achieved in the last few years. 1998 also saw the appearance of the Penguin edition of *The Complete Dead Sea Scrolls in English*. Both books will help readers interested in the Qumran discoveries and in the broader vistas they have opened on post-biblical Judaism and on the Jewish origins of Christianity.

Readers should bear in mind that in describing the life and institutions of the Dead Sea (or Essene) sect the terminology current in Christian religious orders has been used by analogy. This implies that expressions such as 'postulants', 'novices', 'the professed', 'the contemplatives', etc. have no Hebrew equivalents in the texts.

This revised version is dedicated to the memory of Pamela Vermes (she died in 1993), without whose collaboration the 1977 Margaret Harris Lectures, on which the first edition of this book was based, might have never been delivered.

G.V.

Abbreviations

ALUOS	*Annual of Leeds University Oriental Society*
b	*babli* = Babylonian Talmud
BA	*Biblical Archaeologist*
BAR	*Biblical Archaeology Review*
BASOR	*Bulletin of the American Schools for Oriental Research*
Bib	*Biblica*
BJRL	*Bulletin of the John Rylands Library*
CBQ	*Catholic Biblical Quarterly*
CD	Cairo Damascus Rule
CDSSE	G. Vermes, *The Complete Dead Sea Scrolls in English*, London 1998
CRAI	*Comptes rendus de L'Académie des Inscriptions et Belles Lettres*
D	Damascus Rule
DBSuppl	*Supplément au Dictionnaire de la Bible*
DJD	*Discoveries in the Judaean Desert*, Oxford

I. D. Barthélemy and J. T. Milik, *Qumran Cave 1*, 1955
II. P. Benoit, J. T. Milik and R. de Vaux, *Les grottes de Murabba'at*, 1961
III. M. Baillet, J. T. Milik and R. de Vaux, *Les petites grottes de Qumrân*, 1962
IV. J. A. Sanders, *The Psalm Scroll of Qumran Cave II*, 1965
V. J. M. Allegro and A. A. Anderson, *Qumran Cave 4, I (4Q158–4Q186)*, 1968
Va. M. Bernstein et al., *Qumran Cave 4, I (4Q158–186)* (forthcoming)
VI. R. de Vaux and J. T. Milik, *Qumrân Grotte 4, II. 1 Archéologie, II. 2 Tefillin, Mezuzot et Targum (4Q128–4Q157)*, 1977

VII. M. Baillet, *Qumrân Grotte 4, III (4 Q482, 4Q520)*, 1982

VIII. E. Tov, *The Greek Minor Prophets from Nahal Hever*, 1990

IX. P. W. Skehan, E. Ulrich and J. E. Sanderson, *Qumran Cave 4, IV: Palaeo-Hebrew and Greek Biblical Manuscripts*, 1992

X. E. Qimron and J. Strugnell, *Qumran Cave 4, V: Miqsat Ma'ase Ha-Torah*, 1994

XI. E. Eschel et al., *Qumran Cave 4, VI: Poetical and Liturgical Texts*, Part I, 1998

XII. E. Ulrich, F. M. Cross et al., *Qumran Cave 4, VII: Genesis to Numbers*, 1994

XIII. H. Attridge et al., *Qumran Cave 4, VIII: Parabiblical Texts*, Part I, 1994; in fact 1995

XIV. E. Ulrich et al., *Qumran Cave 4, XIV: Deuteronomy, Joshua, Judges, Kings*, 1995

XV. E. Ulrich et al., *Qumran Cave 4, X*, 1997

XVI. E. Ulrich, *Qumran Cave 4, XI, Psalms to Chronicles* (forthcoming, 1999)

XVII. F. M. Cross et al., *Qumran Cave 4, XII* (forthcoming)

XVIII. J. M. Baumgarten, *Qumran Cave 4, XVIII: The Damascus Document (4Q266–273)*, 1996

XIX. M. Broshi et al., *Qumran Cave 4, XIV: Parabiblical Texts*, Part II, 1995

XX. T. Elgvin et al., *Qumran Cave 4, XV: Sapiental Texts*, 1997

XXI. S. Talmon et al., *Qumran Cave 4, XVI: Calendrical texts* (forthcoming)

XXII. G. Brooke et al., *Qumran Cave 4, XVII: Parabiblical Texts*, Part III, 1996

XXIII. F. García Martínez et al., *Qumran Cave 11–2, 11Q2–18, 11Q20–31*, 1998

XXIV. M. J. Winn-Leith, *Wadi Daliyeh – 1: The Wadi Daliyeh Seal Impressions*, 1997

XXV. E. Puech, *Qumrân Grotte 4 – XVIII: Textes hébreux (4Q521–528, 4Q576–579)*, 1998

DSSU	R. Eisenman and M. Wise, *The Dead Sea Scrolls Uncovered*, New York 1993
En.	Enoch
EncJud	*Encyclopaedia Judaica*
ET	English Translation
Flor	Florilegium
H	*Hodayoth* = Hymns
HJP	E. Schürer, G. Vermes, F. Millar et al., *The History of*

	the Jewish People in the Age of Jesus Christ I–III, Edinburgh 1973–87
HTR	*Harvard Theological Review*
HUCA	*Hebrew Union College Annual*
IDB	*Interpreter's Dictionary of the Bible*
IDBS	*Interpreter's Dictionary of the Bible*, Supplement
IEJ	*Israel Exploration Journal*
JBL	*Journal of Biblical Literature*
JJS	*Journal of Jewish Studies*
JNES	*Journal of Near Eastern Studies*
JQR	*Jewish Quarterly Review*
JRS	*Journal of Roman Studies*
JSJ	*Journal for the Study of Judaism*
JSS	*Journal of Semitic Studies*
JTS	*Journal of Theological Studies*
Jub.	Jubilees
LXX	Septuagint
M	*Milḥamah* = War Rule
MMT	*Miqsat Ma'ase ha-Torah* (Some Observances of the Law)
MQC	J. Trebolle Barrera et al. (ed.), *The Madrid Qumran Congress* I–II, Leiden 1992
MT	Masoretic Text
Melch	Melchizedek or Melkizedek
NRT	*Nouvelle Revue Théologique*
NTS	*New Testament Studies*
p	*pesher* = sectarian commentary
PBJS	G. Vermes, *Post-Biblical Jewish Studies*, Leiden 1975
PEQ	*Palestine Exploration Quarterly*
Q	Qumran (1Q, 2Q, etc. = Qumran Cave 1,2 etc.)
RB	*Revue Biblique*
RU	*Revue des Études Juives*
RHR	*Revue de l'Histoire des Religions*
RQ	*Revue de Qumrân*
S	*Serekh* = Community Rule
Sa	Appendix a to *Serekh* = Messianic Rule
Sb	Appendix b to *Serekh* = Benedictions
TDNT	G. Kittel and G. Friedrich (eds), *Theological Dictionary of the New Testament*, Grand Rapids 1963–76

Test	Testimonia
Tg	Targum
TLS	*The Times Literary Supplement*
TS	Temple Scroll
VT	*Vetus Testamentum*
y	*yerushalmi* = Palestinian Talmud
ZAW	*Zeitschrift für die alttestamentliche Wissenschaft*
ZNW	*Zeitschrift für die neutestamentliche Wissenschaft*
ZRGG	*Zeitschrift für Religions- und Geistesgeschichte*

Bibliography

Major editions of Qumran manuscripts

Microfiche edition

E. Tov (ed.), *The Dead Sea Scrolls on Microfiche*, Leiden 1992; *A Companion Volume to the Dead Sea Scrolls Microfiche Edition*, Leiden 1995

CD-Rom edition

T. H. Lim et al., *The Dead Sea Scrolls Reference Library*, Vol. 1(3 CD-ROM), Oxford and Leiden 1997

Photographic edition

Robert H. Eisenman and James M. Robinson (eds), *A Facsimile Edition of the Dead Sea Scrolls*, I–II, Washington 1991

Computer reconstructed edition

B. Z. Wacholder and M. G. Abegg, *A Preliminary Edition of the Unpublished Dead Sea Scrolls* I–III, Washington 1991–1995

Cave 1

M. Burrows, J. C. Trever and W. H. Brownlee, *The Dead Sea Scrolls of St Mark's Monastery*, I, New Haven 1950 (contains Isaiah[a], Habakkuk Commentary); II/2, New Haven 1951 (Manual of Discipline = IQS). There is no II/1

E. L. Sukenik, *The Dead Sea Scrolls of the Hebrew University*, Jerusalem 1954–5 (contains Isaiah[b], War Rule, Thanksgiving Hymns)

D. Barthélemy and J. T. Milik, *Discoveries in the Judaean Desert*, I: *Qumran Cave I*, Oxford 1955 (contains all the fragments from 1Q)

N. Avigad and Y. Yadin, *A Genesis Apocryphon*, Jerusalem 1956

E. Ulrich et al., *Discoveries in the Judaean Desert XXXII: Qumran Cave 1, II: The Isaiah Texts* (forthcoming)

Caves 2–3 and 5–10

M. Baillet, J. T. Milik and R. de Vaux, *Discoveries in the Judaean Desert of Jordan*, III: *Les petites grottes de Qumrân*, Oxford 1962 (contains fragments and the Copper Scroll)

Cave 4

J. M. Allegro and A. A. Anderson, *Discoveries in the Judaean Desert of Jordan*, V: *Qumran Cave 4, I (4Q158–4Q186)*, Oxford 1968 (contains mostly exegetical fragments). For editorial improvements, see J. Strugnell, 'Notes en marge du volume V des *Discoveries in the Judaean Desert of Jordan*', RQ 7, 1970, 163–276

J. T. Milik, *The Books of Enoch: Aramaic Fragments of Qumran Cave 4*, Oxford 1976

R. de Vaux and J. T. Milik, *Discoveries in the Judaean Desert*, VI: *Qumrân Grotte 4, II: I. Archéologie, II. Tefillin, Mezuzot et Targum (4Q128–4Q 157)*, Oxford 1977

M. Baillet, *Discoveries in the Judaean Desert*, VII: *Qumrân Grotte 4, III (4Q482–4Q520)*, Oxford 1982 (contains fragments of the War Rule and remains of liturgical and sapiential compositions)

Carol Newsom, *Songs of the Sabbath Sacrifice: A Critical Edition*, Atlanta 1985

Judith E. Sanderson, *An Exodus Scroll from Qumran: 4QpaleoExod^m and the Samaritan Tradition*, Atlanta 1986

Eileen M. Schuller, *Non-Canonical Psalms from Qumran: A Pseudepigraphic Collection*, Atlanta 1986

P. W. Skehan, E. Ulrich and Judith E. Sanderson, *Discoveries in the Judaean Desert, IX: Qumran Cave 4, IV, Palaeo-Hebrew and Greek Biblical Manuscripts*, Oxford 1992

R. H. Eisenman and M. Wise, *The Dead Sea Scrolls Uncovered*, Shaftesbury and Rockport, Mass. 1992, London 1993

E. Qimron and J. Strugnell, *Discoveries in the Judaean Desert X:*

Qumran Cave 4, V, Miqsat Ma'ase Ha-Torah, 1994

E. Eshel, *Discoveries in the Judaean Desert XI: Qumran Cave 4, VI, Poetical and Liturgical Texts, Part I*, 1998

E. Ulrich, F. M. Cross et al., *Discoveries in the Judaean Desert XII: Qumran Cave 4, VII, Genesis to Numbers*, 1994

H. Attridge et al., *Discoveries in the Judaean Desert XIII: Qumran Cave 4, VIII, Parabiblical Texts, Part 1*, 1994

E. Ulrich and F. M. Cross, *Discoveries in the Judaean Desert XIV: Qumran Cave 4, IX: Deuteronomy, Joshua, Judges, Kings*, 1995

E. Ulrich et al., *Discoveries in the Judaean Desert XV: Qumran Cave 4, X, The Prophets*, 1997

E. Ulrich, *Discoveries in the Judaean Desert XVI: Qumran Cave 4, XI, Psalms to Chronicles* (forthcoming, 1999)

F. M. Cross et al., *Discoveries in the Judaean Desert XVII: Qumran Cave 4, XII* (forthcoming)

J. M. Baumgarten, *Discoveries in the Judaean Desert XVIII: Qumran Cave 4, XIII, The Damascus Document*, 1996

M. Broshi et al., *Discoveries in the Judaean Desert XIX: Qumran Cave 4, XIV, Parabiblical Texts, Part II*, 1995

T. Elgvin et al., *Discoveries in the Judaean Desert XX: Qumran Cave 4, XV, Sapiential Texts, Part I*, 1997

G. Brooke et al., *Discoveries in the Judaean Desert XXII: Qumran Cave 4, XVII, Parabiblical Texts, Part 3*, 1996

E. Puech, *Discoveries in the Judaean Desert XXV: Qumrân Grotte 4, XVIII, Textes hébreux (4Q521–528, 576–579)*, 1998

P. S. Alexander and G. Vermes, *Discoveries in the Judaean Desert XXVI: Qumrân Cave V, XIX: Serekh Ha-Yahad and Two Related Texts*, 1998

E. Chazon et al., *Discoveries in the Judaean Desert XXIX: Qumran Cave 4, XX, Poetical and Liturgical Texts, Part 2* (forthcoming 1999)

S. Talmon et al., *Discoveries in the Judaean Desert XXI: Qumran Cave 4, XVI: Calendrical texts* (forthcoming)

D. Dimant et al., *Discoveries in the Judaean Desert XXX: Qumran Cave 4, XXI: Parabiblical Texts, Part 4* (forthcoming)

J. Strugnell et al., *Discoveries in the Judaean Desert XXXIV: Qumran Cave 4, XXIV, 4 Q Instruction* (forthcoming, 1999)

J. Baumgarten et al., *Discoveries in the Judaean Desert XXXV: Qumran Cave 4, XXV, Halakhic Texts* (forthcoming, 1999)

E. Puech, *Discoveries in the Judaean Desert XXXI: Qumran Cave 4, XXII: Textes en Araméen, tome* 1: 4Q529–549 (forthcoming)

D. Pike et al., *Discoveries in the Judaean Desert XXXIII: Qumran Cave 4, XXIII: Unidentified Fragments* (forthcoming)

P. Alexander, G. Vermes et al., *Discoveries in the Judaean Desert XXXVI: Qumran Cave 4, XXVI: Miscellaneous Texts* (forthcoming)

E. Puech, *Discoveries in the Judaean Desert XXXVII: Qumran Cave 4, XXXVII: Textes en Araméen, tome* 2: 4Q550–555 (forthcoming)

Cave 11

J. A. Sanders, *Discoveries in the Judaean Desert of Jordan, IV: The Psalm Scroll of Qumran Cave 11 (11QPsᵃ)*, Oxford 1965

J. P. M. van der Ploeg, A. S. van der Woude and B. Jongeling, *Le Targum de Job de la grotte XI de Qumrân*, Leiden 1971

Y. Yadin, *Megillat ha-Miqdash I–III*, Jerusalem 1977 (English edition, *The Temple Scroll I–III*, Jerusalem 1983)

E. Qimron, *The Temple Scroll: A Critical Edition with Extensive Reconstructions*, Beer-Sheva and Jerusalem 1996

D. N. Freedman and K. A. Matthews, *The Paleo-Hebrew Leviticus Scroll (11QpaleoLev)*, Winona Lake 1985

F. García Martínez, *Discoveries in the Judaean Desert XXIII: Qumran Cave 11, 11Q218 and 11Q20–22*, Oxford 1998

Nahal Hever

H. M. Cotton and A. Yardeni, *Discoveries in the Judaean Desert XXVII: Aramaic, Hebrew and Greek Documentary Texts from Nahal Hever and Other Sites with an Appendix containing alleged Qumran texts (The Seiyâl Collection II)*, 1997

H. M. Cotton et al., *Discoveries in the Judaean Desert XXXVIII: Miscellaneous Texts from the Judaean Desert* (forthcoming)

Wadi ed-Daliyeh

M. Leith, *Discoveries in the Judaean Desert XXIV: Wadi Daliyeh Seal Impressions I*, 1997

D. Gropp, *Discoveries in the Judaean Desert XXVII: Wadi Daliyeh II, The Samaritan Papyri from Wadi Daliyeh* (forthcoming)

Unidentified Cave

Y. Yadin, *Tefillin from Qumran (XQPhyl 1–4)*, Jerusalem 1969

Damascus Document

M. Broshi, *The Damascus Document Reconsidered*, Jerusalem 1992

General bibliography

1. Qumran bibliographies

B. Jongeling, *A Classified Bibliography of the Finds in the Desert of Judah: 1958–1969*, Leiden 1971

J. A. Fitzmyer, *The Dead Sea Scrolls: Major Publications and Tools for Study*, Missoula, Montana 1975, [2]1977, Atlanta 1990

F. García Martínez and D. W. Parry, *A Bibliography of the Finds in the Desert of Judah 1970–1995*, Leiden 1996

2. General studies and monographs

M. Burrows, *The Dead Sea Scrolls*, New York 1955

T. H. Gaster, *The Dead Sea Scriptures in English Translation*, Garden City, New York 1956, [3]1976

G. Vermes, *Discovery in the Judean Desert*, New York 1956

M. Burrows, *More Light on the Dead Sea Scrolls*, New York 1958

F. M. Cross, *The Ancient Library of Qumran and Modern Biblical Studies*, New York 1958; Grand Rapids [2]1980; Sheffield [3]1996

J. T. Milik, *Ten Years of Discovery in the Wilderness of Judaea*, London 1959

A. Dupont-Sommer, *The Essene Writings from Qumran*, Oxford 1961

G. Vermes, *The Dead Sea Scrolls in English*, London 1962, [2]1975, [3]1987, [4]1995

G. R. Driver, *The Judaean Scrolls. The Problem and a Solution*, Oxford 1965

Edmund Wilson, *The Dead Sea Scrolls 1947–1969*, London 1969

R. de Vaux, *Archaeology and the Dead Sea Scrolls*, London 1973

G. Vermes, *The Dead Sea Scrolls: Qumran in Perspective*, London 1977, Philadelphia 1981, London [2]1982, London [3]1994

G. W. E. Nickelsburg, *Jewish Literature Between the Bible and the Mishnah*, Philadelphia and London 1981

P. R. Davies, *Qumran*, Guildford 1982

B. Z. Wacholder, *The Dawn of Qumran: The Sectarian Torah and the Teacher of Righteousness*, Cincinnati 1983

D. Dimant, 'Qumran Sectarian Literature', in M. Stone (ed.), *Jewish Writings of the Second Temple Period*, Assen and Philadelphia 1984

M. A. Knibb, *The Qumran Community*, Cambridge 1987

P. R. Davies, *Behind the Essenes: History and Ideology in the Dead Sea Scrolls*, Atlanta 1987

P. R. Callaway, *The History of the Qumran Community*, Sheffield 1988

S. Talmon, *The World of Qumran from Within*, Jerusalem and Leiden 1989.

G. J. Brooke (ed.), *Temple Scroll Studies*, Sheffield 1989

L. H. Schiffman (ed.), *Archaeology and History in the Dead Sea Scrolls*, Sheffield 1990

M. O. Wise, *A Critical Study of the Temple Scroll from Qumran Cave 11*, Chicago 1990

H. Shanks (ed.), *Understanding the Dead Sea Scrolls*, New York 1992

F. García Martínez, *Qumran and Apocalyptic: Studies on the Aramaic Texts from Qumran*, Leiden 1992

D. Dimant and U. Rappaport (eds), *The Dead Sea Scrolls: Forty Years of Research*, Leiden 1992

J. Trebolle Barrera and L. Vegas Montaner (eds), *The Madrid Qumran Congress 1991*, Vols. I–II, Leiden 1992

J. A. Fitzmyer, *Responses to 101 Questions on the Dead Sea Scrolls*, London 1992

H. Stegemann, *Die Essener, Qumran, Johannes der Täufer und Jesus*, Freiburg 1993

E. Ulrich and J. C. VanderKam (eds), *The Community of the Renewed Covenant*, Notre Dame 1994

J. C. VanderKam, *The Dead Sea Scrolls Today*, Grand Rapids and London 1994

B. Nitzan, *Qumran Prayer and Religious Poetry*, Leiden 1994

A. Steudel, *Der Midrasch zur Eschatologie aus der Qumrangemeinde (4QMidrEschat^{a-b})*, Leiden 1994

L. H. Schiffman, *Reclaiming the Dead Sea Scrolls*, Philadelphia 1994

F. García Martínez, *The Dead Sea Scrolls Translated: The Qumran*

Texts in English, Leiden 1994

J.-P. Humbert et al., *Fouilles de Khirbet Qumrân et de Ain Feshkha* I, *Album de photographies – Répertoire du fonds photographique – Synthèse des notes de chantier du Père Roland de Vaux OP*, Fribourg and Göttingen 1994

D. D. Swanson, *The Temple Scroll and the Bible: The Methodology of 11QT*, Leiden 1995

G. J. Brooke (ed.), *New Qumran Texts and Studies*, Leiden 1995

J. Maier, *Die Qumran-Essener: Die Texte vom Toten Meer* I–II, Munich 1995

N. Golb, *Who wrote the Dead Sea Scrolls?*, London 1995

J. G. Campbell, *The Use of Scripture in the Damascus Document 1–8, 19–20*, Berlin 1995

P. R. Davies, *Sects and Scrolls: Essays on Qumran and Related Topics*, Atlanta 1996

S. Metso, *The Textual Development of the Qumran Community Rule*, Helsinki 1996

H.-J. Fabry et al., *Qumranstudien*, Göttingen 1996

J. G. Campbell, *Deciphering the Dead Sea Scrolls*, London 1996

M. Wise et al., *The Dead Sea Scrolls. A New Translation*, London and San Francisco 1996

G. Vermes, *The Complete Dead Sea Scrolls in English*, London 1997

S. E. Porter and C. A. Evans (eds), *The Scrolls and the Scriptures*, Sheffield 1997

M. Bernstein et al. (eds), *Legal Texts and Legal Issues . . . in Honour of Joseph M. Baumgarten*, Leiden 1997

F. H. Cryer and T. L. Thompson (eds), *Qumran between the Old and the New Testaments*, Sheffield 1998

J. H. Charlesworth et al. (eds), *Qumran-Messianism*, Tübingen 1998

J. Zimmermann, *Messianische Texte aus Qumran*, Tübingen 1998

P. Flint and J. VanderKam, *The Dead Sea Scrolls after Fifty Years*, I–II, Leiden 1998–99

3. Bilingual edition, vocalized Hebrew text and Qumran Hebrew

J. H. Charlesworth et al. (eds), *The Dead Sea Scrolls: 1. Rule of the Community and Related Document; 2. Damascus Document, War Scroll and Related Documents; 3. Damascus Document Fragments;*

4. *Pseudepigraphic and Non-Masoretic Psalms and Prayers*, Tübingen and Louisville, Ky 1994–7

E. Lohse, *Die Texte aus Qumran, Hebräisch und Deutsch*, Munich 1971

E. Qimron, *The Hebrew of the Dead Sea Scrolls*, Atlanta 1986

F. García Martínez et al., *The Dead Sea Scrolls: Study Edition I–II*, Leiden 1997–9

4. *Aramaic Texts and Qumran Aramaic*

K. Beyer, *Die aramäischen Texte vom Toten Meer*, Göttingen 1984; *Ergänzungsband*, 1995

T. Muraoka (ed.), *Studies in Qumran Aramaic*, Abr-Nahrain, Suppl. 3, Leiden 1992

5. *Advanced introduction*

E. Schürer, G. Vermes, F. Millar and M. Goodman, *The History of the Jewish People in the Age of Jesus Christ*, III, parts 1–2, Edinburgh 1986 (contains detailed classified bibliographies)

6. *The Scrolls and the New Testament*

K. Stendahl (ed.), *The Scrolls and the New Testament*, London 1958

M. Black, *The Scrolls and Christian Origins*, London 1961

J. Murphy-O'Connor (ed.), *Paul and Qumran*, London 1968, New York 1990

M. Black (ed.), *The Scrolls and Christianity*, London 1969

J. H. Charlesworth (ed.), *John and Qumran*, London 1972; New York 1990

G. Vermes, *Jesus and the World of Judaism*, London 1983, Philadelphia 1984

M. Newton, *The Concept of Purity at Qumran and in the Letters of Paul*, Cambridge 1985

N. S. Fujita, *A Crack in the Jar: What Ancient Jewish Documents Tell Us about the New Testament*, New York 1986

J. H. Charlesworth (ed.), *Jesus and the Dead Sea Scrolls*, New York and London 1992

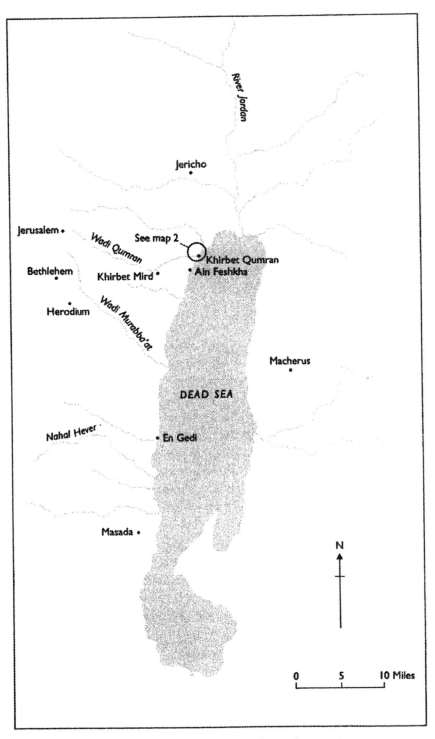

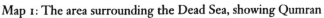

Map 1: The area surrounding the Dead Sea, showing Qumran

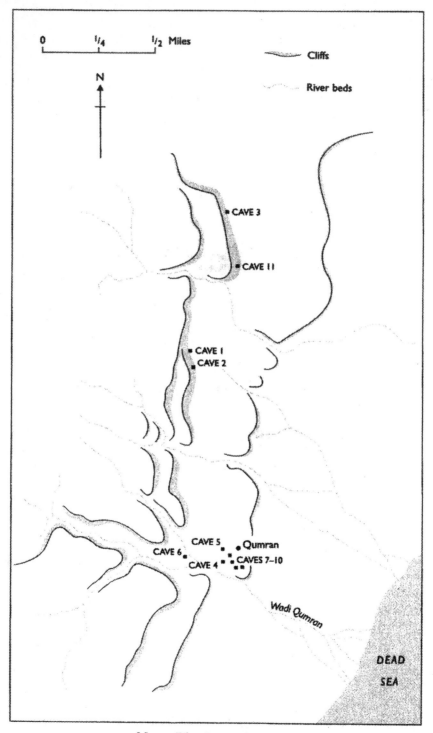

Map 2: The Caves of Qumran

The Dead Sea Scrolls: 1947–1999

On the western shore of the Dead Sea, about eight miles south of Jericho, lies a complex of ruins known as Khirbet Qumran. It occupies one of the lowest parts of the earth, on the fringe of the hot and arid wastes of the Wilderness of Judaea, and is today, apart from occasional invasions by coach loads of tourists, lifeless, silent and empty. But from that place, members of an ancient Jewish religious community whose centre it was, hurried out one day and in haste and secrecy climbed the nearby cliffs in order to deposit their precious scrolls in eleven caves. No one came back to retrieve them, and there they remained undisturbed for almost two thousand years.

The account of the discovery of the Dead Sea Scrolls, as the manuscripts are inaccurately designated, and of half a century of Qumran research, is in itself a fascinating as well as an exasperating story. It has been told many a time, but the extraordinary events of September–November 1991 excuse, and even demand, yet another recounting.

A bird's-eye view of Dead Sea Scrolls research

1. 1947–1967

News of an extraordinary discovery of seven ancient Hebrew and Aramaic manuscripts began to spread in 1948 from Israeli and American sources.[1] The original chance find by a young Bedouin shepherd, Muhammad edh-Dhib, occurred during the last months of the British mandate in Palestine in the spring or summer of 1947, unless it was slightly earlier, in the winter of 1946.[2] In 1949, the cave where the scrolls lay hidden was identified, thanks to the efforts of a bored Belgian army officer of the United Nations Armistice Observer Corps, Captain Philippe Lippens, assisted by a unit of Jordan's Arab Legion, commanded by Major-General Lash. It was investigated by G. Lankester Harding, the English Director of the Department of Antiquities of Jordan, and the French Dominican archaeologist and biblical scholar, Father Roland de Vaux. They retrieved hundreds of leather fragments, some large but most of them minute, additional to the seven scrolls found in the same cave.

Three of the scrolls, an incomplete Isaiah manuscript, a scroll of Hymns and one describing the War of the Sons of Light against the Sons of Darkness, were purchased in 1947 by the Hebrew University's professor of Jewish archaeology, E. L. Sukenik, who proceeded at full speed towards their publication. The other four were entrusted for study and eventual publication by their owner, the Arab metropolitan archbishop Mar Athanasius, head of the Syrian Orthodox monastery of St Mark in Jerusalem, to the resident staff of the American School for Oriental Research in Jerusalem, Millar Burrows, W. H. Brownlee and J. C. Trever. These three took charge of a complete Isaiah manuscript, the Commentary on Habakkuk and the Manual of Discipline, later re-named Community Rule. Finally, after the splitting of British mandatory Palestine into Israel and Jordan, at the École biblique et archéologique française, in Jordanian Jerusalem, two young researchers, the French Dominique Barthélemy and the Pole J. T. Milik, were commissioned in 1951 by de Vaux and Harding to edit the fragments collected in Cave 1.

Between 1951 and 1956, ten further caves were discovered, most of them by Bedouin in the first instance. Two yielded substantial quantities of material. Thousands and thousands of fragments were found in Cave 4 and several scrolls, including the longest, the Temple Scroll, in Cave 11. The previously neglected ruins of a nearby settlement were also excavated by Harding and de Vaux, and the view soon prevailed that the texts, the caves, and the Qumran site were interconnected, and that consequently the study of the script and contents of the manuscripts was to be accompanied by archaeological research.

Progress was surprisingly quick despite the fact that in those halcyon days, apart from the small Nash papyrus, containing the Ten Commandments, found in Egypt and now in the Cambridge University Library, no Hebrew documents dating to late antiquity were extant to provide terms of comparison. Already in 1948 and 1949, Sukenik published two preliminary surveys, in Hebrew, on *Hidden Scrolls from the Judaean Desert* (1948, 1949), and concluded that the religious community involved was the ascetic sect of the Essenes, well-known from the first-century CE writings of Philo, Josephus and Pliny the Elder, a thesis worked out in great detail from 1951 onwards by André Dupont-Sommer in Paris.[3] The first Qumran scrolls to reach the public, and the archaeological setting in which they were discovered, echoed three striking Essene characteristics. The Community Rule, a basic code of sectarian existence, reflects Essene common ownership and celibate life, and the geographical location of Qumran tallies with Pliny's Essene settlement on the north-western shore of the Dead Sea, south of Jericho and north of Engedi. The principal novelty provided by the manuscripts consists in cryptic allusions to the historical origins of the community, launched by a priest, called the Teacher of Righteousness, who was persecuted by a Jewish ruler, designated as the Wicked Priest. The Teacher and his followers were compelled to withdraw into the desert, where they expected the impending manifestation of God's triumph over evil and darkness in the end of days which had already begun.

An almost unanimous agreement soon emerged, on the basis of palaeography and archaeology, dating the discovery to the last centuries of the Second Temple, i.e. second century BCE–first century CE. For a short while there was controversy between de Vaux, who decreed that the pottery and all the finds belonged to the Hellenistic era (i.e., pre-63 BCE), and Dupont-Sommer, who argued for an early Roman (post-63) date. But the finding of further caves and the excavation of the ruins of Qumran brought about on 4 April 1952 de Vaux's dramatic retraction before the French Académie des Inscriptions et Belles-Lettres. His revised archaeological synthesis, presented in the 1959 Schweich Lectures of the British Academy, while admittedly incomplete, is still the best comprehensive statement available today.[4]

A third point of early consensus concerns the chronology of the events alluded to in the Qumran writings, especially the biblical commentaries published in the 1950s, and the Damascus Document. The so-called Maccabaean theory, placing the conflict between the Teacher of Righteousness and the politico-religious Jewish leadership of the day, the Maccabaean high priest or high priests Jonathan and/or Simon, was first formulated in my 1952 doctoral dissertation, published in 1953,[5] soon to be adopted with variations in detail by such leading specialists as J. T. Milik, F. M. Cross and R. de Vaux.[6]

While the editorial task consisted only of publishing the seven scrolls from Cave 1, work was advancing remarkably fast. Millar Burrows and his colleagues published their three manuscripts in 1950 and 1951.[7] Sukenik's three texts appeared in a posthumous volume in 1954/55.[8] In the interest of speed, these editors generously abstained from translating and interpreting the texts, and were content with releasing the photographs and their transcription. The best preserved sections of the Aramaic Genesis Apocryphon followed closely in 1956.[9] Even the fragments from Cave I, handled with alacrity and loving care by Barthélemy and Milik, appeared in 1955.[10] The secrecy rule of later years, restricting access to unpublished texts to a small clique of editors appointed by de Vaux, was not yet invented. In 1952, I was allowed to examine the fragments of the Rule of the Congregation (1QS^a), as may be seen from the inclusion of one of my suggested readings in the final edition.

The scrolls fragments, partly found by the archaeologists, but mostly purchased from the Arabs, who nine times out of ten outwitted their professional rivals, were cleaned, sorted out and displayed in the so-called Scrollery in the Rockefeller Museum, later renamed Palestine Archaeological Museum, to become after 1967 once more the Rockefeller, and if the mass of material disgorged by Cave 4 had not upset the original arrangements, the scandalous delays in publishing in later years need never have happened.

To deal with Cave 4, Father de Vaux improvised, in 1953 and 1954, a team of seven on the whole young and untried scholars. Barthélemy opted out, and the brilliant but unpredictable Abbé Joseph Milik, who later left the Roman Catholic priesthood, became the pillar of the new group. He was joined by the French Abbé Jean Starcky, and two Americans, Monsignor Patrick Skehan and Frank Moore Cross. John Marco Allegro and John Strugnell were recruited from Britain, and from Germany, Claus-Hunno Hunzinger, who soon resigned and was replaced later by the French Abbé Maurice Baillet.

It should have been evident to anyone with a modicum of good sense that a group of seven editors was insufficient to perform such an enormous task on any level, let alone to produce the kind of 'last word' edition de Vaux appears to have contemplated. The second serious error committed by de Vaux was his reliance on his personal, quasi-patriarchal authority, instead of setting up from the start a supervisory body empowered, if necessary, to sack those members of the team who had failed to fulfil their obligations promptly and to everyone's satisfaction.

Yet before depicting the chaos characterizing the publishing process in the 1970s and 1980s, in fairness it should be stressed that during the first decade or so the industry of the group could not seriously be faulted. Judging from the completion around 1960 of a primitive concordance, recorded on hand-written index cards, of all the words appearing in the fragments found in Caves 2 to 10, it is clear that at an early date most of the texts were identified and deciphered. The many criticisms of the subsequent years, focussing on these scholars' refusal to put their valuable findings into the public domain, should not prevent one from acknowledging that this original achievement, in which J. T. Milik had the lion's share, deserves unrestricted admiration.

After the publication of the Cave 1 fragments in 1955, the contents of the eight minor caves (2–3, 5–10) were released in a single volume in 1963.[11] In 1965, J. A. Sanders, an American scholar who was not part of the original team, edited the Psalms Scroll, found in Cave 11 in 1956.[12] Finally, with its typescript completed and despatched to the printers a year before the fatal date of 1967, the first poorly edited volume of Cave 4 fragments saw the light of day in 1968.[13]

2. 1967–1990

With the occupation of East Jerusalem in the Six-Day War, all the scroll fragments housed in the Palestine Archaeological Museum came under the control of the Israel Department of Antiquities. Only the Copper Scroll and a few other fragments exhibited in Amman remained in Jordanian hands. The Temple Scroll, which until then was held by a dealer in Bethlehem, was quickly retrieved with the help of the army intelligence and acquired by the State of Israel. Yigael Yadin, deputy prime minister of Israel in the 1970s, mixing politics with scholarship, managed to complete a magisterial three-volume publication by 1977.[14] A gentlemanly gesture on the part of the Israelis, who decided not to interfere with de Vaux, left him and his scattered troops in charge of the Cave 4 texts. As for the unpublished manuscripts from Cave 11, they were handled by Dutch and American academics.[15]

Father de Vaux, whose anti-Israeli sentiments were no secret, quietly withdrew to his tent and remained inactive until his death in 1971.

Another French Dominican, Pierre Benoit, succeeded him in the editorial chair as it were by natural selection, in 1972. The still non-interfering Israeli archaeological establishment conferred its blessing on him. By then, at my instigation, C. H. Roberts, Secretary to the Delegates of Oxford University Press (= chief executive), decided to demand speedier publication, but Benoit's ineffectual rallying call either elicited no response from his men, or produced empty promises which were never honoured.[16] In a lecture delivered in 1977, I coined the subsequently oft-repeated dictum that the greatest Hebrew manuscript discovery was fast becoming 'the academic scandal *par excellence* of the twentieth century'.[17]

One may ask how and why, after such an apparently propitious beginning, a group of scholars, most of whom were gifted, have turned the editorial work on the Scrolls into such a lamentable story. In my opinion, the 'academic scandal of the century' resulted from a concatenation of causes. The lack of organization and unfortunate choice of collaborators can be blamed on de Vaux. As for the majority of the team members who had other teaching or research jobs to cope with, the overlong part-time effort caused the original enthusiasm to fade and vanish. The most productive of them, J. T. Milik, appears to have been disenchanted by the very cool reception of the highly speculative thesis contained in his 1976 edition of the Aramaic Books of Enoch of Qumran Cave 4. 'Academic imperialism' was also a factor. It was easier to hold that 'These texts belong to us, not to you!' than to admit that the original editors had undertaken more than they could deliver. Add to this the initial unwillingness of the Israelis to shoulder their responsibilities and, as will be shown, their lack of foresight and repeated misjudgments when finally in the late 1980s they began to take an active part in matters of editorial policy. Need I say more?

The inevitable began to happen: in 1980 Patrick Skehan died, followed by Jean Starcky in 1986, without either of them publishing their assignments. Eugene Ulrich and Emile Puech became their heirs, while F. M. Cross and J. Strugnell sublet portions of their texts to doctoral students at Harvard University. Though responsible for some good, and occasionally excellent, monographs, this unfortunate practice further delayed progress, as writers of dissertations like to keep their cards close to their chests until their PhDs are in the bag.

In 1986, a year before his death, Pierre Benoit resigned as editor-in-chief and the depleted international team elected as his successor the talented but tardy John Strugnell, who in thirty-three years failed to produce a single volume of text. In 1987, at a public session of a Scrolls Symposium held in London, I urged him to publish at once the photographic plates, while he and his acolytes carried on with their work at their customary snail's pace. This request was met with a one-syllable answer: no. To the surprise of many, for by that time they should have known better, the Israel Antiquities Authority (or IAA) acquiesced in Strugnell's appointment. His grandiose schemes never bore fruit. In 1990, after a compromising interview given by him to an Israeli newspaper, in which he was reported as having made disparaging remarks not only about Israelis, but also about the Jewish religion, which he called horrible, his fellow-editors persuaded him to tender his resignation. It was accepted on health grounds by the IAA. Belatedly even the Israelis saw the light, and *de facto* terminated the thirty-seven-year-old disastrous reign of the international team.

3. 1990–1999

After John Strugnell's withdrawal, the very capable Emanuel Tov, professor of biblical studies at the Hebrew University, was appointed chief editor, the first Jew and the first Israeli to head the Qumran publication project. He auspiciously began his activities by redistributing the unpublished texts among freshly recruited collaborators. The new editorial team, of which I too am a member, consists of some sixty scholars compared to the original seven! Unfortunately, Tov did not feel free to cancel the 'secrecy rule', introduced and strictly enforced by de Vaux and his successors, prohibiting access to unpublished texts to all but a few chosen editors. However, the protective dam erected around the fragments by the international team collapsed in the fall of 1991 under the growing pressure of public opinion, mobilized in particular by Hershel Shanks in the columns of the widely read *Biblical Archaeology Review* (*BAR*). The first landmark event leading towards full freedom was the publication in early September by *BAR*'s parent body, the Biblical Archaeology Society, of seventeen Cave 4 manuscripts reconstructed with the help of a computer by Ben Zion Wacholder and Martin Abegg[18] from the Preliminary Concordance, alluded to earlier, which was privately issued in twenty-five copies (in theory only for the use of the official editors) by John Strugnell in 1988.[19] Later in the same month came the announcement by William A. Moffet that the Huntington Library of San Marino, California, a renowned research institution, would confine to dust a forty-year old closed shop by opening its complete photographic archive of the Qumran Scrolls to all qualified scholars. The Huntington was presented with a set of negatives by Elisabeth Bechtel, a renowned Californian Scroll Maecenas, who managed to obtain not one, but two series of photographs from the Jerusalem Department of Antiquities, one for the Biblical Manuscript Institute founded by her in Claremont, and another for herself. The latter ended up in the vaults of the Huntington five years before Mrs Bechtel's death in 1987.

The IAA and the official editors attempted to resist, but by the end of October they were forced to recognize that the battle was lost and all restrictions had to be lifted. Almost at once, the Scroll photograph archives at the Oxford Centre for Postgraduate Hebrew Studies and at the Ancient Biblical Manuscripts Center at Claremont, previously legally compelled to restrict access only to persons approved by Jerusalem, were also thrown open to all competent research scholars. Moreover, in November 1991 the Biblical Archaeology Society published a two-volume photographic edition by Robert Eisenman and James Robinson of the bulk of the Qumran fragments.[20] How they obtained the material remains unclear. This new policy has had an essentially beneficial effect on Qumran studies. Since vested interests are no longer protected, the rate of publication has noticeably accelerated and learned periodicals are flooded with short papers by scholars claiming fresh discoveries. Free competition is likely to expedite the official edition itself. The first Cave 4 volume of biblical texts, announced as imminent by Father Benoit in 1983, actually appeared – pace the 1992 date on the cover page – on 4 March 1993.[21] Scholarship and the general public are the beneficiaries of the new era of liberty. Only the selfish and the procrastinators stand to lose. In fact, the official publication is now proceeding at a fast pace.

Postscript

In January 1996, two Israeli archaeologists, H. Eshel and M. Broshi, investigated man-made caves close to the settlement which, in their opinion, were used as sleeping quarters by the members of the sect.

Also another search, organized in early 1996 by James Strange of the University of South Florida, discovered two ostraka, or inscribed potsherds, on the Qumran site itself. They include a document attesting the transfer of a servant, by the name of Hisday, of a house and the produce of an orchard to an Eleazar son of Nahmani by a certain Honi in fulfilment of an oath to the 'Community' (*yahad*). If the decipherment of the original editors is accepted, this ostrakon connects for the first time a sectarian text with the Qumran site itself.[22] However, their reading is far from certain.[23]

The present state of Dead Sea Scrolls studies

Between 1947 and 1956, the eleven Qumran caves yielded a dozen scrolls written on leather and one embossed on copper. To these we have to add fragments on papyrus or leather, the precise number of which is unknown but probably in the order of six figures. Over eight hundred original documents are fully or partly represented. The Cave 4 list alone contains 555 titles.[24] Most scrolls are written in Hebrew, a smaller portion in Aramaic and only a few attest the ancient Greek or Septuagint version of the Bible. The claim that some tiny Greek fragments from Cave 7 represent the New Testament is unsound.

Among the texts previously known, all the books of the Hebrew Scriptures are extant at least in fragments save Esther, the absence of which may be purely accidental. Even Daniel, the most recent work to enter the Palestinian canon in the mid-second century BCE, is testified to by eight manuscripts. There are also remains of Aramaic and Greek scriptural translations.

Furthermore, the caves have yielded some of the Apocrypha, i.e. religious works missing from the Hebrew Bible but included in the Septuagint. Caves 4 and 11 attest the Book of Tobit in Aramaic and in Hebrew, Psalm 151, described in the Greek version as a supernumerary psalm, and the Wisdom of Jesus ben Sira or Ecclesiasticus in Hebrew.

Part of the latter, chapters 39–44, has also survived at Masada, hence dates not later than 73/74 CE, when the stronghold was captured by the Romans, and two mediaeval manuscripts, discovered in the store-room (geniza) of a synagogue in Cairo in 1896, have preserved about two-thirds of the Greek version.

A third category of religious literature, the Pseudepigrapha, though popular in some Jewish circles, failed to attain canonical rank either in Palestine or in the Diaspora. Some of them, previously known in Greek, Latin, Syriac translations, have turned up in their original Hebrew (e.g. the Book of Jubilees) or Aramaic (e.g. the Book of Enoch). A good many further compositions pertaining to this class have also come to light, such as fictional accounts relating to Joseph, Amram or Moses, and apocryphal psalms, five of which have survived also in Syriac, others revealed for the first time at Qumran.

The sectarian Dead Sea Scrolls, thought to have been composed or revised by the Qumran community, constitute with one exception[25] a complete novelty. This literature comprises rule books, Bible interpretation of various kinds, religious poetry, wisdom compositions in prose and in verse, sectarian calendars and liturgical texts, one of them purporting to echo the angelic worship in the heavenly temple. Some curious miscellanea should be added: the Copper Scroll alluding in cryptic language to sixty-four caches of precious metals and scrolls, including another copy of this same inventory written without riddles, and several 'horoscopes' or more precisely documents of astrological physiognomy, a literary genre based on the belief that the temper, physical features and fate of an individual depend on the configuration of the heavens at the time of the person's birth, and a text (*brontologion*) predicting prodigies if thunder is heard on pre-set days of certain months with the moon passing through given signs of the zodiac.

After a first few gaffes committed before the excavation of the site, the paleographical, archaeological and literary-historical study of the evidence produced a general consensus among scholars concerning (*a*) the age, (*b*) the provenance, and (*c*) the significance of the discoveries. Holders of fringe opinions have recently tended to explain this consensus as tyranically imposed from above by Roland de Vaux and his henchmen. The truth, however, is that the *opinio communis* has resulted from a natural evolutionary process – from arguments advanced by single individuals, often unconnected with the international team, which others found persuasive – and not from an almighty *establishment* forcing an official view down the throats of weaklings.

1. The dating of the manuscripts

Palaeography was the first method employed to establish the age of the texts. Despite the paucity of comparative material, experts independently arrived at dates ranging between the second century BCE and the first century CE. By the 1960s, in addition to the Qumran texts, they could make use also of manuscripts from Masada (first century CE), as well as from the Murabba'at and other Judaean desert caves yielding first- and second-century CE Jewish writings. A rather too rigid, but useful, comprehensive system was quickly construed by F. M. Cross.[26] While admittedly controversial if unsupported either by actual dates in the manuscripts themselves (a phenomenon, alas, unknown at Qumran) or by external criteria, these palaeographical conclusions were to receive a twofold boost from archaeology and radiocarbon dating. The archaeological thesis, based *inter alia* on the study of pottery and coins, was formulated by R. de Vaux (cf. note 4). He assigned the occupation of Qumran to the period between the second half of the second century BCE and the first war between Jews and Romans (66–70 CE).

Radiocarbon tests were first applied to the cloth wrapping of one of the scrolls as early as 1951. The date suggested was 33 CE, but one had to reckon with a 10% margin of error each way.[27] However, with the improved techniques of the 1990s, eight Qumran manuscripts were subjected to Accelerator Mass Spectometry or AMS. Six of them were found definitely pre-Christian, and only two straddled the first century BCE – first century CE dividing line.[28] Most importantly, with a single exception – the Testament of Qahat being shown to be about 300 years earlier than expected – the radiocarbon dates confirm in substance those proposed by the palaeographers. Unfortunately, the manuscripts tested in 1990 did not include historically sensitive texts. But the IAA has apparently invited the same Institut für Mittelenergiephysik of Zurich to analyse further manuscripts which, if given a pre-30 CE date, would render any direct Christian association highly unlikely.[29]

In sum, the general scholarly view today places the Qumran scrolls roughly between 200 BCE and 70 CE, with a small portion of the texts possibly stretching back to the third century BCE, and the bulk of the extant material dating to the first century BCE.

2. *The provenance of the manuscripts*

With negligible exceptions, scholarly opinion recognized already in the 1950s that the scrolls found in the caves and the nearby ruined settlement were related. To take the obvious example, Cave 4 with its 555 documents lies literally within a stone's throw from the buildings. At the same time, the Essene identity of the ancient inhabitants of Qumran gained general acceptance.

Today the Essene theory is questioned by some, but usually for unsound reasons. They adopt a simplistic attitude in comparing the two sets of evidence, namely the classical sources (Philo, Josephus and Pliny the Elder) and Qumran, and any disagreement or contradiction between them is hailed as final proof against the Essene thesis. Yet, if its intricacies are handled with sophistication, it is still the best *hypothesis* today, and I remain unrepentant in upholding it.[30] Indeed, it accounts best for such striking peculiarities as common ownership of property and the lack of reference to women in the Community Rule; the probable co-existence of celibate and married sectaries (in accordance with Flavius Josephus's account of two kinds of Essenes); and the remarkable coincidence between the geographical setting of Qumran and Pliny the Elder's description of an Essene establishment near the Dead Sea between Jericho and Engedi.[31] I of course admit that the Scrolls and the archaeological data surrounding them do not always fully agree with the Greek and Latin notices, and that both the Qumran and the classical accounts need to be interpreted and adjusted, bearing in mind that the Scrolls represent the views of initiates against those of more or less complete outsiders. But since none of the competing theories associating the Qumran group with Pharisees, Sadducees, Zealots or Jewish Christians can withstand critical scrutiny, I believe my statement formulated in 1977 is still valid:

> The final verdict must . . . be that of the proposed solutions the Essene theory is relatively the soundest. It is even safe to say that it possesses a high degree of intrinsic probability.[32]

3. The significance of the Qumran Scrolls

The uniqueness of the Qumran discovery was due to the fact that with the possible exception of the Nash papyrus referred to earlier, no Jewish text in Hebrew or Aramaic written on perishable material could previously be traced to the pre-Christian period. Before 1947, the oldest Hebrew text of the whole of Isaiah, contained in the Ben Asher codex from Cairo, dated to 895 CE, as against the complete Isaiah Scroll from Cave 1, which is about a millennium older. The Apocrypha and Pseudepigrapha, save the Hebrew Ben Sira and the Aramaic fragments of the Testament of Levi, survived only in translation. The sectarian writings found in the caves, apart from the already mentioned Damascus Document, count as a total novelty.

To begin with, the Qumran scrolls and the other Judaean Desert finds have created a new discipline: ancient, i.e., pre-mediaeval, Hebrew *codicology*. We now possess concrete evidence that scribes carefully prepared, often lined, the leather or papyrus on which they were to write with vegetable ink, kept in ink-wells. Longer compositions were written on scrolls, on one side of the sheets, some of them numbered, which were subsequently sown together. Papyrus documents were often re-used, with a different text inscribed on the verso. Short works, e.g. letters, were recorded on small pieces of writing material: leather, papyrus, wood or potsherd. By contrast, no book or codex, with pages covered with script on both sides and bound together, has come to light at Qumran, or in any other Judaean Desert site.

The Qumran finds have also substantially altered our views concerning the *text* and *canon* of the Bible. The many mediaeval Hebrew scriptural manuscripts, representing the traditional or Masoretic text, are remarkable for their almost general uniformity. Compared to the often meaningful divergences between the traditional Hebrew text and its ancient Greek, Latin, or Syriac translations, the few variant readings of the Masoretic Bible manuscripts, ignoring scribal errors, mainly concern spelling. By contrast, the scriptural scrolls, and especially the fragments, are characterized by extreme fluidity: they often differ not just from the customary wording, but when the same book is attested by several manuscripts, also among themselves. In fact, some of the fragments echo what later became the Masoretic text; others resemble the Hebrew underlying the Greek Septuagint; yet others recall the

Samaritan Torah or Pentateuch, the only part of the Bible which the Jews of Samaria accepted as scripture. Some Qumran fragments represent a mixture of these, or something altogether different. It should be noted, however, that none of these variations affects the scriptural message itself. In short, while largely echoing the contents of biblical books, Qumran has opened an entirely new era in the textual history of the Hebrew Scripture.[33]

The Community's attitude to the biblical canon, i.e., the list of books considered as Holy Scripture, is less easy to define, as no such list of titles has survived. Canonical status may be presumed indirectly either from authoritative quotations or from theological commentary. As regards the latter, the caves have yielded various interpretative works on the Pentateuch (the Temple Scroll, Pentateuchal Paraphrases, the Genesis Apocryphon, and a smaller commentary or commentaries on Genesis), and the Prophets (e.g. Isaiah, Habakkuk, Nahum, etc.), but only on the Psalms among the Writings, i.e., the third traditional division of the Jewish Bible. From the texts available in 1988, I collected over fifty examples of Bible citations used as proof in doctrinal expositions, thus indicating that they were thought to possess special religious-doctrinal importance.[34]

On the other hand, the Psalms Scroll from Cave 11 contains seven apocryphal poems, including chapter 51 of the Wisdom of Jesus ben Sira, not annexed to, but interspersed among, the canonical hymns. This may be explained as a liturgical phenomenon, a collection of songs chanted during worship; but it may, and in my view probably does, mean that at Qumran the concept 'Bible' was still hazy, and the 'canon' open-ended, which would account for the remarkable freedom in the treatment of the text of scripture by a community whose life was nevertheless wholly centred on the Bible.

Of the two *Apocrypha* attested at Qumran, the original Tobit reflects the longer version of the original Greek text.[35] Nevertheless, one can note that four out of the five Cave 4 manuscripts are in Aramaic and only one in Hebrew. So the long-debated original language of this book is still uncertain, but Aramaic has become the likeliest candidate. On the other hand, the Hebrew poem from Ben Sira 51 has a patently better chance of reflecting the original than either the Greek translation by the author's grandson, preserved in the Septuagint, or the Hebrew of the mediaeval Cairo Geniza manuscripts, because the Qumran version alone faithfully reflects the acrostic character of the composition with the lines starting with the successive letters of the Hebrew alphabet, *aleph, bet, gimel*, etc.[36]

Qumran has also added to the *Pseudepigrapha* several new works dealing with biblical figures such as Joseph, Qahat, Amram, Moses, Joshua, Samuel. Among the works in this category previously known, the Aramaic fragments of Enoch deserve special mention because they appear to attest only four out of the five books of the Ethiopic Enoch.[37] Book 2 (i.e., chapters 37–72), which describes the heavenly apocalyptic figure called *son of man*, a subject on which New Testament scholars have wasted a considerable amount of ink without even approaching the vaguest consensus, is missing at Qumran. The Aramaic Enoch does not therefore support their speculations any more than do the Greek manuscripts, which are also without chapters 37–72 of the Ethiopic Enoch.[38]

The contribution of the Scrolls to general *Jewish history* is negligible, and even to the *history of the community* is fairly limited. The chief reason for this is that none of the non-biblical compositions found at Qumran belongs to the historical genre. The sectarian persons and events mentioned in the manuscripts are depicted in cryptic language as fulfilment of ancient prophecies relating to the last age. The chief sources of sectarian history, the Damascus Document and the Bible commentaries or *pesharim*, identify the community's principal enemies as the kings of Yavan (Greece) and the rulers of the Kittim (Romans). Also, the Nahum Commentary's historical perspective extends from Antiochus (no doubt Epiphanes, *c.*170 BCE) to the conquest by the Kittim (probably 63 BCE). Names familiar from Jewish or Graeco-Roman history appear here and there. The Nahum Commentary alludes, in addition to Antiochus, to another Syrian Greek king, Demetrius (most likely Demetrius III at the beginning of the first century BCE). A very fragmentary historical calendar from Cave 4 contains the phase 'Aemilius killed', meaning no doubt Aemilius Scaurus, governor of Syria at the time of Pompey's conquest of Jerusalem in 63. The same document also mentions Jewish rulers of the Maccabaean-Hasmonaean era (second-first centuries BCE), Shelamzion or Alexandra-Salome, widow and successor of Alexander Jannaeus (76–67 BCE); Hyrcanus and John (Yohanan), either John Hyrcanus I (135/4–104 BCE) or more likely II (63–40 BCE), and King Jonathan, Alexander Jannaeus or, in my opinion, more likely Jonathan Maccabaeus (161–143/2 BCE).[39] In one respect, despite the absence of detail, the evidence is telling: all these characters belong to the second or the first half of the first century BCE. So also do most of the coins discovered at Qumran.

The mainstream hypothesis, built on archaeology and literary analysis, sketches the history of the Scrolls community (or *Essene* sect) as follows. Its pre-history starts in Palestine, some claim also Babylonian antecedents, with the rise of the Hasidic movement, described in the First Book of the Maccabees (I Macc. 2.42–44; 7.13–17) at the beginning of the second century BCE. Sectarian (Essene) history itself originated in a clash between the Wicked Priest or Priests (Jonathan and/or possibly Simon Maccabaeus) and the Teacher of Righteousness, the anonymous priest who was the spiritual leader of the community. The sect consisted of the survivors of the Hasidim, linked with a group of dissident priests who, by the mid-second century, came under the leadership of the sons of Zadok, associates of the Zadokite high priests. This history continues at Qumran, and no doubt in many other Palestinian localities, until the years of the first Jewish rebellion against Rome, possibly 68 CE, when the settlement is believed to have been occupied by Vespasian's soldiers. Whether the legionaries encountered sectarian resistance – such a theory would be consonant with Josephus's reference to an Essene general among the revolutionaries,[40] and to a massacre of the Essenes by the Romans[41] – or whether the threatening presence of the contingents of Zealot-Sicarii, who had already expelled the Essenes from Qumran, provoked a Roman intervention, are purely speculative matters. One fact is certain, however. No one of the original occupants of Qumran returned to the caves to reclaim their valuable manuscripts.

A variation on this theme, called the Groningen hypothesis, postulates a series of six Wicked Priests, and identifies the community with an Essene splinter group.[42] The Zealot theory, elaborated in the 1950s in Oxford by Sir Godfrey Driver and Cecil Roth,[43] is hard to reconcile with the evidence as a whole, as the latter predates the Zealot period. There are also the various conjectures linking the Scrolls to primitive Christianity, first modestly advanced in England by Jacob Teicher of Cambridge in the early 1950s (Jesus = Teacher of Righteousness – Paul = Wicked Priest),[44] continued more and more loudly with media connivance by J. M. Allegro with his ponderings on the role of a hallucinogenic fungus in the creation of the church,[45] and recently revived by Barbara Thiering, for whom John the Baptist is Teacher of Righteousness, while the married, divorced and remarried Jesus, father of four children, plays the Wicked Priest,[46] and lastly by Robert Eisenman, who ignores Jesus and assigns the part of the Teacher of Righteousness to James, the brother of Jesus, keeping Paul as the Wicked Priest.[47] In my opinion these fail the basic credibility test: these theories do not spring from, but are foisted on, the texts.[48]

Norman Golb of Chicago is responsible for another forceful attack on the common view, repeated in a series of papers since 1980, which culminated in a hefty volume, *Who wrote the Dead Sea Scrolls?*[49] The target of his criticism is the provenance of the scrolls found at Qumran. According to him, the manuscripts originated in a Jerusalem library (or libraries), the contents of which were concealed in desert caves when the capital was besieged between 67 and 70 CE. The chief corollary of the hypothesis is that the Essenes had nothing to do either with the Qumran settlement – in Golb's opinion a fortress[50] – or with the manuscripts.

The early assumption of Scroll scholars that every non-biblical Dead Sea text was an Essene writing[51] might have justified Norman Golb's scepticism to some extent. But nowadays specialists distinguish between Qumran manuscripts written by members of the Essene sect and others either predating the community, or simply brought there from outside. Emanuel Tov, for instance, has drawn a dividing line on scribal grounds between scrolls produced at Qumran and the rest.[52] However, in my view, the soft underbelly of the Jerusalem hypothesis is revealed, apart from the patent weakness of the archaeological interpretation (for Qumran is not a fortress), by the composition of the manuscript collection itself, definitely pointing towards a sectarian library. If Cave 4 is taken as representative, whereas several biblical books (Kings, Lamentations, Ezra and Chronicles) are attested only in *single* copies and others as important as Numbers, Joshua, Judges, Proverbs, Ruth and Ecclesiastes in *two* copies, we find *ten* copies of the Community Rule and *nine* of the Damascus Document. Over a *dozen* manuscripts contain sectarian calendars, yet not one mainstream calendar figures among the 555 compositions found in that cave! So, if the texts discovered at Qumran came from the capital, can their source have been an *Essene* library of Jerusalem?[53]

As for the relationship of the Scrolls to the *New Testament*, it can be presented under a threefold heading. Fundamental similarities of language, ideology, attitude to the Bible, etc. may be due to the Palestinian religious atmosphere of the epoch, without entailing any direct influence. More specific features, such as monarchic administration (i.e. single leaders, overseers at Qumran, bishops in Christian communities) and the practice of religious communism in the strict discipline of the sect and at least in the early days in the Jerusalem church would suggest a direct causal connection. If so, it is likely that the young and inexperienced church modelled itself on the by then well-tried Essene society.

In the study of the historical Jesus, the charismatic-eschatological aspects of the Scrolls have provided the richest gleanings for comparison. For example, the Prayer of Nabonidus, known since the mid-1950s,[54] which recounts the story of Nabonidus' cure by a Jewish exorcist who forgave his sins, provides the most telling parallel to the Gospel account of the healing of a paralytic in Capernaum whose sins Jesus declared forgiven.[55]

The second example is the so-called Resurrection fragment (4Q521).[56] In this poem, the age of the eschatological kingdom is characterized, with the help of Psalm 146.7–8 and Isaiah 61.1, by the liberation of captives, the curing of the blind, the straightening of the bent, the healing of the wounded, the raising of the dead and the proclamation of the good news to the poor. Likewise, in the Gospels, victory over disease and the devil is viewed as the sure sign of the initial manifestation of God's reign. Jesus is reported to have announced:

> If it is by the finger of God that I cast out demons, the Kingdom of God has come upon you (Luke 11.20).

Similarly, to John the Baptist's enquiry whether Jesus was the final messenger the following reply is sent:

> Go and tell John what you hear and see: the blind receive their sight and the lame walk, lepers are cleansed and the deaf hear, and the dead are raised up, and the poor have good news preached to them (Matt. 11.4–5).

Note furthermore that the Community Rule 4.6 lists healing as the chief eschatological reward and that according to the Palestinian Aramaic paraphrases of Genesis 3.15, the days of the Messiah will bring an ultimate cure to the children of Eve wounded by the serpent in the garden of Eden.[57]

If one had to single out the most revolutionary novelty furnished by Qumran, the choice of its contribution to our understanding of the genesis of Jewish literary compositions would surely be justified. Comparative study of biblical manuscripts, where no two copies of the same text are identical, and of sectarian works attested in a number of sometimes startlingly different redactions, has revealed, in one leading scholar's words, 'insufficiently controlled copying',[58] but in my view the phenomenon would better be described as scribal creative freedom. Qumran manuscripts of scripture, and even more of the Community Rule and the War Scroll, indicate that diversity, not uniformity, reigned there and then, and that redactor-copyists felt free to improve the composition which they were reproducing. Or to quote myself,

> The Dead Sea Scrolls have afforded for the first time direct insight into the creative literary-religious process at work within that variegated Judaism which flourished during the last two centuries of quasi national independence, before the catastrophe of 70 CE forced the rabbinic successors of the Pharisees to attempt to create an 'orthodoxy' by reducing dangerous multiplicity to a simple, tidy and easily controllable unity.[59]

Looking at the Qumran discoveries from an overall perspective, it is – I believe – the student of the history of Palestinian Judaism in the intertestamental era (150 BCE–70 CE) who is their principal beneficiary. For such an expert, the formerly quite unknown sectarian writings of the Dead Sea literature have opened new avenues of exploration in the shadowy era of the life of Jesus, the rise of Christianity and the emergence of Rabbinic Judaism. From the Jewish side, it was previously poorly documented. The rabbis of the first and second centuries had not permitted religious writings of that epoch to go down to posterity unless they fully conformed to their ideas, and although some of these texts were preserved by Christians (viz. the Apocrypha and many of the Pseudepigrapha), the fact that they had served as a vehicle for church apologetics caused their textual reliability to be suspect. But the Scrolls are unaffected by either Christian or Rabbinic censorship, and once their evidence is complete, historians will be thoroughly acquainted, not with just another aspect of Jewish beliefs or customs, but with the whole organization, teaching and aspirations of a religious community flourishing during the last centuries of the Second Temple.

The Scrolls have understandably awakened intense interest in the academic world, but why have they appealed so strongly to the imagination of the non-specialist? I would say, the outstanding characteristic of our age appears to be a desire to reach back to the greatest attainable purity, to the basic truth free of jargon. Affecting the whole of our outlook, it has necessarily included the domain of religious thought and behaviour, and with it in the Western world the whole subject of Judaeo-Christian culture and spirituality. A search is being made for the original meaning of issues with which we have become almost too familiar and which with the passing of the centuries have tended to become choked with inessentials, and it has led not only to a renewed preoccupation with the primitive but fully developed expression of these issues in the scriptures, but also to a desire for knowledge and understanding of their prehistory.

The laws and rules, hymns and other liturgical works as well as the Bible commentaries of the Qumran Community respond to this need in that they add substance and depth to the historical period in which Jewish Christianity and Rabbinic Judaism originated. They reveal one facet of the spiritual ferment at work among the various Palestinian religious parties at that time, a ferment which culminated in a thorough re-examination and reinterpretation of the fundamentals of the Jewish faith. By dwelling in such detail on the intimate organization of their society, on the role attributed to their Teacher, and on their ultimate hopes and expectations, the sect of the Scrolls has exposed its own resulting synthesis. This in its turn has thrown into relief and added a new dimension to its dissenting contemporaries. Thus, compared with the ultra-conservative rigidity of the Essene Rule, Rabbinic Judaism reveals itself progressive and flexible, and the religion preached and practised by Jesus of Nazareth stands out invested with religious individuality and actuality. Also, by comparison to all three, the ideology of the Gentile church sounds a definitely alien note.[60] Yet at the same time, the common ground from which they all sprang, and their affinities and borrowings, show themselves more clearly than ever before. It is no exaggeration to state that neither of these religious movements can properly be understood independently of the others.

Essenism is dead. The brittle structure of its stiff and exclusive brotherhood was unable to withstand the national catastrophe which struck Palestinian Judaism in 70 CE. Animated by the loftiest of ideals and devoted to the observance of 'perfect holiness', it yet lacked the pliant strength and the elasticity of thought and depth of spiritual vision which enabled Rabbinic Judaism to survive and flourish. And although the Teacher of Righteousness clearly sensed the deeper obligations implicit in the Mosaic Law, he was without the genius of Jesus the Jew, who succeeded in uncovering the essence of religion as an existential relationship between human beings and human beings and God.

2

Authenticity and Dating of the Scrolls

Nowadays the authenticity and antiquity of the Dead Sea Scrolls are no longer in dispute, indeed they are taken for granted. But this was not the case in the late 1940s, when the world of learning still remembered an earlier claim of the same kind concerning another biblical manuscript. Not only had that 'discovery' turned out to be a fraud; some specialists had almost been deceived by it. Moses William Shapira, a Jerusalem antique dealer, acquired notoriety in 1883 when he produced fifteen leather strips inscribed with archaic Hebrew characters which he said he had bought from Arabs who had found them in Transjordan. He took his fragments (from the Book of Deuteronomy) to Germany and tried unsuccessfully to find a buyer there. Raising his price to a million pounds (which was worth rather more at that time than it is now), he travelled undeterred to London, where he had the satisfaction of getting his manuscript exhibited in the British Museum. But his hopes were short-lived. A cursory inspection persuaded the French epigraphist, C. Clermont-Ganneau, that the text was a forgery. It had been written on pieces of leather cut from the margins of synagogue scrolls, and the letters had been copied from the mid-ninth-century BCE inscription of Mesha, king of Moab, discovered in Transjordan a few years earlier in 1868.

Clermont-Ganneau's evaluation was most unwelcome to the British public, who had looked forward to possessing a Pentateuch text almost as old as the Exodus from Egypt. Among other things, it would have discomfited once and for all those ungodly people who would not accept that Deuteronomy was composed by Moses himself. Nevertheless, though not without much hesitation, the officially appointed expert Hebraist C. D. Ginsburg was obliged to concur with the judgment of his foreign colleague and declare the document fraudulent. In the following year Shapira committed suicide, but understandably his ghost has continued to haunt later scholars faced with alleged manuscript finds.[1]

Is it in any case wise to be so sure that the Dead Sea Scrolls are authentic?[2] More explicitly, is it reasonable to accept the story of the Taamire tribesmen that their texts came from the Dead Sea caves? If so, were they actually deposited there in antiquity, or did the Arabs plant them there to make them look genuine?

That the Scrolls came from the caves can now be demonstrated fairly easily: the undisturbed sites of Caves 3, 5, 7, 8, 9 and 10, all of which yielded manuscript fragments, were discovered, not by the Bedouin, but by Father de Vaux and his team of searchers. Furthermore, an exploration of the hiding-places first found by the Taamires uncovered yet more scraps overlooked by them, some of which were part of the very manuscripts already removed by the Bedouin.

As for the theory that the Scrolls were planted to deceive the archaeologists, this cannot stand up to serious scrutiny. It is not impossible to imagine that experienced forgers – which the Taamire Bedouin were not – might have introduced a few fragments into the caves which they would afterwards name as the source of their texts. But to organize six (out of eleven) hiding-places, to provide each of them with fragments and one of them with the valuable Copper Scroll, to block the entrances so that they would appear as if abandoned for centuries, to arrange the interiors so that they looked genuinely antique, finally to hope that credulous archaeologists would find the caves and be persuaded by the fragments to accept all the manuscripts offered to them for sale as authentic – the very idea is absurd.

The scientific technique of radio-carbon analysis also helped to establish the authenticity and age of the discovery. The cloths in which the Scrolls were wrapped were subjected to a carbon-14 test and the date obtained was 33 CE. Unfortunately, in the early 1950s an inevitable margin of error could add or deduct about two hundred years to or from this figure, but even so the cloths were shown to be not more recent than 230 CE, and possibly as old as 170 BCE.[3]

The sceptic may suggest that the date of the wrappings need not necessarily be that of the manuscripts (which cannot be tested short of burning them!). But the fact that a Scroll fragment in an advanced state of decomposition was found adhering to one of these cloths is evidence that the manuscripts and wrappings genuinely belong together. A second test was performed in 1990–91 by the Institut für Mittelenergie-physik of Zurich. Fourteen manuscripts from the Judaean Desert (8 from Qumran, 2 from Masada, 1 from Wadi Daliyeh, 1 from Wadi Seyal, 1 from Wadi Murabba'at and 1 from Khirbet Mird) were sub-jected to Accelerator Mass Spectometry, yielding the following cali-brated results:

Daliyeh	405–354 BCE
	306–231 BCE
Testament of Qahat	388–353 BCE
Pentateuchal paraphrase	339–324 BCE
	209–117 BCE
1QIsaiah[a]	335–327 BCE
	202–107 BCE
Testament of Levi	191–155 BCE
	146–120 BCE
4QSamuel[c]	192–63 BCE
Masada apocryphal Joshua	169–93 BCE
Masada sectarian document	33 BCE–74 CE
Temple Scroll	97 BCE–1 CE
Genesis Apocryphon	73 BCE–14 CE
Thanksgiving Hymns	21 BCE–61 CE
W. Seyal	28–122 CE
W. Murabba'at	69–136 CE
Khirbet Mird	676–765 CE.[4]

The test has largely confirmed, except for the Testament of Qahat, the dates suggested by the palaeographers. These were: Testament of Qahat, 100–75 BCE; Pentateuchal paraphrase, 125–100 BCE; 1QIsaiah[a], 125–100 BCE; Testament of Levi, late second–early first century BCE; 4Q Samuel, 100–75 BCE; Temple Scroll, late first-century BCE–early first-century CE; Genesis Apocryphon, late first century BCE–early first century CE; Thanksgiving Hymns, 50 BCE–70 CE. Note further that one of the Daliyeh papyri mentions the date 352–351 BCE; the Murabba'at papyrus is dated 134 CE and the Mird text 744 CE.

After settling these points, three separate questions still remain to be answered. First, when were the Scrolls placed in hiding? Second, when were they written? Third, when were the original documents, of which the Scrolls are copies, themselves composed?

Archaeology provides an answer to the first enquiry. It also reveals the chronological framework of the sect's history. The second, the problem of the age of the different handwritings on Scrolls and fragments, is determined by the scientific study of ancient Hebrew scripts or palaeography. And finally, the literary content and especially the historical allusions supply pointers to the respective periods of Jewish history to which the various works belong.

It should be noted that none of the Qumran documents is dated. Nor do the biblical manuscripts have colophons, i.e. a statement appended to the text, revealing when the copyist completed his work. If they did, or if they referred to identifiable contemporaneous events, there would be no problem. The Bar Kokhba documents, by contrast, give precise dates. For example, document 42, published by Y. Yadin, opens with the words, 'On the first day of Iyyar in the first year of the redemption of Israel b[y Simeo]n bar Kosiba, Prince of Israel.'[5] There is therefore no doubt that this text was drawn up in April 1 3 2 CE. No such direct historical indications are included in the Qumran texts, however, and we have to rely solely on their indirect and cryptic hints, deciphering them and associating them as best we can with otherwise known persons or happenings.

Archaeology and the Scrolls

Archaeology is not an exact science, as the dogmatic and erroneous assertions made by the explorers of Cave I plainly demonstrate. The interpretation of data revealed during an excavation depends not only on the correct identification of the material objects uncovered, but also on the solidity of the working hypothesis into which individual facts are inserted.

In 1949, Father de Vaux, whilst admitting that the shape of the jars found in the cave was unparalleled, assumed initially that almost all the potsherds were Hellenistic, i.e. from the end of the second or the beginning of the first century BCE, and that the few specimens of Roman pottery belonged to the third century CE and were irrelevant to the dating of the Scrolls. 'No manuscript,' he felt entitled to write, 'is posterior to the first century BCE, while some of them may be older.' [6] He then concluded that all the Scrolls were hidden during the reign of the Jewish priest-king Alexander Jannaeus (103–76 BCE).[7] His fellow-archaeologist W. F. Albright disagreed. He preferred the second half of the first century BCE, and even allowed for the possibility of a date as late as the destruction of Jerusalem in 70 CE. Other literary and historical critics, chief among them A. Dupont-Sommer, argued in the same vein.[8]

The following general account of the archaeological work at Qumran will show how the five seasons of excavation between 1951 and 1956 helped to correct this initial bias in the matter of dating.

It was established first of all that an eighth-century BCE settlement had been destroyed and abandoned at the end of the seventh century BCE, and that a modest fresh occupation had begun in the second half of the second century (150–140 BCE). Some of the older remains had been restored and new rooms added at that time. This early phase, thought to have been of relatively short duration and known as Period Ia, apparently came to an end some time during the rule of John Hyrcanus I (134–104 BCE).

Period Ib is distinguished by an increase in building activity in the form of a substantial enlargement of the occupied area. The complex now included a two-storey tower, a large assembly hall, a refectory, workshops and extensive water installations. Roland de Vaux could consequently write: 'Khirbet Qumran is not a village or a group of houses; it is the establishment of a community.'[9] Coins discovered in this layer of the ruins indicate that Period Ib corresponded to that of the Hasmonaean government of Palestine from the time of John Hyrcanus I (134–104 BCE) to Antigonus Mattathias (40–37 BCE) and on to the beginning of the reign of Herod the Great (37–4 BCE). Its end was marked by an earthquake and, in view of de Vaux's theory, based on traces of burning, that Khirbet Qumran was destroyed by fire and earthquake, it is tempting to identify the latter with the catastrophe described by the first-century CE Jewish historian Flavius Josephus as having occurred in 31 BCE: 'Meanwhile the battle of Actium took place between Caesar and Antony, in the seventh year of Herod's reign, and there was an earthquake in Judaea, such as had not been seen before' (*Ant.* 15.121).

Father de Vaux's archaeological reconstruction of the history of the site includes at this point an interval during which the settlement was unoccupied, though to defend this hypothesis he had to explain the presence of ten coins of Herod, probably dating to later than 31 BCE, by suggesting that they were brought to the site at the time of its re-occupation after Herod's death. But in fact it is quite possible that the place was continuously inhabited, however sparsely, until the beginning of the Christian era.

Period II opens with the rebuilding of Qumran after its devastation. One of the most suggestive finds connected with this era, the remains of a table made of mud brick and covered with plaster, with two ink wells near by, one of them still containing traces of ink, led de Vaux to maintain that they were part of a *scriptorium*, i.e. a room used for copying manuscripts.[10]

Apart from the ten Herodian coins already mentioned, the numismatic evidence relating to Period II points firmly to the first century CE. The coins begin with Herod Archelaus (4 BCE–6 CE) and finish with the first revolution of 66–70 CE. Ninety-four bronze pieces struck by the rebels have survived, eighty-three dating to the 'second year' (68–69 CE): the dates of the rest are illegible. Now in the summer of 68 CE, the Roman armies led by the future emperor Vespasian captured Jericho, only eight miles north of Qumran. Father de Vaux therefore concluded that the Qumran establishment must also have fallen to the Romans at the same time in June 68 CE.

Roman coins found in the layer known as Period III indicate that the site was held by a Roman garrison, probably the Tenth or *Fretensis* Legion, until the end of hostilities; for it should be borne in mind that the Zealots continued to resist in the Judaean desert until the fall of Masada in 74 CE, four years after the conquest of Jerusalem.[11]

Assuming that this historical reconstruction is correct, and that the Romans assaulted Qumran in 68 CE and expelled its occupants, who were either members of the Dead Sea sect or some other group of militant Jewish revolutionaries in possession of the site because of its strategic importance, it is highly probable that the Dead Sea Scrolls were concealed at that time in face of the expected danger. The establishment in any case of the summer of 68 CE as the *terminus ad quem* of the Qumran settlement has a number of important consequences, both in regard to the dating of the Scrolls, but also, as will be seen, for our knowledge of the history of the Dead Sea Community.

1. All the manuscripts, and consequently all the events to which they allude, are to be considered as prior to 68 CE.

2. The period of occupation of the Qumran site – c.150–140 BCE to 68 CE – provides the most likely chronological framework into which the literary works attributable to the sect are to be inserted.

3. These time-limits do not exclude the possibility that the Community owned further manuscripts written earlier.

4. The persons and events associated with the origins of the sect should probably be placed in the middle of the second century BCE and are unlikely to have belonged to the second half of the first century CE.[12]

Palaeography and the Scrolls

As has been said, the dating of the concealment of the manuscripts has merely determined that all the Scrolls and fragments preceded 68 CE. It remained now for palaeography to define their age more closely.[13]

At its best, this branch of science offers no more than an approximation to the truth, and Hebrew palaeography in particular, when first called on to aid with the dating of the Scrolls, was still very much in embryo. Furthermore, it had in those years to rely on only a limited amount of comparative material assembled from Egyptian Aramaic papyri, Palestinian Jewish inscriptions (mostly on ossuaries), and a single biblical document, the Nash papyrus, none of which, apart from the latter, were specially well suited *a priori* for the task in hand. Letters engraved or scratched on stone or plaster are usually shaped differently from those traced with pen and ink, and papyri are often written in a hastily scribbled cursive script bearing little resemblance to the calligraphy expected of scribes of literary works. Before Qumran, however, there were simply no Hebrew literary manuscripts in existence predating the Middle Ages. As for the closest parallel to the Scrolls, the Nash papyrus with its extract from Deuteronomy 5.6–6.5 (the Ten Commandments and the *Shema'* or 'Hear O Israel'), the dates proposed for it before the Dead Sea discoveries varied from the second century BCE to the second century CE.[14]

In such circumstances, the palaeographers invited to pronounce on the date of the Scrolls were confronted, one would have thought, with serious difficulties. Yet not only did they not shrink from advancing firm opinions – in my view, often far too firm – but they arrived at datings, independently of each other, which were roughly the same and which

soon appeared compatible with the time-scale suggested by archaeology. They noted that the script of the Scrolls antedated that of the
early third-century CE Jewish inscriptional material from Dura Europos
on the Euphrates.[15] The slight fluctuation in the use of the five final
letters peculiar to the square Hebrew alphabet indicated the end of the
Second Temple era, namely from the second century BCE to 70 CE, and
the letters of the Qumran manuscripts displayed definite similarities to
ossuary inscriptions dating to the first century BCE and CE. Their verdict, therefore, was that the Scrolls were to be ascribed to between 200
BCE and the first century CE.

Since those heroic days, the discovery of the Bar Kokhba documents
and the Masada manuscripts and ostraca or inscribed potsherds has
transformed Hebrew palaeography. The papyri and other texts found at
Murabba'at and Nahal Hever, many of them dated to the early second
century CE, prompt the palaeographer to estimate that the Qumran
script is older than theirs. The Masada texts, on the other hand, show a
script similar to that of the Scrolls. But as the fortress fell in 74 CE, they
were demonstrably contemporaneous with the Qumran library.[16]

One of the consequences of this improvement in palaeographical
knowledge, an advance that has enabled scholars to elaborate systematically the history of the square Hebrew alphabet, has been that several
experts have felt confident that some of the Qumran biblical fragments
go back to the third century BCE, the century preceding the foundation
of the Qumran establishment. They find the earliest manuscripts to be
those from Cave 4; a fragment of I Samuel, another of Exodus and
another of Jeremiah are dated by them to *c.* 225–200 BCE, while a fragment of Ecclesiastes is placed to 175–150 BCE.[17]

From this same palaeographical point of view the Dead Sea Scrolls
fall into three categories: pre-Hasmonaean, Hasmonaean and Herodian.
The biblical fragments from between 225 and 150 BCE belong to the
first of these groups. The Hasmonaean category (150–30 BCE) is represented by the large Isaiah manuscript, the Community Rule from Cave
1, and the oldest copy of another sectarian document, the Damascus
Document from Cave 4. The bulk of the extant texts, however, is
Herodian (30 BCE–70 CE), e.g., most of the biblical commentaries, the
second Isaiah Scroll, the Hymns, the War Rule, the Genesis Apocryphon
from Cave 1, the Psalms Scroll and the Job Targum from Cave 11.

Some of the biblical manuscripts from Qumran employ in the narrative, or in the writing of the Tetragram YHWH and other divine names, the ancient Hebrew or Phoenician script, an alphabet in general use among Jews until the Babylonian exile but eventually replaced by the square Hebrew or Aramaic lettering. This archaizing phenomenon in the text of the Scrolls is comparable to the revival of the ancient characters in the legends on Hasmonaean coins and was no doubt inspired by nationalistic sentiments. The choice, on the other hand, of a different script for the divine names reflects Jewish usage of the time. A Greek papyrus fragment of Deuteronomy dated to the second century BCE gives the Tetragram in square Hebrew letters, a custom considered by Origen in the third century CE to be old and characteristic of the best codices of the Greek Bible.[18]

Thus palaeography and archaeology have confirmed each other's findings in such a way that it can be asserted with a high degree of verisimilitude that the Scrolls are to be dated to a period extending from the second century BCE to the first century CE.

Historical allusions in the Scrolls

The final aspect of the problem of dating concerns internal criteria such as the mention of persons and events which fix the historical perspective of the writer of a document, but since a special chapter is to be devoted to the reconstruction of the sect's history, the present enquiry will be restricted to a few telling data.

The Qumran texts are notoriously poor in chronologically identifiable facts. No historical documents proper figure among them, and they recount the story of their own movement cryptically in the form of Bible interpretation. Nevertheless, a few indications do exist that are immediately meaningful. There is, for example, the negative pointer that no mention is made of the destruction of the Second Temple. The inauguration of the eschatological worship described in the second column of the War Scroll is envisaged as taking place in the existing Temple of Jerusalem. Positively, on the other hand, the few historical characters referred to by name belong either to the second or first century BCE. The Nahum Commentary speaks of a Greek king called Antiochus who captured Jerusalem, and of another, Demetrius, who tried without success to perform the same feat. The first personage was Antiochus IV

Epiphanes, the Seleucid ruler of Syria (175–164 BCE), and the second was no doubt Demetrius III Eucaerus (92–89 BCE). Again, a very fragmentary calendar from Cave 4 contains the names of Shelamzion, the Hebrew for the queen Alexandra-Salome (76–67 BCE), John and Hyrcanus, probably John Hyrcanus II(63–40 BCE). It alludes also to an Aemilius who was responsible for a massacre, i.e. M. Aemilius Scaurus, the first Roman governor of Syria (65–62 BCE). A poetic fragment mentions King Jonathan, i.e. Alexander Jannaeus (103–76 BCE), or, more likely, Jonathan Maccabaeus (153/2–143/2 BCE).

Less specific but still significant is the information contained in the Scrolls that during the initial phase of the Community's history Jerusalem was governed by priestly rulers, men identifiable within our chronological context as members of the Maccabaean-Hasmonaean dynasty (153–37 BCE). These Jewish rulers were to be defeated by a foreign enemy, the Kittim, led, according to the Commentaries on Habakkuk and Nahum, by commanders, a terminology suggestive of republican Rome. By contrast, the War Scroll places at their head a king, an allusion applicable to Rome after 27 BCE when Augustus became emperor.

In sum, the clearest of the historical allusions confirm the principal conclusions reached independently by archaeology and palaeography: namely, that the period in question covers at least the second and first centuries BCE, but possibly also the first century CE.

The evidence is thus broadly based and perfectly convergent. The Scrolls and fragments found in the eleven Qumran caves were deposited there during the first war of the Jews against Rome, probably in 68 CE. The large majority of them were copied or composed during the occupation of the Qumran settlement by the Dead Sea Community, which first took up residence there in about 150–140 BCE. Palaeographical evidence suggests, however, that a few of the biblical manuscripts can be traced back further, some of them to the beginning of the third century BCE. Qumran, in other words, has provided the world with the oldest Hebrew writings preserved on leather or papyrus in existence, a priceless library of biblical and post-biblical Jewish literature whose effect has been totally to transform our knowledge of inter-testamental Judaism.

3

The Qumran Library

The non-biblical Dead Sea Scrolls have been reliably rendered into almost every European tongue and there is no better approach to them than by reading the texts themselves. A list of complete translations appears in the General Bibliography, though for excerpts quoted in this book I use the fourth edition of my own volume, *The Complete Dead Sea Scrolls in English*. The introductory comments to the most important individual Scrolls forming the present chapter are intended for those who wish to familiarize themselves with these non-canonical writings.

The works are classed under five headings: Rules; poetic and liturgical texts; wisdom texts; Bible interpretation; miscellaneous compositions. A full list of all the Dead Sea Scrolls is provided in a catalogue at the end of this book (pp. 192–217).

For a useful bibliography, see J. A. Fitzmyer, *The Dead Sea Scrolls. Major Publications and Tools for Study*; F. García Martínez and D. W. Parry, *A Bibliography of the Finds in the Desert of Judah 1970–1995*.

The Rules

1. The Community Rule (1QS; 4Q255–264; 4Q502; 5Q11,13).

Known also as Manual of Discipline (and in Hebrew as *Serekh ha-Yahad*), this Scroll from Cave 1 has been assigned, according to the evidence of the writing used, to the first half of the first century BCE. Fragments of ten manuscripts representing the same document were also found in Cave 4 and two small fragments in Cave 5. Eleven columns long, 1QS bears the marks of editorial alterations, particularly in columns 8 and 9, introduced in the course of its transmission. It is reasonable to suppose therefore that the actual composition may date back to the second half of the second century BCE.

The work, which appears to have served as a handbook of instruction for the Master or Guardian of the community, opens with a general outline of the sect's aims and purpose (1.1–18), followed by an account of the ceremony of entry into the Covenant. Priests and Levites (1.18–3.12) invoke blessings on those who have joined the sect and elected to live a holy life, and curses on those others who have decided to cast in their lot with Satan.

> May He bless you with all good and preserve you from all evil! May He lighten your heart with life-giving wisdom and grant you eternal knowledge! May He raise His merciful face towards you for everlasting bliss! (2.2–4).

> May He deliver you up for torture at the hands of vengeful Avengers! May He visit you with destruction by the hands of the Wreakers of Revenge! Be cursed without mercy because of the darkness of your deeds! (2.5–7).

Another section advises the Master how to assess the spiritual condition of the people in his charge, how to distinguish the 'kind of spirit which they possess', the spirit of truth or falsehood, or the spirit of light or darkness (3.13–4.26).

The main Rule begins at 1QS 5.1. The important fragmentary scroll, 4QS^d (4Q258), actually starts at this point. This principal section, to which 1QS 1–4 serves as a liturgical introduction, is concerned with statutes relating to the common life under the leadership of the sons of Zadok, the priests (but they are not mentioned in 4QS^d and 4QS^b), the various stages of progress within the sect, and a detailed penal code intended to remain in force until the Messianic age.

The Scroll ends with directives addressed to the Master, the sect's teaching on the times for worship (9.12–10.8), and finally with the Master's own hymn of thanksgiving (10.9–11.22).

For the *editio princeps*, see M. Burrows et al., *The Dead Sea Scrolls of St Mark's Monastery*.

2. Community Rule Fragments from Cave 4 (4QS^{d/e})

4QS^d = 4Q258 is the best-preserved of the ten 4QS manuscripts. Seven columns of the text have survived. Column 1, with a wide margin on the right, is almost certainly the beginning of the scroll. It corresponds to

1QS 5.1. The last identifiable passage represents 1QS 11. 7. Column 1 provides a shorter and smoother version of the Rule than 1QS. The more fragmentary 4QS[b] (= 4Q256) supports 4QS[d] (= 4Q258). The opening line is different and 'the Priests, the Sons of Zadok' repeatedly fail to be mentioned. For both occurrences of the phrase in 1QS, the two 4QS manuscripts read 'the Congregation' *(ha-rabbim),* an alternative likely to possess historical implications.

Three fragmentary columns of 4QS[e] = 4Q259 contain damaged sections of 1QS 7–9. The text translated comes from columns 2 and 3 and represents an important doctrinal section of 1QS (8.4–9.11) in an abridged form. Not only are some of the interlinear additions to 1QS absent, suggesting their later editorial nature, but 4QS[e] (4Q259) jumps from 1QS 8.15 to 9.12, thus omitting the mention of the 'Prophet and the Messiah of Aaron and Israel' (1QS 9.11). It would seem that the copyist of this manuscript substituted 4Q319 (the calendrical document of Otot) for the text corresponding to 1QS 10–11.

1QS col.5	4QS[d] (4Q258)
And this is the Rule for the men of the Community who have freely pledged thernselves to be converted from all evil and to cling to all His commandments according to His will. They shall separate from the congregation of the men of injustice and shall unite, with respect to the Law and possessions, under the authority of the sons of Zadok, the Priests who keep the Covenant, and of the multitude of the men of the Community who hold fast to the Covenant. Every decision concerning doctrine, property and justice shall be determined by them.	Teaching for the Master concerning the men of the Law who have freely pledged themselves to convert from all evil and hold fast to all that He has commanded. And they shall separate from the congregation of the men of injustice and shall unite with respect to doctrine and property, and they shall be under the authority of the Congregation concerning all matters of doctrine and property.

For the *editio princeps* of 1QS, see M. Burrows et al., *The Dead Sea Scrolls of St Mark's Monastery Vol.II, Fasc.* 2: *Plates and transcription of the Manual of Discipline.* For the Cave 4 material, see P. S. Alexander and G. Vermes, *DSD* XXVI. For a preliminary edition, see J. H. Charlesworth, *The Dead Sea Scrolls I*, 1–51, 72–83.

The Community Rule is one of several Qumran legislative codes, but apart from these, has no parallel in inter-testamental Jewish literature. It may on the other hand be seen as a forerunner of the so-called 'church orders' such as the Didache or Teaching of the Twelve Apostles, the Apostolic Constitutions, and the earliest rules of Christian monasticism, all of which are to be placed between the second and the fourth century.

3. *The Damascus Document (CD)*

The Damascus Rule or Zadokite Document had been preserved in two incomplete mediaeval manuscripts of the tenth (MS A) and twelfth centuries (MS B) and were first discovered in the Cairo Geniza in 1896 by Solomon Schechter, who published them in 1910. Now, however, we have fragments of the same work from Caves 4 (4Q265–73), 5 (5Q12) and 6 (6Q15) of Qumran, and these are dated to the first half of the first century BCE and largely correspond to the recension contained in MS A.

The Cairo version of the Damascus Document opens with an exhortation (A1.1–8.21; B1.1–2.34 [= 19.1–20.34]) to the followers of the sons of Zadok to remain faithful to the Covenant made by those who retreated from Judaea to the Land of Damascus. They are assured by means of a theological interpretation of the history of Israel that God always rewards fidelity and punishes apostasy. Valuable historical allusions to the origins of the Community also emerge from this sermon, and these will be discussed in Chapter 6.

> For when they were unfaithful and forsook Him, He hid His face from Israel and His Sanctuary and delivered them up to the sword. But remembering the Covenant of the forefathers, He left a remnant to Israel and did not deliver it up to be destroyed. And in the age of wrath, three hundred and ninety years after He had given them into the hand of king Nebuchadnezzar of Babylon, He visited them, and caused a plant-root to spring from Israel and Aaron to inherit His land and to prosper on the good things of His earth. And they perceived their iniquity and recognized that they were guilty men, yet for twenty years they were like blind men groping for the way. And God

observed their deeds, that they sought Him with a whole heart, and He raised for them a Teacher of Righteousness to guide them in the way of His heart (1.3–11).

The second section, the Statutes (9.1–16.19), consists of laws arranged according to their subject matter: on vows and oaths, on the tribunal, on witnesses and judges, on purification by water, on sabbath observances, on ritual cleanness and uncleanness. To a large extent they are sectarian re-interpretations of biblical precepts, but rules relating to the organization and institutions of the Community are also included. A fragmentarily preserved penal code is appended, similar to that contained in the Community Rule. An intermediary version appears in one of the Cave 4 texts (4Q266).

The Qumran fragments have revealed that the Geniza manuscripts do not represent the whole original composition or always follow the authentic order of contents; in particular, the beginning and the end are missing. But in addition, several sections have been omitted from the first part of the statutes concerned with priestly purity, diseases, marriage, agriculture, and tithes, Gentiles and magic as well as the ritual for the feast of the renewal of the Covenant, which is placed in the third month, coinciding with the Feast of Weeks or Pentecost. Moreover, it should also be noted that pages 15 and 16 of the Cairo MS A should precede page 9.

The Exhortation which opens the work corresponds to a literary *genre* well known in both Jewish and Christian writings (e.g. Testaments of the Twelve Patriarchs, IV Maccabees – Hebrews, I Peter). The Statutes, on the other hand, with their systematic grouping of laws, prefigure the Mishnah, the Tosefta and the Talmud, i.e. the rabbinic codes compiled between 200 and 500 CE.

4. Damascus Document Fragments from Cave 4 (4QD)

The 4Q material (4Q265–273) represents 1. a prologue missing from CD and substantial legal sections which follow the broken ending of the Statutes of CD. These laws relate to 2. the admission or dismissal of candidates; to 3. criteria for disqualifying priests; to 4. detailed rulings concerning skin disease; to 5. laws pertaining to gleanings and to the agricultural priestly dues; to 6. a penal code partly overlapping with

1QS 7; and the ritual for the dismissal of unworthy members used in the ceremony marking entry into and expulsion from the Covenant celebrated in the third month, no doubt on the Feast of Weeks or Pentecost; and the hybrid 4Q265, in which the Community Rule and the Damascus Document merge.

For the *editio princeps* of CD, see S. Schechter, *Fragments of a Zadokite Work*, Cambridge 1910, reprinted with a Prolegomenon by J. A. Fitzmyer, 1970. For the *editio princeps* of 4QD, see J. M. Baumgarten, *DJD* XVIII. See also M. Broshi, *The Damascus Document Reconsidered*; and J. H. Charlesworth (ed.), *The Dead Sea Scrolls II*, 4–79.

5. The Messianic Rule (1QSa = 1Q28a)

Sometimes designated as the Rule of the Congregation, this short two-columned appendix to the Community Rule prescribes for the Last Days when the sect's affairs would be in the hands of the two Messiahs of Israel and Aaron. Addressed to the whole congregation of Israel, including women and children, under the authority of the priests the sons of Zadok (mentioned also in the Damascus Document and 1 QSb, but omitted in 4QSᵇ and 4QSᵈ), it decrees a programme for the individual reaching from childhood education, to marriage, and to adult participation in matters of litigation and in the sect's militia.

The document further outlines how sectaries were to move upward towards higher positions of authority, and gives various causes for disqualification from doing so.

The function of the Levites is defined as that of an executive body, and a list is provided of the 'men of renown' called to council meetings. The closing lines are devoted to a description of the Messianic assembly and meal.

When the common table shall be set for eating and the new wine [poured] for drinking, let no man extend his hand over the first-fruit of bread and wine before the Priest; for (it is he) who shall bless the first-fruits of bread and wine, and shall be the first [to extend] his hand over the bread. Thereafter, the Messiah of Israel shall extend his hand over the bread (2.17–21).

For the *editio princeps*, see D. Barthélemy, *DJD* I, 107–18.

6. *The War Scroll (1QM, 4Q491–496)*

The nineteen incomplete columns of this manuscript, to which should be added remains of six further Cave 4 scrolls (4Q 491–496), attesting a fair amount of differences, are concerned with the eschatological war which the sectaries believed would be waged during the last forty years of their epoch. The work is nevertheless not a military manual, as has been mistakenly claimed, but a theological consideration of a perpetual struggle between good and evil in which the opposing forces are of equal strength and to which only God's intervention can bring an end. The author places the spiritual battle within an imaginary historical context and provides the armies of angels and demons with earthly allies: the Sons of Light are represented by the children of Levi, Judah and Benjamin; the Sons of Darkness, by the Gentiles headed by the final enemy, the Kittim. Jerusalem is foreseen as reconquered after six years of the war, and the Temple worship restored, and plans for a defeat of all the foreign nations are elaborated in the seventh year. Another thirty-three years of combat would, however, remain.

> During the remaining thirty-three years of the war, the men of renown, those summoned to the Assembly, together with the heads of family of the congregation, shall choose for themselves fighting-men for all the lands of the nations. They shall arm for themselves warriors from all the tribes of Israel to enter the army year by year when they are summoned to war (2.6–8).

Columns 3 and 4 describe in stirring language the trumpets and standards and their inscriptions (e.g. on the trumpets of ambush, 'The hidden powers of God can destroy wickedness'); column 5, the disposition of the lines of battle and the weapons; column 6, the movements of infantry and cavalry.

The weapons and tactics portrayed seem to reflect the Roman art of warfare, and reference to the 'king' of the Kittim would suggest the Roman imperial era. The most likely date for the composition of this work is consequently the end of the first century BCE or, more probably, the first half of the first century CE. But in spite of the writer's familiarity with real Roman warfare, the unreality of his story is obvious if only for the fact that the fighters are elderly or middle-aged, and the auxiliaries young and strong.

> The men of the army shall be from forty to fifty years old. The inspectors of the camps shall be from fifty to sixty years old. The officers shall be from forty to fifty years old. The despoilers of the slain, the plunderers of booty, the cleansers of the land, the keepers of the baggage, and those who furnish the provisions shall be from twenty-five to thirty years old (7.1–3).

Ritual purity was to be maintained strictly in the camps. Women and young boys were to be forbidden access to them and the physically unfit and ritually unclean were not to be permitted to take part in the fighting.

A further eight columns enlarge on a battle liturgy, with priests and Levites blowing the trumpets and the rams' horns and reciting prayers; and the final five (15–19) project in vigorous language the vision of the closing phase of the war and the victory of the Sons of Light.

> The Priests shall sound to marshal them into the divisions of the formation; and at the sound of the trumpets the columns shall deploy until [every man is] in his place. Then the Priests shall sound a second signal on the trumpets for them to advance, and when the [foot-] soldiers approach throwing distance of the formation of the Kittim, every man shall seize his weapon of war. The Priests shall blow the trumpets of Massacre, [and the Levites and all] the blowers of rams' horns shall sound a battle alarm, and the foot-soldiers shall stretch out their hands against the host of the Kittim; [and at the sound of the alarm] they shall begin to bring down the slain. All the people shall cease their clamour, but the Priests shall continue to blow [the trumpets of Massacre and the battle shall be fought against the Kittim] (17.10–15).

Compared to the first fourteen columns, these last five are repetitious because they apply to the battle against the Kittim the rules and ordinances laid down earlier in general terms. But this does not necessarily imply that the document is not a literary unity. It may be understood as entailing an introduction (col. 1), general rules (cols 2–14) and a sketch of the ultimate battle (cols 15–19). A better explanation distinguishes a primitive composition (cols 1, 15–19) inspired by Daniel 11.40–12.3 of a battle against the Kittim, from an account of a series of wars against all the different Gentile nations conducted according to highly developed religious rules.

An interesting parallel to the military symbolism of the War Scroll may be found in the New Testament, in Ephesians 6.10–17.

For the *editio princeps*, see E. L. Sukenik, *The Dead Sea Scrolls of the Hebrew University*; M. Baillet, *DJD VII*. Cf. also J. H. Charlesworth (ed.), *The Dead Sea Scrolls II*, 80–203.

7. *The Book of War (4Q285)*

A collection of small fragments akin to the War Scroll probably reflects the missing end of 1QM. They include allusions to the archangel Michael, the Prince of the Congregation identified as the Branch of David, i.e. the victorious Messiah, and to the defeated and slain Kittim.

The very mutilated passage, claimed erroneously to refer to a suffering Messiah, in all probability speaks of the triumphant Branch of David. It is related to 4Q285 (see p. 80).

> [As it was said by] Isaiah the Prophet, [*The thickets of the forest*] *will be* [*cut down with an axe and Lebanon by a majestic one will f*]*all. And there shall come forth a shoot from the stump of Jesse* [. . .] the Branch of David and they will enter into judgment with [. . .] the Prince of the Congregation, the Br[anch of David] will kill him [. . . by strok]es and by wounds. And a Priest [of renown (?)] will command [. . . the s]lai[n] of the Kitti[m . . .] (4Q285, fr. 5).

For a preliminary edition see G. Vermes, 'Seminar on the Rule of War', *JJS* 43, 1992, 85–90; *CDSSE*, 187–9. The *editio princeps* by P. S. Alexander and G. Vermes is due out shortly (*DJD XXXVI*).

8. *The Temple Scroll (11Q TS)*

The Temple Scroll covers sixty-seven columns. According to its editor, Y. Yadin, the script is Herodian *(c.* 30 BCE–70 CE), but the composition itself dates either to the end of the second or to the first century BCE.

The beginning of the manuscript is very mutilated. The first section (cols 3–45) describes the Temple. Next follow purity regulations (cols 46–51) and laws relating to sacrifices, vows and apostasy (cols 51–54). A significant unit deals with the statute of the king (cols 56–59), following by miscellaneous regulations (cols 60–66).

Most of the legislation comes from Exodus, Leviticus and Deuteronomy, but the laws are often reworded and rearranged and placed directly on God's lips.

For the *editio princeps* see Y. Yadin, *The Temple Scroll* I–III. For 4Q365a, see S. White, *DJD* XIII, 1994, 319–33. Cf. also E. Qimron, *The Temple Scroll*, Jerusalem 1996.

9. *Communal ceremony (4Q275)*

This small fragment describes the ceremony of the Renewal of the Covenant (cf. 1QS).

> [And the Guardian will come] and the elders with him . . . and they will be introduced into the genealogy . . .

For a preliminary edition, see B. Z. Wacholder and M. G. Abegg, *A Preliminary Edition of the Unpublished Dead Sea Scrolls* III, 83. *Editio princeps*, P. S. Alexander and G. Vermes, *DJD* XXVI, 214–46.

10. *Four lots (4Q279)*

The four 'lots' of the Community alluded to in this tiny fragment are described in CD 14.5–6 as Priests, Levites, Israelites and Proselytes.

> [The first] lot belongs [to the Pries]ts, the sons of Aaron . . . And] the fourth lot will belong to the Prosely[tes] . . .

For a preliminary edition, see B. Z. Wacholder and M. G. Abegg, *A Preliminary Edition of the Unpublished Dead Sea Scrolls* III, 89. *Editio princeps*, P. S. Alexander and G. Vermes, *DJD* XXVI, 221.

11. 4QTohorot B–C (4Q276–277)

These fragments deal with the biblical law of the 'Red heifer' (Num. 19), the ashes of which were used for the cleansing of impurity resulting from contact with a dead body. The subject is also treated in MMT (4Q394 frs. 3–7 i,16–20).

4Q276

[And the priest wears the garments] in which he is not ministering in the Sanctuary. . . . renders the garments guilty. And he slaughtered [the] heifer before Him. He shall carry her blood in a clay vessel which is [not brough]t near the altar. And with his finger he shall sprinkle some of her blood seven [times towa]rds the front of the tent of meeting.

For a preliminary study, see J. M. Baumgarten, 'The Red Cow Purification Rites in Qumran Texts', *JJS* 46, 1995, 112–19.

12. 4QTohorot G (4Q284a)

Four fragments of a document in a late Hasmonaean – early Herodian script deal with matters of uncleanness affecting fruits. The phrase 'liquids of the Congregation' recalls 1QS 6.20; 7.20.

Fr. 1

. . . And let him no]t gather them . . . may not touch the liquids of the Congregation, for these [render unclean the] basket and the figs [and the pomegranates, if] their [liq]uids . . . if their ju[ice] oozes out wh[en he squee]zes them all and [a man] who has not been brou[ght into the C]ovenant has gathered them.

For a preliminary study, see J. M. Baumgarten, 'Liquids and Susceptibility to Defilement in New 4Q Texts', *JQR* 85, 1994, 93–6.

13. Some Observances of the Law (MMT = Miqṣat Maʿase ha-Torah 4Q394–399)

Six badly worn manuscripts represent a legal document of some 120 lines which was addressed to a single leader and argues about the calendar, ritual purity as well as marriage and intermarriage rules echoing here and there the teaching of the Sadducees. The leader is compared to King David and the three parties involved are 'we', 'you' and 'they'.

> We have also written to you concerning some of the observances of the Law, which we think are beneficial to you and your people. For [we have noticed] that prudence and knowledge are with you. Understand all these (matters) and ask Him to straighten your counsel and put you far away from thoughts of evil and counsels of Belial.

For the *editio princeps*, see E. Qimron and J. Strugnell, *DJD* X, 62–3.

14. The Wicked and the Holy (4Q181)

This appears to be a fragment of a liturgical text concerned with the destinies of the damned and the elect.

> In conformity with their congregation of uncleanness, (they are to be separated) as a community of wickedness until (wickedness) ends.
>
> In accordance with the mercies of God, according to His goodness and wonderful glory, He caused some of the sons of the world to draw near (Him) . . . to be counted with Him in the com[munity of the g]ods as a congregation of holiness (1.2–4).

For the *editio princeps*, see J. M. Allegro, *DJD* V, 79–80.

15. Purity matters A (4Q274)

This manuscript, one of ten documents discussing uncleanness, deals with fluxes and bleeding.

> A woman with a seven-day issue of blood shall not touch a man with a flux, nor any vessel touched by a man who has a flux, nor anything he has sat on (1.4–5).

For a preliminary edition see J. M. Baumgarten, 'The Laws about Fluxes in 4QTohora^a', in D. Dimant et al. (eds), *Time to Prepare the Way in the Wilderness*, Leiden 1996, 1–8.

16. *Exhortation by the Master addressed to the Sons of Dawn (4Q298)*

Eight fragments of a manuscript written in a cryptic alphabet contain an exhortation to a group, designated as 'Sons of Dawn' by the 'Master' *(maskil)*, the title of the teacher in charge of instruction in the Community (cf. Community Rule). It is suggested that 'the Sons of Dawn' (not yet 'Sons of Light') are newcomers to the sect at the earliest stages of their initiation.

4Q298 frs. 1–2i

[Wor]d of the Master which he spoke to all the sons of Dawn. Liste[n to me all men of heart (= intelligence) and understand my word. [And seeke]rs of righteousness, h[ea]r my word in all that proceeds from [my] lips. Those who [k]now have sear[ch]ed [th]ese (matters) and [have] returned [to the path] of life.

For a preliminary study, see Stephen Pfann, '4Q298: The Maskil's Address to All Sons of Dawn', *JQR* 85, 1994, 203–35.

17. *Rebukes (4Q477)*

These fragments contain a list of community members rebuked for offences against the rules. Individual sectaries are named as Yohanan son of Ar[ ], Hananiah Notos and Hananiah son of Sim[on]. The rebukes probably originated with witnesses of the offence who reported it to the Guardian (cf. CD 9. 2–4; 16–20).

Fr. 2

II . . . who . . . [wh]o acted wickedly . . . the Congregation . . . Yohanan son of Ar . . . [they rebuked because] he was short-tempered . . . with him . . . the iniquity with him and also and also the spirit of pride was with [him] . . . [blank] They rebuked Hananiah Notos because he . . . [to dis]turb the spirit of the Communi[ty . . . and] also to mingle the . . . they rebu[k]ed because evil . . . was with him and also because he was not . . . and also because he loved his bodily nature (or: showed preference to his near kin) . . . [blank]. And [they rebuked] Hananiah son of Sim[on] . . .

For a preliminary study, see E. Eshel, 'The Rebukes by the Overseer', *JJS* 45, 1994, 111–22.

18. Remonstrances (4Q471ᵃ)

This small fragment, written in Herodian script, contains reproofs addressed to a group of wicked Jews. The second half of the fragment can be interpreted in a positive sense alluding to a last-minute mass conversion of unfaithful Jews before the final battle.

. . . You have been unfaithful to His covenant . . . [You] said: Let us fight His wars for He has redeemed us . . . Your [mighty men] shall be humbled. And they did not know that He has despised . . . you shall show yourselves mighty in war. And you have been reckoned . . . You shall seek righteous judgment and the work . . . you shall exalt yourselves.

For a preliminary study, see Esther Eshel and Menahem Kister, 'A Polemical Qumran Fragment', *JJS* 43, 1992, 277–81.

Poetic and liturgical texts

19. The Hymns (1QH, 4Q427–432)

The Hymns or *Hodayot* Scroll consists of eighteen columns, none of them complete, and a number of fragments. Its bad state of preservation has prevented scholars from determining exactly how many poems are included, and estimates vary from between twenty-five to forty. The script proves it to belong to the first century CE, confirmed by radiocarbon dating.

The compositions, which resemble biblical Psalms, are individual prayers of thanksgiving normally beginning with 'I thank Thee, O Lord'. The two central religious ideas conspicuous throughout the whole collection are salvation and knowledge. The following two examples are characteristic.

> I thank Thee, O Lord,
>   for Thou hast [fastened] Thine eye upon me.
> Thou hast saved me from the zeal
>   of lying interpreters,
> and from the congregation of those
>   who seek smooth things.
> Thou hast redeemed the soul of the poor one
>   whom they planned to destroy
> by spilling his blood because he served Thee.
>
> (2 [10].31–33)

> I [thank Thee, O Lord],
>   for Thou hast enlightened me through Thy truth.
> In Thy marvellous mysteries,
> and in Thy loving kindness to a man [of vanity,
> and] in the greatness of Thy mercy to a perverse heart,
>   Thou hast granted me knowledge.
>
> (7[15].26–27)

The subject-matter of most of the Hymns is of a general sort, but a few appear to reflect the experiences of a religious teacher persecuted by his enemies and abandoned by his disciples. These may be references to the Teacher of Righteousness, but no certainty can be reached. One passage seems to allude to a revolt within the sect against his authority.

> [All who have ea]ten my bread
>   have lifted their heel against me,
> and all those joined to my Council
>   have mocked me with wicked lips.
> The members of my [Covenant] have rebelled
>   and have murmured round about me;
> they have gone as talebearers
>   before the children of mischief
> concerning the mystery which Thou hast hidden in me.
>
> (5 [13].23–25)

We can only speculate on the purpose of a collection of individual Hymns, but assuming that they were recited by the Guardian and the new members of the Community during the Feast of the Renewal of the Covenant on the Feast of Weeks, it is worth recalling that the Therapeutae, or Egyptian 'contemplative Essenes', each chanted hymns, one after the other, during their Pentecostal vigil (cf. below, p. 159).

For the *editio princeps* see E. L. Sukenik, *The Dead Sea Scrolls of the Hebrew University*.

20. *Apocryphal Psalms [I] (11QPs^a = 11Q5, 4Q88)*

In the substantial vestiges of this manuscript, dated on palaeographical grounds to the early first century BCE, are preserved forty-one canonical Psalms, a poem identical with II Samuel 23.1–7, four apocryphal Psalms previously known from Greek, Latin and Syriac translations, and in addition three new compositions and a prose supplement.

The known apocryphal Psalms are Psalm 151 (11QPs^a 28.3–14), a variant recension of the corresponding poem in the Psalter of the Greek Bible on the election of David; Psalm 154 (11 QPs^a 18.1–16), extant also in Syriac, a hymn praising God's wisdom; and Psalm 155(11 QPs^a 24.3–17), a supplication also attested in Syriac. The fourth composition (11QPs^a 21.11–17; 22.1) glorifies divine Wisdom and corresponds to the Greek Ecclesiasticus 51.13–19, 30 and to the relevant section of the Hebrew Ben Sira from the Cairo Geniza.

Of the previously unknown Psalms, the first is entitled by the editor 'A Plea for Deliverance' (11QPs^a 19.1–18).

> I was destined to death because of my sins,
>   and my iniquities sold me to the underworld.
> But YHWH, Thou hast saved me
>   according to Thy great mercies,
> and according to the multitude
>   of Thy deeds of justification.

The second new Psalm (11 QPs^a 22.1–18) celebrates Zion and is an acrostic poem, i.e. one in which the first character of each line represents the successive letters of the Hebrew alphabet (*aleph, beth, gimel*, etc.).

I remember thee, O Zion, as a blessing,
By all my might, I love thee:
   may thy memory be blessed for ever.
Great is Zion's hope:
   may peace and thine awaited salvation come.

The third Psalm in this category is addressed to the Creator (11 QPs^a 26.9–15).

Great and holy is YHWH,
   the holiest for all generations.
Majesty goes before Him,
   and behind Him the roar of many waters.
Grace and truth surround His face,
   truth, judgment and justice support His throne.

The prose supplement (11 QPs^a 27.2–11) is a record of David's poetic achievements crediting him not with the traditional figure of 150 Psalms but with 3600, together with 364 Songs for the daily Sacrifice, 52 Songs for the Sabbath offering, 30 Songs for festivals, and 4 Songs for exorcism.

In all, they were 4050. All these he uttered through prophecy which was given him from before the Most High (27.10–11).

For the *editio princeps,* see J. A. Sanders, *DJD* IV. Cf. J. Starcky, 'Psaumes apocryphes de la grotte 4 de Qumrân', *RB* 73, 1966, 353–74.

21. *Non-canonical Psalms (4Q380–381)*

Two poorly preserved manuscripts contain apocryphal Hebrew religious poetry resembling biblical Psalms. These poems bore titles, three of which have been preserved: 'Psalm of Obadiah', 'Hymn of the Man of God' and 'Prayer of Manasseh, King of Judah when the King of Assyria imprisoned him'. The attributions are no doubt pseudepigraphic.

4Q380

. . . [Jeru]salem, that is [the city
chosen by the L]ord from everlasting to [everlasting.]
. . . the holy ones
[for the na]me of the Lord is called on her,
[and his glory] is seen on Jerusalem and Zion.
Who will utter the name of the Lord,
and who makes all his praises heard?
The Lord [remem]bered him in his favour and visited him
that he might show him the prosperity [of] his [cho]sen ones, making
him rejoice in the gladness of his nation (cf. Ps. 106. 2,4–5).

For a preliminary edition, see Eileen Schuller, *Non-Canonical Psalms from Qumran: A Pseudepigraphic Collection*.

22. *Apocryphal Psalms [II] (4Q88)*

The last four columns of a fragmentary Psalms manuscript from Cave 4 have preserved three apocryphal poems. The first of these is identical with 11Q5 22. Of the other two, the first (col. 9) focusses on the final judgment and the second (col. 10) is a hymn to Judah.

9 . . . Congregation
and they shall praise the name of the Lord,
for He has come to judge every action,
to remove the wicked from the earth
[so that the sons] of iniquity shall not be found.
The heavens [shall give] their dew
and there shall be no . . . [within] their [boundarie]s.

10 . . . Then heaven and earth shall exult together.
Let all the stars of the evening twilight exult.
Rejoice, Judah, rejoice!
Rejoice, rejoice and be glad with gladness!
Celebrate your feasts and pay your vows
for there is no Belial in your midst.

For a preliminary edition, see J. Starcky, 'Psaumes apocryphes de la grotte 4 de Qumrân', *RB* 73, 1966, 353–71.

23. *(11QPsap^a = 11Q11)*

Badly worn remains of five columns of a Scroll with apocryphal psalms, at least partly devoted to exorcism, have survived in Cave 11. In col. 1, the name of Solomon implies that the poems was attributed to him. The repeated use of the term 'demons' and mention of 'healing' suggest the genre of the composition. In col. 3 a 'powerful angel' is mentioned who seems to be charged with defeating the demon and casting it to the 'great abyss' and the 'nethermost [hell]'. Col. 5, 3–13 has been recognized as the canonical Psalm 91, preceded by small remains of the exorcistic poem of col. IV and followed by a liturgical formula, 'And they shall an[swer, Amen, amen.] Selah.' All the lacunae of col. 4 have been conjecturally filled by E. Puech in a French rendering. His presentation will be reproduced here in English; it provides a possible general understanding of the text, but with no guarantee that any of the restored details is correct.

4 . . .
To David. O[n words of incanta]tion.
[Cry out al]l the time in the name of the Lor[d] towards heave[n when]
   Beli[al] comes to you.
[And sa]y to him: Who are you? [Be afraid of] man and of the seed of
   the ho[ly ones].
Your face is a face of [nothin]g and your horns are horns of dr[eam].
[You ar]e [d]arkness and not light; [injustic]e and not righteousness.
[The prin]ce of the h[os]t [is against you];
   the Lord [will cast] you [to] the nethermost [hell] . . .

For preliminary editions, see J. P. M. van der Ploeg, 'Un petit rouleau de psaumes apocryphes (1 1QPsAp^a)', in G. Jeremias et al. (eds), *Tradition und Glaube. K. G. Kuhn Festschrift*, Göttingen 1971, 128–39; E. Puech, 'Les deux derniers psaumes davidiques du rituel d'exorcisme, 11QPsAp^a IV 4–V 14', in D. Dimant and U. Rappaport (eds), *The Dead Sea Scrolls: Forty Years of Research*, 64–89; cf. esp. 68–9. For the *editio princeps*, see J. P. M. van der Ploeg in DJD XXIII, 198–200.

24. *Hymnic Fragment (4Q255 recto)*

Fragment of a poem depicting the Community as a plant.

> . . . For the Master . . .
> a plant of delight, a plant in His garden and in His vineyard.
> Its branches bear fruit and will increase . . .

For a preliminary edition, see B. Z. Wacholder and M. G. Abegg, *A Preliminary Edition of the Unpublished Dead Sea Scrolls* III, 369.

25. *A Messianic Apocalypse (4Q521)*

A collection of fragments, dating probably to the beginning of the first century BCE, represents a poem, related to late biblical poetry, in which the Messiah, the Kingdom of God, healing and bodily resurrection are brought together.

> . . . [the hea]vens and the earth will listen to His Messiah,
> And glorious things which have never been the Lord will
> accomplish . . .
> For He will heal the wounded, and revive the dead, and bring good
> news to the poor.
> (Frg. 2,2.1, 11–12)

For the *editio princeps*, see E. Puech, DJD XXV, 10–18.

26. *Jerusalem and King Jonathan (4Q448)*

This fragment, written in a very difficult semi-cursive script, comprises three columns, the first being a Hallelujah psalm, partly identical with Ps.154, and the second praising the Holy City and King Jonathan, either Alexander Jannaeus or, more likely, Jonathan Maccabaeus.

> Holy City for King Jonathan and for all the congregation of Thy people Israel, who are in the four corners of heaven. May the peace of them all be on Thy Kingdom! May Thy name be blessed! (col. B. 1–9).

For a preliminary study see E. Eshel, H. Eshel and A. Yardeni, 'Qumran Composition containing Part of Ps.154 and a Prayer for the Welfare of King Jonathan and his Kingdom', *IEJ* 42, 1992, 199–229; G. Vermes, 'The So-called King Jonathan Fragment', *JJS* 44, 1993, 294–300; E. Puech, 'Jonathan, le Prêtre Impie et les débuts de la communauté de Qumrân', *RQ* 17, 1996, 241–70.

27. *Calendars of priestly courses (4Q320–330)*

Eleven fragmentary manuscripts from Cave 4 present in various forms the peculiar 'solar' calendar of the Qumran community. Some documents from 4Q (320 and 321) attempt to combine this calendar with the various priestly courses, with the dates of the full moon, the date of the solar month and the equivalent date of the lunar calendar of mainstream Judaism. E. g. (The full moon falls): 'On the 5th (day) in the week of Jedaiah, corresponding to the 29th day of the lunar month, which falls on the 30th day of the 1st solar month.' The badly mutilated remains of 4Q322–324b record the names of political figures, Jewish and Roman, as well as dated historical events in a calendar of priestly courses. E. g.: '. . . [in] the seventh [mon]th . . . in the week of Gamul . . . Aemilius killed . . .'

Mishmarot A (4Q320) Fr. 1

(There is full moon) On the 4th (day) in the week [of the sons of G]amul in the first month of *[the firs]t year.*
[On the 5th (day) in (the week of) Jedai]ah, (corresonding) to the 29th (day of the lunar month, which falls) on the 30th (day) of the 1st (solar month).

For a preliminary edition, see B. Z. Wacholder and M. G. Abegg, *A Preliminary Edition of the Unpublished Dead Sea Scrolls* I, 60–101.

28. *Calendrical signs (Otot)*

The so-called Otot or 'Signs' document was copied as the continuation of 4QS^e (4Q259). 4Q319 represents a calendrical system based on the weekly rotation of the twenty-four priestly courses during a six-year period and constructed into six consecutive Jubilees, i.e. 294 years. The 'sign' which recurs every three years probably identifies the years in which the shorter lunar year of 354 days is supplemented by means of the intercalation of an extra month of 30 days (3 x 354+30 = 1092) to equal the length of three 'solar' years of 364 days each (3 x 364 = 1092).

> I The sign of Gamul: in the (year) of Release (= the first sabbatical year).
> (Second sabbatical cycle):
> The si]gn [of Shecaniah: in the thi]rd (year).
> The sign of [G]amul: in the sixth (year).
> (Third sabbatical cycle):
> The sign [of Shecaniah: in the second (year).
> The sign of G]amul: [in the fifth (year).

For a preliminary study, see U. Glessmer, 'The Otot-texts (4Q319) and the Problem of Intercalations in the Context of the 364-day Calendar', *'Qumran Studies': Schriften des Institutum Judaicum Delitzschianum* III, Göttingen 1995, 125–64.

29. Lamentations (4Q179, 4Q501)

In Cave 4, the remains were found of poems resembling the biblical Book of Lamentations. Both are thought to date to the second half of the first century BCE.

> [How] solitary [lies] the city,
>   . . .
> the princess of all people is desolate
> like a forsaken woman. . . (4Q 179, frg.2.4–5)

For the *editio princeps*, see J. M. Allegro, *DJD* V, 75–7; M. Baillet, *DJD* VII, 79–80.

30. The Words of the Heavenly Lights (4Q504–506)

These liturgical prayers for recitation on the various days of the week are preserved in three fragmentary manuscripts, palaeographically dated to the mid-second century BCE.

Hymns for the Sabbath Day . . .
Give thanks . . .
[Bless] His holy Name unceasingly
 . . . all the angels of the holy firmament (7.4–6).

For the *editio princeps*, see M. Baillet, *DJD* VII, 137–75.

31. *Songs of the Holocaust of the Sabbath (4Q400–407, 11Q5–6)*

Remains of eight Cave 4, two Cave 11 manuscripts and a large fragment
from Masada contain angelic praises of God to be chanted on the first
thirteen Sabbaths of the year. The poems describe the heavenly Temple,
the divine Throne-Chariot and the various participants of the celestial
liturgy. They are inspired by Ezekiel 1.10 and 40–48; 4Q405 20
furnishes an early post-biblical attestation of *Merkabah* mysticism. The
composition probably belongs to the first century BCE.

> In the name [of the mighty deeds of] the gods,
>   the sixth sovereign Prince shall bless
>   with seven words of His marvellous mighty deeds
>   all who are mighty in wisdom.
> He shall bless all the perfect of way
>   with seven marvellous words
>   to be in attendance for [ever] (4Q403 1.21–22).

Preliminary edition: Carol Newsom, *Songs of the Sabbath Sacrifice*,
1985.

32. *A liturgical prayer (1Q34^bis)*

This badly damaged text is probably part of the liturgy of the Renewal
of the Covenant.

> And Thou didst renew for them Thy Covenant (founded) on a glori-
> ous vision and on the words of Thy Holy [Spirit], on the works of
> Thy hands and the writing of Thy Right Hand, that they might know
> the foundations of glory and the steps towards eternity (2.6–7).

For the *editio princeps*, see J. T. Milik, *DJD* I, 152–5.

33. A liturgical work (4Q392)

A liturgical writing reminiscent of the Thanksgiving Hymns seems to relate the story of the creation.

> He created darkness [and l]ight in His, and in His dwelling is the most perfect light, and all gloominess ceases before Him. It is not for Himself, the distinction between light and darkness, for He has distinguished them for the sons of man: light during the day by means of the sun; night: moon and stars (4–7).

For a preliminary edition, see B. Z. Wacholder and M. G. Abegg, *A Preliminary Edition of the Unpublished Dead Sea Scrolls* II, 38–9.

34. Prayers for festivals (4Q507–509)

In this badly damaged manuscript are included prayers to be recited on the Day of Atonement, the Feast of the First Fruits, etc. The text is dated to the first century CE.

> *Prayer for the Day of Atonement* Remember O Lord
> the feast of mercies and the time of return (?) . . .
> Thou hast established it for us as a feast of fastings,
> an everlasting precept . . . (4Q 508, frg. 2).

For the *editio princeps*, see M. Baillet, *DJD* VII, 175–215.

35. Daily prayers (4Q503)

A liturgical work on papyrus assembles evening and morning benedictions for each day of the month.

> On the sixth of the month in the evening they shall bless. Answering they shalt [say]: Bles[sed be the God] of Israel (3.16–17).

For the *editio princeps*, see M. Baillet, *DJD* VII, 105–36.

36. *The blessings (1QSb = 1Q28b)*

A series of liturgical blessings forms a second appendix to the Community Rule or 1QS (the first being the Messianic Rule, cf. above, pp. 37–8). They were to be recited by the Master, who was to bless, first, all the members of the Covenant, then the High Priest (or possibly the Priestly Messiah), then the Zadokite priests, and finally the Prince of the Congregation (the Messiah of Israel?). The manuscript is dated to *circa* 100 BCE.

> Words of blessing. The Mas[ter shalt bless] the sons of Zadok the Priests, whom God has chosen to confirm His Covenant for [ever, and to inquire] into all His precepts in the midst of His people, and to instruct them as He commanded . . .
>
> May the Lord bless you from His holy [Abode]; may He set you as a splendid jewel in the midst of the congregation of the saints (3.22–26).

For the *editio princeps*, see J. T. Milik, *DJD* I, 118–29.

37. *Blessings (4Q286)*

4QBerakhot[a] (4Q286) provides continuous passages which parallel Community Rule 2 and War Rule 13, and the style of 4Q286 1 also recalls the Songs of the Holocaust for the Sabbath (4Q400–7). 4QBerakhot is probably an independent version of the ceremony of the renewal of the covenant included in 1QS 2.3–17.

> Fr. 1
>
> II. The seat of Thy splendour and the footstool of Thy glory in the [h]eights of Thy standing and Thy holy stepping-place. And Thy glorious chariots, their cherubim and their wheels and all [their] companies . . .
>
> Fr. 2
>
> [they shall] all [bless in com]munity Thy holy name.

Cf. B. Nitzan, '4QBerakhot (4Q286–290): A Preliminary Report', in G. J. Brooke (ed.), *New Qumran Texts and Studies*, 53–71.

38. Liturgical curses (4Q280–282; 286–287)

The first of these two fragments is a parallel to Community Rule 2 and contains the name Melkiresha, one of Belial's titles.

[Be cur]sed, Melkiresha, in all the thou[ghts of your guilty inclination! May] God [deliver you up] for torture at the hands of the vengeful Avengers! (2.2–3).

The second fragment corresponds to Community Rule 2 and War Rule 13. The curses are preceded by blessings of the party of God.

Afterwards [they] shall damn Satan and all his guilty lot. They will answer and say, Cursed be [S]atan in his hostile design, and damned in his guilty dominion! (10.2, 2–3).

For a preliminary edition, see J. T. Milik, '*Milki-ṣedeq* et *Milki-resha*', *JJS* 23, 1972, 130–5; B. Nitzan, '4QBerakhot (4Q286–90)', in J. G. Brooke (ed.), *New Qumran Texts and Studies*, 53–71.

39. Order of divine office (4Q334)

Cave 4 has yielded five fragments of a liturgical work, listing the number of songs and words of praise to be sung during the night and during the day on consecutive days of the month.

Fr. 2

[And on the eighth of it (of the month) at night: e]ight [so]ngs and forty- . . . [w]ords of prai[se, and during the day: . . . songs and] sixtee[n wor]ds [of praise. And on the nint]h of it at night: [eight songs and] fort[y-t]wo [words of praise, and during the d]ay: . . . songs [and . . . words of praise].

For a preliminary edition, see B. Z. Wacholder and M. G. Abegg, *A Preliminary Edition of the Unpublished Dead Sea Scrolls* III, 124.

40. *Confessional ritual (4Q393)*

Fragmentary remains of a communal confession of sins recall the language of Psalm 51, Jeremiah and Deuteronomy, and resemble confession prayers in Ezra 9. 5–15; Daniel 9.4–19; 1QS 1.2–2.1.

> I . . . in our iniquities . . . they [stiff]ened the neck. Our God, hide Thy face from [our] si[ns and] blot out [al]l our iniquities and create in us a new spirit, O Lord. . . . II . . . Thy people and Thine inheritance shall not be forsa[k]en and let no man walk in the stubbornness of his evil heart. And where is Strength? And on whom shalt Thou cause Thy face to shine without his being purified?

For a preliminary study, see Daniel Falk, '4Q393: A Communal Confession', *JJS* 45, 1994, 184–207.

41. *Purification ritual (4Q512)*

A papyrus manuscript, datable to the early first century BCE, includes prayers for the removal of ritual uncleanness.

> Answering he will say: Blessed art Thou, [God of Israel], who hast delivered me from all my sins: and purified me from impure indecency . . .

For the *editio princeps*, see M. Baillet, *DJD* VII, 263–86.

42. *The triumph of righteousness (1Q27, 4Q299–301)*

These fragments, which may derive from a sermon, expound the theme of the battle between good and evil.

> And this shall be the sign for you that these things shall come to pass. When the breed of iniquity is shut up, wickedness shall then be banished by righteousness as darkness is banished by the light (1.5–6).

For the *editio princeps*, see J. T. Milik, *DJD* I, 102–5; for a preliminary edition, see L. H. Schiffmann, '4QMysteries^a', in Z. Zevit (ed.), *Solving Riddles*, Winona Lake 1995, 207–60.

Wisdom texts

43. *The seductress (4Q184)*

In this Wisdom poem the dangers and temptations of error and false doctrine are symbolized by the harlot. Paleographically the manuscript dates to the first century BCE, but the composition is probably pre-Qumran.

> She will never re[st] from wh[orin]g,
>   her eyes glance hither and thither.
> She lifts her eyelids naughtily
>   to stare at the virtuous man and join him,
>   and at an important man to trip him up,
>   at upright men to pervert their way (1.13–14).

For the *editio princeps*, see J. M. Allegro, *DJD* V, 82–5.

44. *Exhortation to seek Wisdom (4Q185)*

A teacher encourages his 'people' and 'sons' to meditate on the power of God revealed in the history of Israel.

> Now pray hearken to me, my people,
> heed me, O you Simple;
> become wise through the might of God.
> Remember His miracles which He did in Egypt
> and His marvels in the land of Ham (1.13–15).

For the *editio princeps*, see J. M. Allegro, *DJD* V, 85–7.

45. *Parable of the tree (4Q302a)*

The topic of this badly damaged fragment seems to be a giant 'good' tree which, nevertheless, produces thorns.

> Sages, reflect on this.
> If a man has a good tree
> [which grows] as far as heaven

[and its branches reach (?)]
to the ex[tremitie]s of the lands,
yet it [pr]oduces thorny fruits (?) . . .

For a preliminary edition, see B. Z. Wacholder and M. G. Abegg, *A Preliminary Edition of the Dead Sea Scrolls* II, 229.

46. *A sapiential work (i) (4Q413)*

Two fragments have preserved the first four lines of a column from a Wisdom composition.

And they will understand the ways of man
and the works of the sons of ma[n].
[According to] God's [loving kindness] towards man,
He has enlarged his inheritance in the knowledge of His truth,
and according to His rejection of every ev[il man,]
one who [walks after] his ears and his eyes shall not live.

For a preliminary study, see E. Qimron, 'A Work concerning Divine Providence: 4Q413', in Z. Zevit et al. (eds), *Solving Riddles . . .*, 191–202.

47. *A sapiential work (ii) (4Q415–418, 423, 1Q26)*

A substantial wisdom composition, probably dating to the seeond century BCE, has survived in six fragmentary manuscripts. The work is sectarian and displays a terminology akin to the Community Rule, the Damascus Document and the Thanksgiving Hymns.

4Q417, fr. 1 i (= 4Q416, fr. 2 i)

Let [instr]uction not depart from your heart
and God will be for you, yourself.
Widen . . . in your head,
for who is more insignificant than a poor man.
Do not be jolly while in mourning
lest you labour all your life.
Look at the approaching mystery

and grasp the sources (or: begetters) of salvation,
and know who is to inherit glory or injustice.

For a preliminary edition, see B. Z. Wacholder and M. G. Abegg, *A Preliminary Edition of the Dead Sea Scrolls* II, 1992, 44–154.

48. A sapiental work (iii): ways of righteousness (4Q420–421)

Two badly fragmented copies of a Wisdom composition portray the behaviour of the righteous man in universal terms.

4Q420 fr. I (4Q421 fr. I ii)

II to practise righteousness in the ways of God (4Q42 11 ii)
. . . he shall not reply before he has heard,
nor shalt he speak before he has gained understanding.
He shall patiently respond and . . . shall issue words.
He shall seek truth (and) judgment
and by searching righteousness he shall find its outcome.

For a preliminary edition, see B. Z. Wacholder and M. G. Abegg, *A Preliminary Edition of the Dead Sea Scrolls* II, 1992, 159–62.

49. A sapiential work (iv) (4Q424)

This poem instructs the righteous man not to entrust wisdom to the unworthy.

Do not send a blind man to bring a vision to the upright;
li[kewise] do not send a man who is hard of hearing to enquire
into judgment,
for he will not smooth out a quarrel between people (Frg. 3,3–4).

For a preliminary edition, see B. Z. Wacholder and M. G. Abegg, *A Preliminary Edition of the Dead Sea Scrolls* II, 1992, 174–6.

50. Bless, my soul (4Q434)

Called after its opening words, this poem, preserved in five manuscripts (4Q 434–438), resembles the Thanksgiving Hymns, but is devoid of sectarian features.

> Bless, my soul, the Lord
> for all His marvels for ever
> and may His name be blessed.
> For He has delivered the soul of the poor (Frg. 1,1–2).

For a preliminary edition, see B. Z. Wacholder and M. G. Abegg, *A Preliminary Edition of the Dead Sea Scrolls* III, 1995, 310–17.

51. Songs of the sage (4Q510–511)

These sapiential poems include exorcism of evil spirits.

> And I, the Master, proclaim the majesty
> of His beauty to frighten and ter[rify]
> all the spirits of the destroying angels and
> the spirits of the bastards, the demons, Lilith . . . (4Q510, 4–5).

For the *editio princeps*, see M. Baillet, *DJD* VII, 215–62.

52. Beatitudes (4Q525)

The characteristic feature of this Wisdom poem is that the blessing of virtues is followed not by the reward granted to those who practise them, but by antithetic parallelism.

> [Blessed is] . . . with a pure heart and does not slander with his tongue. Blessed are those who hold to [Wisdom's] precepts and do not hold to the ways of iniquity (Frg. 3,1–2).

For a preliminary edition, see E. Puech, 'Un hymne essénien en partie retrouvé et les béatitudes', *RQ* 13, 1988, 69–88. For the *editio princeps*, see E. Puech, DJD XXV, 122–6.

53. The two ways (4Q473)

The fragment is akin to the Instruction on the two Spirits in 1QS
3.13–4.25.

> . . . and He has placed [before you] t[wo] ways, one which is goo[d
> and one which is evil] . . .

For the *editio princeps,* see T. Elgvin, *DJD* XXII, 289–94.

Bible interpretation and apocryphal works

Five types of biblical commentary have been recovered from the
Qumran caves.

The least developed form of exegesis is contained in the so-called 'Re-
worked Pentateuch' texts. The Temple Scroll may also be assigned to
this group, as well as the Aramaic and Greek translations of the Hebrew
Scriptures from Caves 4 and 7. The second type, represented by the
Genesis Apocryphon, sets out to render the Bible story more intelligible
and attractive. In a somewhat similar manner, a commentary on Genesis
from Cave 4 (4Q252) attempts to adjust the chronology of the Flood to
the specific sectarian calendar of the Qumran community. The third
type of commentary departs from the biblical text and creates a new
story. Among others, the Admonition associated with the Flood
(4Q370, 185) comes into this category. The fourth form of exegesis
applies prophetic texts to the past, present, and future of the sect.
Normally the commentator expounds a biblical book verse by verse, e.g.
Habakkuk (1QpHab), but some works, e.g. A Midrash on the Last Days
(4Q174), assemble passages from different parts of Scripture in order to
develop a common theme. Finally, free compositions modelled on the
Bible, e.g. Jubilees (4Q216–228), or circulating together with the Bible,
e.g. the Para-Danielic fragments (4Q243–245), and works attributed to
Noah (1Q19, etc.), the Patriarchs Levi (4Q213–214, 537–541), Moses
(4Q374–377, 390), etc., constitute a fourth category of exegesis. The
Aramaic and Hebrew manuscripts of Tobit (4Q196–200) also pertain
to this class.

54. Aramaic Bible translations (Targums)

A small scroll from Cave 11 has preserved in Aramaic much of the last seven chapters of Job. This text, together with small remains from Cave 4 of Leviticus (4Q156) and of another manuscript of Job (4Q157), represent the oldest extant Aramaic renderings of the Hebrew Bible. The translation of Job frequently differs from the customary text of the Hebrew Bible, but it is unclear whether the divergences are merely due to the difficulty of translating poetry, or to a Hebrew original not identical with the traditional Scripture.

Hebrew Job 40.12	11 QarJob
Look on every one that is proud	And every proud spirit
and bring him low;	you will smash;
and tread down the wicked	and extinguish the wicked
where they stand.	below them.

For the *editio princeps of* 11Q10, see J. P. M. van der Ploeg et al., *Le Targum de Job de la grotte XI de Qumrân*: DJD XXIII, 160–2. For the Targums of Leviticus and Job (4Q156, 157), see J. T. Milik, *DJD VI*, 85–91.

55. Greek Bible translations and other Greek texts

The Greek documents found in Caves 4 and 7 are remarkably few. Those which have been identified with certainty belong to the Greek translation of the Bible, mostly the Pentateuch. Cave 4 has yielded remains of two scrolls of Leviticus (4Q119,120), one of Numbers (4Q121) and Deuteronomy (4Q122), dating to the second or the first century BCE. They represent the traditional text of the Septuagint with minor variations. The remaining two Greek texts in Cave 4 date roughly to the turn of the era. One (4Q126) cannot be identified and the other (4Q127) is probably a paraphrase of Exodus. Among the nineteen minute fragments found in Cave 7, two have been identified as relics of Exodus (7Q1) and the Letter of Jeremiah (7Q2). Both are dated to about 100 BCE. The rest have been declared by the editors to be unidentifiable. A fringe opinion, rejected by all the major experts, holds that they are the earliest New Testament texts.

For the *editio princeps* of the 4Q and 7Q material, see P. W. Skehan and E. Ulrich, *DJD* IX, 161–97, 219–42; M. Baillet et al., *DJD* III, 142–6. For the latest refutation of the New Testament identification, see E. Puech, 'Des fragments grecs de la grotte 7 et le Nouveau Testament?', *RB* 102, 1995, 570–84. For the identification of several 7Q fragments as representing the Greek version of Enoch, see G. W. Nebe, '7Q – Möglichkeit und Grenze einer Identifikation', *RQ* 13, 1988, 629–33; E. A. Muro, 'The Greek Fragments of Enoch from Qumran Cave 7', *RQ* 18, 1997, 207–12; E. Puech, 'Sept fragments grecs de la letter d'Hénoch dans la grotte 7 de Qumrân', *RQ* 18, 1997, 313–23.

56. Reworked Pentateuch (4Q158, 4Q364–367)

Five badly preserved manuscripts have been classified as re-workings of the Pentateuch incorporating interpretative supplements. All the manuscripts may be dated on palaeographical grounds to the first century BC E.

4Q158, frs. 1–2

And the Lord said] to Aaron, Go to me[et Moses in the wilderness. So he went and met him at the mountain of God and kissed him. And Moses told Aaron all] the words of the Lord with which he had s[ent] him and all [the signs which he had charged him to do. And] *the Lord [spoke] to me saying, When thou bringest out the [people of Israel] . . . to go as slaves and behold these are [four hundred and] thirty [years] . . .*

For the *editio princeps,* see J. M. Allegro in *DJD* V, 1–6, and E. Tov and S. White in *DJD* XIII, 187–351.

57. Paraphrase of Genesis and Exodus (4Q422)

Nine fragments of a manuscript written in Hasmonaean characters contain a paraphrase of Gen. 1–4, 6–9 and of the opening chapters of Exodus.

III . . . But He hardened [his] (Pharaoh's) heart [to] sin so that the m[en of Isra]el might know for eternal gene[rations]. And He changed their [wate]rs to blood. Frogs were in all their land and lice in all their territories, gnats in their houses and they struck all their . . . And He smote with pestile[nce all] their flock and their beasts He delivered to de[at]h.

For the *editio princeps,* see T. Elgvin and E. Tov, *DJD* XIII, 417–41.

58. The Genesis Apocryphon (1QapGen)

The Genesis Apocryphon, called the Lamech Scroll before it was unrolled, is a fragmentary paraphrase in Aramaic of the Genesis story. Substantial sections are missing both from the beginning and from the end of the manuscript. The writing of the Scroll is dated to the first half of the first century BCE, and the composition itself to the early first, or possibly second, century BCE. From the literary point of view, it is the Bible re-written, i.e. made colourful by supplementary stories and interpretations.

The first section (col. 2) recounts the miraculous birth of Noah to Bathenosh. Lamech, her husband, suspects that the child may be the result of Bathenosh's intercourse with an angel, and although she denies this, Lamech sends Methuselah, his father, to visit Enoch, Lamech's grandfather in Paradise, to learn the truth from him.

> My heart was then greatly troubled within me, and when Bathenosh, my wife, saw that my countenance had changed . . . Then she mastered her anger and spoke to me, saying, 'O my lord, O my [brother, remember] my pleasure! I swear to you by the Holy Great One, the King of [the heavens] . . . that this seed is yours and that [this] conception is from you . . . and by no stranger, or Watcher or Son of Heaven (2.11–16).

After several damaged columns (cols 3–18) telling the story of various episodes in Noah's life and also the beginning of the history of Abraham, the main part of the Scroll, corresponding to Genesis 12.8 to 15.4, gives an account of the Patriarch's stay in Canaan, and of a journey to Egypt that ended with Sarah's abduction by Pharaoh and a visitation of plagues and afflictions on the Egyptian king by God until Pharaoh returned Sarah safely to her husband (cols 19–20).

When Harkenosh (an Egyptian prince) heard the words of Lot, he went to the king and said, 'All these scourges and afflictions with which my lord the king is scourged and afflicted are because of Sarai, the wife of Abram. Let Sarai be restored to Abram her husband, and this scourge and the spirit of festering shall vanish from you' (20.24–26).

On leaving Egypt, Abraham is described as worshipping God at Bethel and being shown from a mountain top the land his seed is to inherit. He is then ordered to take symbolical possession of it by walking its boundaries. This promised land includes the entire Near East, from the Mediterranean to the Euphrates, and from the Taurus-Amanus range of mountains in Southern Turkey to the Persian Gulf and the Arabian peninsula. At the close of his journey, Abraham settles in Hebron until the invasion of the land of Canaan by the five Mesopotamian kings; the account here closely follows Gen. 14. The narrative ends with the patriarch complaining that because of his childlessness his wealth will be inherited by a servant. God, however, promises him a natural heir (cols 21–2).

For the *editio princeps*, see N. Avigad and Y. Yadin, *A Genesis Apocryphon*. Cf. J. C. Greenfield et al., 'The Genesis Apocryphon Col.XII', *Abr-Nahrain*, Suppl.3, 1992, 70–7; M. Morgenstern et al., 'The Hitherto Unpublished Columns of the Genesis Apocryphon', *Abr-Nahrain* 33, 1995, 30–52.

59. A Genesis Commentary (4Q252–254)

Two fragments of a non-continuous paraphrase of Genesis represent sectarian exegesis. The first intends to adapt the biblical chronology of the Flood to the sectarian solar calendar and discusses the story of Abraham. The second, dwelling on the blessing of Judah (Gen. 49.10), restricts the legitimacy of the holder of the royal throne to true descendants of David, thereby outlawing the Hasmonaean priest-kings.

And the waters of the Flood arrived on the earth in the six-hundredth year of the life of Noah, in the second month – on the first day of the week – on the seventeenth (of the month). On that day all the fountains of the great deep burst forth and the windows of the heavens were opened. And rain fell on the earth forty days and forty nights – until the twenty-sixth day of the third month, the fifth day of the week (Frg. 1.3–7).

Whenever Israel rules, there shall [not] fail to be a descendant of David upon the throne. For the *ruler's staff* is the Covenant of Kingship, [and the clans] of Israel are the *divisions*, until the Messiah of Righteousness comes, the Branch of David (Frg. 2.1–4).

For the *editio princeps*, see G. Brooke, *DJD* XXII, 185–236.

60. *The Book of Jubilees (4Q220, 225–228)*

The pseudepigraphon, previously known from a complete Ethiopic and partial Greek, Latin and Syriac translations, has surfaced mostly in small fragments in its Hebrew original in the Qumran caves. Remains of three Hebrew manuscripts (4Q225–227) have preserved a writing akin to Jubilees or representing a discrepant version of it. Palaeographically, 4Q225 is dated to the turn of the era; 4Q226 to the second half, and 4Q227 to the final decades, of the first century BCE. The author recounts the sacrifice of Isaac with details which differ from the Genesis story and display close parallels to the post-biblical representation of the Akedah or Binding of Isaac, anticipating features known from the Palestinian Targums and Pirqe de-Rabbi Eliezer. 4Q225 provides the earliest (pre-Christian) evidence for the rabbinic story of Isaac's voluntary self-sacrifice which is thought to have supplied a model for the formulation by New Testament writers of the teaching on the sacrificial death of Jesus. Cf. G. Vermes, *Scripture and Tradition in Judaism*, 1961, 193–227. Cf. also G. Vermes, 'New Light on the Akedah from 4Q225', *JJS* 47, 1996, 140–6.

4Q220

[And do not go a]fter idols and after . . . and do not [eat any bl]ood of a wild or domestic animal or a bird which [flies] . . . [And if you sac]rifice a peace offering as a burnt offering, sacrifice it for (God's) pleasure. And sprinkle their blood on the alt[ar. And all] the flesh of the burnt offering you will offer on the alt[ar] together with the flour mixed with [o]i[l] of its meal offering.

61. 4Q225 (4Q226)

I . . . And a son was born afterwards [to Abraha]m and he called his name Isaac. And the prince Ma[s]temah came [to G]od and accused Abraham on account of Isaac. And [G]od said [to Abra]ham, 'Take your son, Isaac, [your] only (son) [whom] you [love] and offer him to me as a burnt offering on one of the . . . mountains [which I will tell] you.' And he ro[se and he we]n[t] from the wells to Mo[unt Moriah]. . . . And Ab[raham] lifted up II his [ey]es [and behold there was] a fire. And he placed [the wood] on Isaac, his son, and they went together]. And Isaac said to Abraham, [his father, 'Behold there is the fire and the wood, but where is the lamb] for the burnt offering?' And Abraham said to [Isaac, his son, 'God will provide a lamb] for himself. Isaac said to his father, 'T[ie me well' . . .

For the *editio princeps* of 4Q216–228, see J. C. VanderKam and J. T. Milik, *DJD* XIII, 1–185.

62. The Prayer of Enosh and Enoch (4Q369)

Ten fragments have survived of a manuscript written with Herodian characters, recording prayers associated with Enosh, who according to Gen. 4.26 was the first human to call on the name of the Lord, and with Enoch.

Frg. 1

I . . . of Thy marvels, for from old times Thou hast ordered for them His judgment until the age of determined judgment through all everlasting commandments. *vacat*
[Kenan was from the fourth generation and Mehalalel] his [son] was the fifth generation . . . [and Jared his son. And Jared his son was sixth generation and Enoch] his son. Enoch was seven[th] generation . . .]

For the *editio princeps*, see H. Attridge and J. Strugnell, *DJD* XIII, 353–62.

63. The Book of Enoch (4Q201–202, 204–212) and the Book of Giants (1Q23–4, 2Q26, 4Q203, 530–533, 6Q8)

Various Qumran caves have yielded the original Aramaic text of the Book of Enoch, previously known from a complete Ethiopic and a partly preserved Greek translation. Qumran Cave 4 has yielded seven copies of the writing attested by the Ethiopic, and four further copies of the related Book of Giants, dependent on chapter 6 of Enoch. Palaeographically, all of them date to the last two centuries of the pre-Christian era. The astronomical section is more developed than the text from which the Ethiopic Enoch was made, while the Book of Parables with its Son of Man speculation is completely lacking at Qumran. The bulk of the fragments is tiny. The Book of the Giants is missing from the Ethiopic, but circulated in Manichaean, Talmudic and mediaeval Jewish literature.

4Q201 1(I Enoch 6.7–7.1)

III . . . And these are [the names of their chiefs. Shemihazah wh[o was their head, Arataqo]ph, his second; Ramta[el, third] to him; Kokabe[l, fourth to him; . . . el, fif]th to him; Ramae[l, sixth to him;] Daniel, seve[nth to him; Ziqiel, eigh]th to him; Baraqel, nin[th to him]; Asael, tenth [to him; Hermoni, eleven]th to him; Matarel, twelf[th to him]; Ananel, thirteenth [to him]; Stawel, [fo]urteenth to him; Shamshi[el, fif]teenth to him; Shahriel, [s]ixteenth to him; Tummiel, seven[teenth to him]; Turiel, eighteenth to him; Yomiel, nine[teenth] to him; [Yehaddiel, twentieth to him.] These are the chiefs of the chiefs of tens. The[se and] their [ch]iefs [took for them-selves] wives from all those whom they chose and [they began to go in to them and defile themselves with them and to teach them sorcery and [magic] . . . And they became pregnant by them and bo[re giants] . . .

The Book of Giants

4Q530

. . . [Then all the giants . . .] were terrified [and] c[al]led Mahawai and he came to th[em]. And the giants as[ked him] and sent him to

Enoch, [the interprete]r [scribe] and said to him, Go . . . listen to his voice and say to him that he should expl[ain to you and] inter[p]ret the dreams . . .

For a preliminary edition, see J. T. Milik, *The Books of Enoch: Aramaic Fragments of Qumran Cave 4.*

64. *The Book of Noah (1Q19, 4Q534–6, 6Q8, 19)*

Several groups of small fragments from Qumran Caves 1, 4 and 6 are relics of a Book of Noah mentioned in Jubilees. 1Q19 represents a Hebrew version, 6Q8 and 19 an Aramaic Noah narrative. 1Q19, 6Q8 and 1QapGen deal with the miraculous birth of Noah, as does also 4Q534.

1Q19fr.3

. . . [to] his father. And when Lamekh (Noah's father) saw the . . . [the child made] the rooms of the house [shine] like the rays of the sun
. . .
to frighten the . . .

4Q534

I . . . And then he will acquire wisdom and learn und[erstanding] . . . vision to come to him on his knees. And with his father and his ancestors . . . life and old age. Counsel and prudence will be with him, and he will know the secrets of man. His wisdom will reach all the peoples, and he will know the secrets of all the living. And all their designs against him will come to nothing, and (his) rule over all the living will be great. His designs [will succeed], for he is the Elect of God.

For a preliminary edition of 4Q534, see J. Starcky, 'Un texte messianique araméen', *Mémorial du Cinquantenaire 1914–1964*, Paris 1964, 51–66; for 4Q536, see K. Beyer, *Die aramäischen Texte vom Toten Meer. Ergänzungsband*, 126–7.

65. Words of the Archangel Michael (4Q529, 6Q23)

In this poorly preserved Aramaic fragment Michael addresses the angels in general and the archangel Gabriel in particular about a vision. Since the speaker refers to Shem and Ham, sons of Noah, and to the construction of a wicked city, it is likely that the building of the tower of Babel is meant.

> I Words of the book which Michael spoke to the angels . . . He said: I found there divisions of fire [and I saw there] nine mountains: two to the eas[t, and two to the west, and two to the north and two to the so]uth. I saw there the angel Gabriel . . .

For a preliminary edition, see K. Beyer, *Die aramäischen Texte vom Toten Meer. Ergänzungsband,* 127–8.

66. Sermon on the Exodus and the Conquest of Canaan (4Q374)

One of the fragments of a writing, palaeographically dated to the last third of the first century BCE, deals with the exodus from Egypt and the occupation of Canaan. The speaker may be Joshua.

> Fr. 2
>
> II . . . And the nations rose up in anger . . . in their actions and in the uncleanness of the deeds of . . . and there was no remnant for [them] and none who escaped and for their posterity . . . And he made a plantation for u[s] his elect in the land that is the most desirable of all the lands . . . And he made him as a god over the mighty and as a cause of dread for Pharaoh . . . they melted and their heart trembled and their entrails dissolved.

For the *editio princeps, see* Carol Newsom, *DJD* XIX, 99–110.

67. A narrative based on Genesis and Exodus (4Q462–464)

Palaeographically dated to the mid-first century BCE, 4Q462 represents a historical narrative on the theme that after repeated oppression God is to remember Jerusalem.

4Q462

. . . And behold they were handed over to Egypt for the second time in the period of the kingship, and [they] were safeguarded . . . [and the inhabitants of Philistia and Egypt will become a booty and a ruin. And he will make it stand . . . the fierceness of her face will be changed to brightness and her soiled garments [to] . . . And he will remember Jerusalem . . .

For the *editio princeps, see* M. S. Smith, *DJD* XIX, 195–209.

68. A Flood apocryphon (4Q370)

Based on Genesis 6–9, these fragments offer a re-written account of the story of Noah with an ethical exhortation.

'Whoever does my will, let him eat and be satisfied', says [the Lo]rd. 'And let them bless [My holy] name. But, behold, they have done what is wicked in my eyes,' said the Lord (2.2–3).

For the *editio princeps, see* Carol Newsom, *DJD* XIX, 85–97.

69. The ages of the creation (4Q180)

This badly worn document includes a reference to the myth of the fallen angels (Gen. 6.1–4).

And the interpretation concerns Azazel and the angels who [came to the daughters of men; and] they bore to them giants (1.7–8).

For the *editio princeps*, see J. M. Allegro, *DJD* V, 77–9.

70. Testament of Levi (i) (4Q213–214, 1Q21)

Among the numerous small fragments representing the Aramaic Testament of Levi, 4Q213a contains sections of a prayer of Levi. As the best part of the same text survives also in Greek in a manuscript from Mt Athos, it is possible to complete most of the prayer.

4Q213a

I [Then] I raised [my eyes and face] towards heaven [and opened my mouth and spoke. And I stretched out] the fingers of my hands and my hands . . . for truth towards the holy ones and I prayed and said, Lord, Thou [knowest every heart, and T]hou alone knowest all the thoughts of [the heart. And now my sons are with me. Give me all] the paths of truth, and distance [from me, O Lord, the evil spirit and the e[vil inclination] and fornication and repulse [pride from me] . . .

For the *editio princeps* see M. E. Stone and J. C. Greenfield, *DJD* XXII, 27–32.

71. *Testament of Levi (ii) (4Q213–214, 4Q 537–541)*

Levi is the protagonist of this Aramaic writing, dated to the end of the second century BCE, but the testament is probably that of his father, Jacob. The eschatological priest alluded to clashes with the wicked of his age.

> He will atone for all the sons of his generation and will be sent to all the sons of his [peo]ple. His word is like a word of heaven, and his teaching is according to the will of God (Frg. 9 I 2–34).

For a preliminary edition, see E. Puech, 'Fragments d'un apocryphe de Lévi', in Barrera and Montaner (eds), *Madrid Qumran Congress* II, 1992, 499–501.

72. *Testament of Naphtali (4Q215)*

Fragments, containing the Hebrew Testament of Naphtali, overlap with the Greek version but are not identical with it.

> She conceived and bore Bilhah, my mother, and Hannah called her name Bilhah, for when she was born, she was in a hurry to suck (Frg. 1.4–5).

For the *editio princeps*, see M. E. Stone, *DJD* XXII, 73–82.

73. A Joseph Apocryphon (4Q372)

In this Hebrew polemical, anti-Samaritan writing, the story of the Patriarch Joseph is recounted.

And for all this, Joseph was thrown to un[known] lands, to a strange nation, and they were dispersed in the whole world.

For a preliminary edition, see E. Schuller, '4Q372: A Text about Joseph', *RQ* 14, 1989–90, 348–76.

74. Testament of Qahat (4Q542)

Part of the deathbed literature of the Second Temple period, this Aramaic work resembles the Testaments of the Twelve Patriarchs, and reveals a priestly perspective. Palaeographically it is dated to the second century BCE, but the carbon-14 text places it to the fourth or third century BCE.

So hold to the word of Jacob, your father, and seize the laws of Abraham and the righteousness of Levi and mine. And be holy and pure of all fornication in the community.

For a preliminary edition, see E. Puech, 'Le Testament de Qahat', *RQ* 15, 1991–2, 23–54.

75. The Testament of Amram (4Q543–48)

Five incomplete copies are extant of this Aramaic composition purporting to be the deathbed admonition made by Amram, the father of Moses, to his children. The context is that of Exodus. Amram speaks of a dream in which he sees Melkiresha (i.e. Satan, cf. p. 57 above) and addresses the chief of the Sons of Light, probably Melkizedek (cf. pp. 89–90 below).

Copy of the words of the vision of Amram, son of Qahat, son of Levi, al[l that] he explained to his sons and enjoined on them on the day of [his] death, in his one hundred and thirty-seventh year, which was the

year of his death, [in] the one hundred and fifty-second year of Israel's
exile in Egypt (4Q54 5, 1–4).

For a preliminary edition, see J. T. Milik, '4Q visions d'Amram'. *RB* 79,
1972, 77–97.

76. *The Words of Moses (1Q22)*

This composition, inspired by Deuteronomy, takes the form of a
farewell speech by Moses and is characterized by the stress laid on the
choice of Levites and priests as teachers of the Law.

> [God spoke] to Moses in the [fortieth] year after [the children of]
> Israel had come [out of the land of] Egypt, in the eleventh month, on
> the first day of the month, saying: '[Gather together] all the congre-
> gation and go up to [Mount Nebo] and stand [there], you and Eleazar
> son of Aaron. Inter[pret to the heads] of family of the Levites, and to
> all the [priests], and proclaim to the children of Israel, the words of
> the Law which I proclaimed [to you] on Mount Sinai' (1.1–4).

For the *editio princeps*, see J. T. Milik, *DJD* I, 91–7.

77. *A Moses Apocryphon A (4Q373, 2Q22)*

Three small Cave 4 fragments which partly overlap with 2Q22 represent a historical narrative in which Og, king of Bashan, is named.
According to S. Talmon, the topic of the fragment is probably the defeat
of Og by Moses, richly elaborated by Targum, Midrash and Talmud.

> 4Q373 1–2 (2Q22)
>
> . . . all his servants Og . . . his height was . . . and a half cubits and
> two [cubits were his breadth . . .] a spear like a cedar tree . . . a shield
> like a tower. The nimble-footed . . . he who removed them seven
> stades. [I] did not stand . . . and I did not change. The Lord our God
> broke him.

For a preliminary edition, see Eileen Schuller, 'A Preliminary Study of
4Q373', in Barrera and Montaner (eds), *Madrid Qumran Congress* II,
515–30.

78. *Moses Apocryphon B (4Q375–376)*

Akin to the Words of Moses, this writing determines how to treat a man suspected of being a false prophet.

> And the prophet who will arise and speak in your midst [defection, turn]ing you away from your God, shall be put to death (Frg. 1.4–5).

For the *editio princeps* see J. Strugnell, *DJD* XIX, 111–36.

79. *Moses Apocryphon C (4Q377)*

In this apocryphal account an elder called Eliab curses the Jews for failing to observe the Law while Moses was with God on the mountain.

> II . . . And Eliab(?) answered and said: Hearken, congregation of the Lord, and listen, all the assembly! . . . to al[l His] wor[ds] and judgments. Cursed be the man who does not stand by, keep and prac[tise] all the comman]dments of the L[ord (issued) by the mouth of Moses, His anointed, and follow the Lord, the God of our fathers, He who commanded us from the mountains of Sinai.

For a preliminary edition, see B. Z. Wacholder and M. G. Abegg, *A Preliminary Edition of the Dead Sea Scrolls* III, 1995, 164–6.

80. *Plan for the conquest of the Holy Land (4Q522, 5Q9)*

Two mutilated columns of a narrative appear to relate the future conquest of the Holy Land. It appears to be connected with 5Q9, which mentions Joshua. Col. 1 of 4Q522 consists of a list of localities, several of which appear in Joshua 15–21 (e.g. Beer Sheba, Bealoth, Keilah, Adullam, etc.) and Judges 1 (Ashkelon, Kitron). Col. 2 predicts the conquest of Zion by David and the building of the Temple.

> II . . . For behold a son is born to Jesse, son of Perez, son of Ju[dah] . . . [He is to take] the Rock of Zion and from there he is to possess the Amorites . . . to build a house for the Lord, the God of Israel. Gold and silver cedars and cypress trees will he br[ing from] Lebanon to build it.

For a preliminary edition, see *DSSU*, 89–92.

81. Pseudo-Moses (4Q390)

An apocryphal divine address to Moses announcing the future of Israel. Palaeographically Herodian (late first century BCE – first century CE), the work may date to the second half of the second century BCE.

> And from the completion of that generation in the seventh jubilee of the devastation of the land they will forget the precept, and the appointed time, and the Sabbath and the Covenant (Frg. 1.7–8).

For a preliminary edition see D. Dimant, 'New Light from Qumran on the Jewish Pseudepigrapha', in Barrera and Montaner (eds), *Madrid Qumran Congress* II, 405–47.

82. A Joshua Apocryphon (i) or Psalms of Joshua (4Q378–379)

This badly mutilated composition represents a rewritten account of the story of Joshua in the form of a farewell speech. It contains admonitions, curses and prayers, a prayer listing the twelve tribes of Israel, songs, and a praise mentioning Abraham, Isaac, Jacob, Moses, Eleazar and Ithamar. 4Q379 22 is quoted in 4QTestimonia (4Q175).

> 4Q379 12
>
> they [cr]ossed (the Jordan) on dry ground (cf. Josh.4.22) in [the fi]rst month of the forty-f[irst] year of their exodus from the lan[d] of Egypt (cf. Josh.4.19). That was a jubilee year at the beginning of their entry into the land of Canaan. And the Jordan overflows its banks from the f[our]th (?) month until the wheat harvest . . .

For the *editio princeps, see* Carol Newsom, *DJD* XXII, 237–88.

83. The Vision of Samuel (4Q160)

Seven badly mutilated fragments seem to describe a vision of Samuel in the house of Eli (cf. I Sam. 3).

> Samuel lay in front of Eli. And he arose and opened the d[oors . . .] to announce the oracle to Eli. Eli answered and [said, . . .] Let me know the vision of God (1.3–5).

For the *editio princeps* see J. M. Allegro, *DJD* V, 9–11.

84. A paraphrase on Kings (4Q382)

154 papyrus fragments have survived from a paraphrase of the Books of Kings containing names such as Jezebel, Ahab, Obadiah, Elijah, Elisha.

Frg. 104

. . . Thou hast forsaken them to the hand of their kings and hast made them stumble among the people[s] . . . Didst Thou give them [the Law?] by the hand of Moses . . .

For the *editio princeps*, see S. Olyan, *DJD* XIII, 363–416.

85. An Elisha Apocryphon (4Q481A)

Three minute fragments reproduce the Hebrew text of 2 Kings 2.14–16 with periphrastic supplements.

Fr. 2

. . . [And] Elisha went up. [When the sons of the prophets who were over at Jericho] saw [him over against them, they said, The spirit of Elijah rests over Elish]a. And they came to meet Elisha, [and bowed to the ground before him.

For the *editio princeps*, see J. Trebolle, *DJD* XXII, 305–9.

86. A Zedekiah Apocryphon (4Q470)

Fragments of an 'early Herodian' manuscript depict favourably king Zedekiah as conversing with the archangel Michael. 4Q470 prefigures Josephus, who praises Zedekiah's 'goodness and sense of justice' *(Antiquities* 10, 120).

Fr. 1

Michael . . . Zedekiah [shall en]ter into a covenant on [th]at day . . . to practise and to cause all the Torah to be practised. [At] that time M[ich]ael shall say to Zedekiah. . . . I will make with you [a cov]e[nant] before the assembly [to p]ractise . . .

For the *editio princeps* of 4Q470, see Erik Larson, Lawrence H. Schiffman and John Strugnell, *DJD* XIX, 235–44.

87. Commentaries on Isaiah (4Q161–165)

These are four fragments, each representing a Qumran *pesher*, or fulfilment interpretation of prophecy. 4Q161, akin to 4Q285 (see p. 40), comments on the Messianic passage Isa. 2 ('And there shall come forth a rod from the stem of Jesse', etc.). 4Q162–3 allude to the enemies of the sect, described as 'scoffers' and the 'seekers after smooth things'. 4Q164 identifies the Community with the heavenly city of Jerusalem.

> Referring to the last days, this saying concerns the congregation of those who seek smooth things in Jerusalem (4Q163, 2.10–11).

For the *editio princeps* see J. M. Allegro, *DJD* V, 11–30.

88. A Jeremiah Apocryphon C (4Q384–385B)

These fragments belong to an apocryphal account of the life of Jeremiah in Babylon and in Egypt. The script probably dates to the end of the first century BCE.

> II . . . And Jeremiah lamented . . . lamentations ov]er Jerusalem . . . *vacat* [And the word of the Lord was addressed to] Jeremiah in the land of Tahpanes which was in the land of Eg[ypt . . . Go to] the sons of Israel and the sons of Judah and Benjamin [. . . and speak to them saying,] Day by day seek my decrees and ke[ep] my commandments . . . and do not follow] the i[d]ols of the gentiles [after] which wa[lked . . . for] they will not sa[ve y]ou . . .] nor . . .

For a preliminary study, see D. Dimant, 'An Apocryphon of Jeremiah from Cave 4 (4Q385^B)', in G. J. Brooke (ed.), *New Qumran Texts and Studies*, 1–30. For the *editio princeps* of 4Q384, see M. Smith, *DJD* XIX, 136–52.

89. *The New Jerusalem (4Q554–5, 5Q15)*

Fragments of a visionary Aramaic writing inspired by Ezekiel 40–48 have been found in Cave I (1Q32), 2 (2Q24) and 11Q18 as well. They portray the Jerusalem of the end of time, with its measurements, avenues, streets, houses, rooms, etc.

> [And the] mid[dle street passing through the mid]dle of the city, its [width measures] thirt[een] ree[ds] and one cubit 92 cubits. And all t[he streets of the city] are paved with white stone . . . marble and jasper (5Q15, 1.5–7).

For the *editio princeps* see J. T. Milik, *DJD* III,184–93.

90. *Second Ezekiel[a] (4Q385, 391)*

Dated to the mid-first century BCE, this work, surviving in five or six manuscripts, retells conversations between God and Ezekiel.

> [And I said, 'Lord,] I have seen many from Israel who have loved Your name and walked [in] the ways [of righteousness, and] when will [these] things come to pass? And how will their piety be rewarded?' And the Lord said to me, 'I will make the sons of Israel see and they will know that I am the Lord' (Frg. 2.1–3).

For a preliminary edition see D. Dimant, '4Q Second Ezekiel', *RQ* 13, 1988, 45–58.

91. *Tobit (4Q196–200)*

Prior to Qumran finds, Tobit existed in a long and a short Greek recension. Cave 4 has revealed remains of four Aramaic and one Hebrew manuscripts. They represent the Semitic original from which the longer Greek recension and the Old Latin version were made. The Aramaic is likely to be the original language of the composition.

4Q196, Fr. 2

(ii,1) And in the days of [ki]ng Esarhaddon, when I returned to my home and Hannah my wife and Tobiah my son were restored to me, on the day of the Festival of Wee[ks, I] had an excellent meal and I reclined to [ea]t.

(2) And they put a table in front of me and I saw the many delicacies placed on it, [and I] said [to Tob]iah my son, My son, go and bring all those among our brot[hers whom you] can find . . .

For the *editio princeps* of 4Q196–200, see J. A. Fitzmyer, *DJD* XIX, 1–79.

92. *The Prayer of Nabonidus (4Q242)*

The Prayer is an important fragment of an Aramaic work related to the Book of Daniel with its story of the miraculous recovery of the Babylonian king Nebuchadnezzar (605~562 BCE) in Dan. 4. The Qumran document describes the healing of rhe last ruler of Babylon, Nabonidus (555–539 BCE), by a Jewish exorcist.

I was afflicted [with an evil ulcer] for seven years . . . and an exorcist pardoned my sins. He was a Jew from among the [children of the exile of Judah, and said,] 'Recount this in writing to [glorify and exalt] the Name of the [Most High God'] (1.3–5).

For the *editio princeps* see J. Collins, *DJD* XXII, 83–93.

93. *Pseudo-Danielic Writings (4Q 243–245)*

Aramaic remains of a composition belonging to the Danielic cycle have survived in Cave 4.

The children of Israel chose themselves rather than [God and they sacrificed their sons to the demons of idolatry. God was enraged against them and determined to surrender them to Nebu[chadnezzar, King of Ba]bel and to devastate their land (17–18).

For the *editio princeps* see J. Collins et al., *DJD* XXII, 95–164.

94. An Aramaic Apocalypse (4Q246)

Extracts from this Aramaic fragment, sometimes referred to as the 'Son of God' text, were disclosed by J. T. Milik in a lecture given at Harvard University in 1972 and have been published on the basis of that lecture by J. A. Fitzmyer. The work appears to be historico-eschatological and like the War Scroll (1.2–4), contains allusions to the king of 'Assyria' and to 'Egypt'. One of the characters, designated as 'son of God' but represented as being distinct from the triumphant 'people of God', is in my view the historico-apocalyptic head of the last world empire who was to deify himself. E. Puech is of a similar opinion. Milik is said to have identified the 'son of God' as the Seleucid ruler Alexander Balas (150–145 BCE). Fitzmyer prefers to see in him the son of a Jewish king, depicted messianically. For David Flusser he is the anti-Christ and F. García Martínez thinks that he is the heavenly Melkizedek.

I (7) . . . he will be great on earth

   (8) . . . will make. . . and all will serve

   (9) . . . he will be called (or call himself) [grea]t . . . and by his name he will be designated (or designate himself).

II (1) The son of God he shall be proclaimed (or proclaim himself) and the son of the Most High they will call him. Like the sparks

   (2) of the vision, so will be their kingdom. They will reign for years on

   (3) the earth and they trample all. People will trample people and one province on another province

   (4) until the people of God will arise and all will rest from the sword.

For the *editio princeps* see E. Puech, *DJD* XX,165–84.

95. Apocryphal Weeks (4Q247)

A fragment consisting of seven mutilated lines, and palaeographically dated to the last decades of the first century BCE, appears to belong to an apocalyptic account of world history, divided into weeks of years and possibly centred on the Temple of Jerusalem.

[de]temined [end] . . . [And afterwards will co]me the fif[th] . . . four-hundred [and thirty years] Solo[mon] (built the Temple). (It was destroyed in the time) [of Zede]kiah king of Judah . . . (It was restored by) the Levites and the people of the Lan[d] . . . (Final stage) . . . kin[g] of the Kittim . . .

For a preliminary study, see J. T. Milik, *The Books of Enoch: Aramaic Fragments of Qumran Cave 4*, 256.

96. Conquest of Egypt and Jerusalem by a king (4Q248)

The story told in this mutilated fragment resembles the account of Daniel 11 concerning the 'King of the North' who invades Egypt and ill-treats Jerusalem.

. . . in Egypt and Zion and . . . Therefore they shall eat . . . their [s]ons and their daughters in a siege in . . . [And] (the Lord) shall cause [His] wind to pass [through] their courtyards and . . . he shall come to Egypt and sell her dust and . . . to the holy city and shall capture her with all [her ..] And he shall turn against the lands of the nations and shall return to Egyp[t] . . .

For a preliminary edition, see B. Z. Wacholder and M. G. Abegg, *A Preliminary Edition of the Dead Sea Scrolls* III, 1995, xvi, 33; M. Broshi and E. Eshel, 'The Greek King is Antiochus IV', *JJS* 48, 1997, 120–9.

97. The four kingdoms (4Q552–553)

These poorly preserved documents allude to the story of the four empires (Dan. 7–8) in the form of a metaphor of four trees.

4Q552

[I saw an angel] II standing on whom light (shone) and four trees [stood by] him. And the trees rose and moved away from him. And he said to [me: Do you see] this shape? And I said: Yes. I see it and consider it. And I saw the tree . . . placed. And I asked it: What is your name? And it said to me: Babel.

For a preliminary edition, see K. Beyer, *Die aramäischen Texte vom Toten Meer,* 108–9.

98. Proto-Esther (?) (4Q550)

A number of badly damaged fragments of an Aramaic writing report events said to have occured in the Persian court, thus recalling the biblical story of Esther. The script is dated to the second half of the first century BCE.

4QProto-Esther[a]

. . . In that hour the king could not go to sleep (literally, his spirit was stretched) [and he commanded that the b]ooks of his father be read before him. And among the books there was a scroll [the mou]th of which [was] s[ealed] with seven seals by the signet-ring of his father Darius the heading of which . . . [Dar]ius the king to the officials of the kingdom, Peace.

For a preliminary edition, see J. T. Milik, 'Les modèles araméens du livre d'Esther dans la grotte 4 de Qumrân', *RQ* 15, 1992, 321–406.

99. Commentary on Hosea (4Q166–167)

The prophet's metaphor of the unfaithful wife is interpreted as referring to Israel and her Gentile lovers.

Interpreted, this means that He smote them with hunger and nakedness that they might be shamed and disgraced in the sight of the nations on which they relied. They will not deliver them from their miseries (2.12–14).

Another fragment mentions the 'furious young lion' (cf. below, 4Q169), described also as 'the last Priest' who attacked 'Ephraim'.

For the *editio princeps* see J. M. Allegro, *DJD* V, 131–2.

100. Commentary on Micah (1Q14)

In this very badly preserved document the commentator reads into Micah allusions to the sect, to the Teacher of Righteousness, and to the 'Spouter of Lies', an enemy of the movement.

> [Interpreted, this concerns] the Teacher of Righteousness who [expounded the Law to] his [Council] and to all who freely pledged themselves to join the elect of [God to keep the Law] in the Council of the Community (Frg. 8; 10.6–8).

For the *editio princeps* see J. T. Milik, *DJD* I, 77–80.

101. Commentary on Nahum (4Q169)

The four fragmentary columns of the Nahum Pesher constitute one of the most important sources for the reconstruction of the sect's history. The commentary mentions by name the Seleucid kings Antiochus and Demetrius, accuses a Jewish ruler of crucifying his opponents, and also records a split among the enemies of the Community, Ephraim and Manasseh. The allusions are discussed fully in Chapter 6.

> Interpreted, this concerns the furious young lion [who executes revenge] on those who seek smooth things and hangs men alive, [a thing never done] formerly in Israel (1.5–8).

For the *editio princeps* see J. M. Allegro, *DJD* V, 37–42.

102. Commentary on Habakkuk (1QpHab)

Application of the first two chapters of Habakkuk to the sect's history makes of this commentary a principal historical source of information. In it, the Chaldean enemy becomes the Kittim (Romans) sent by God to punish the 'last (Hasmonaean) priests of Jerusalem' for the injustice done to the Teacher of Righteousness by the ruling Wicked Priest. For a further discussion, see Chapter 6. It is worth noting that the Tetragram is written in the archaic script (cf. above, p. 29–30). The script may be assigned to the end of the first century BCE.

Interpreted, this concerns the Wicked Priest who pursued the Teacher of Righteousness to the house of his exile that he might confuse him with his venomous fury. And at the time appointed for rest for the Day of Atonement, he appeared before them to confuse them, and to cause them to stumble on the Day of Fasting, their Sabbath of repose (11.4–8).

For the *editio princeps* see M. Burrows et al., *The Dead Sea Scrolls of St Mark's Monastery I.*

103. *Commentary on Zephaniah (1Q15; 4Q170)*

Minute fragments of Zephaniah commentaries have been found in Caves 1 and 4, but the interpretative sections are never long enough for translation. As in the Habakkuk Commentary, here too the Tetragram appears in archaic Hebrew letters.

For the *editio princeps* see J. T. Milik, *DJD* I, 80; J. A. Allegro, *DJD* V, 42.

104. *Commentary on Psalms (4Q171, 173)*

Two 'Herodian' manuscripts contain interpretations of Psalms, mostly of Psalm 37, but remains of Ps. 45 and 127 have also been preserved. In the exegesis of Ps. 37 the fate is described of the good and the evil as reflected in the history of the Community and its opponents, Ephraim and Manasseh. The conflict between the Teacher of Righteousness and the Wicked Priest occupies a central place. The Tetragram is again written in archaic letters.

Interpreted, this concerns the wicked of Ephraim and Manasseh, who shall seek to lay hands on the Priest and the men of his Council at the time of trial which shall come upon them. But God will redeem them from out of their hand. And afterwards they shall be delivered into the hand of the violent among the nations for judgment (2.17–19).

For the *editio princeps* see J. M. Allegro, *DJD* V, 42–53.

105. Midrash (or Commentary) on the Last Days (4Q174)

Two fragmentary columns have survived of 4Q Florilegium. In it, excerpts from Exodus 15, Amos 9, Psalm 1, Isaiah 8, Ezekiel 44 and Psalm 2 are combined so that they reinterpret the story of the building of the Temple by Solomon (II Sam. 7.10–14) in such a way as to introduce the establishment of the Community and the coming of the Davidic Messiah.

> *I [shall be] his father and he shall be my son.* He is the Branch of David who shall arise with the Interpreter of the Law [to rule] in Zion [at the end] of time (1.11–12).

Further tiny but identifiable fragments comment on Deuteronomy 33.8–11, 12, 19–21.

For the *editio princeps* see J. M. Allegro, *DJD* V, 53–7.

106. A Messianic anthology (4Q175)

The Testimonia or scriptural texts considered as the foundation of the messianic teachings of the Community consist of five Bible quotations arranged in four groups. The biblical text in the last group is accompanied by a citation from a sectarian writing.

The first group combines Deuteronomy 5.28–29 with Deut. 18.18–19 ('I will raise up a prophet like you from among their brethren', etc.). The second gives the oracle of Balaam from Numbers 24.15–17 (which includes 'A star shall come out of Jacob and a sceptre shall rise out of Israel', etc.). The third repeats the blessing of the Levites by Moses and, implicitly, of the priestly Messiah in Deuteronomy 33.8–11 ('Bless his power, O Lord, and delight in the work of his hands', etc.). The fourth unit opens with Joshua 6.26, then expounds this text with the help of the sectarian Psalms of Joshua (4Q379) as applying to the principal opponents of the Community.

> When Joshua had finished offering praise and thanksgiving, he said: *Cursed be the man who rebuilds this city! May he lay its foundation on his first-born, and set its gate upon his youngest son!* Behold, an accursed man, a man of Satan, has risen to become a fowler's net to his people and a cause of destruction to all his neighbours. And [his

brother| arose |and ruled|, both being instruments of violence. They have rebuilt |Jerusalem and have set up| a wall and towers to make of it a stronghold of ungodliness . . . (1.21–26).

For the *editio princeps* see J. M. Allegro, *DJD* V, 57–60.

107. *Commentary on Biblical Laws (4Q159, 4Q513–514)*

Known also as 'Ordinances', this document reinterprets a variety of biblical precepts. For example, Deut. 23.25–26 ('When you go into your neighbour's standing grain, you may pluck the ears with your hand') is understood to mean that a poor Jew may eat corn plucked in a field but not take it home. He may, however, do so with grain collected from a threshing floor. Exodus 30.11–16 (38.26–28) is interpreted as imposing the duty of a single payment of ransom money; nothing is said here of the annual Temple tax traditionally associated with this passage. Leviticus 25.39–46, prohibiting the buying of compatriots as slaves, forbids in this commentary their sale to Gentiles. Deuteronomy 22.5 enlarges on the unlawfulness of wearing clothes of the opposite sex, and 22.13–14 legislates on the case of a husband claiming that his wife was not a virgin at the time of their wedding.

And they shall examine her [concerning her] worthiness, and if he has not lied concerning her she shall be put to death. But if he has humiliated her [false]ly, he shall be fined two minas, and shall not divorce her all his life (4Q159, 2.8–10).

For the *editio princeps* see J. M. Allegro, *DJD* V, 6–9; M. Baillet, *DJD* VII, 287–98.

108. *The Melkizedek Document (11Q13)*

These thirteen fragments, dated to the first century BCE, are the remains of an eschatological midrash, i.e. a commentary on diverse scriptural themes relating to the end of time. They are based on Leviticus 25.13, Deuteronomy 15.2 and Isaiah 61.1 and were found in Cave 11. The deliverance proclaimed is seen as part of the general restoration of property in every fiftieth or Jubilee year, a restoration regarded in the Bible as a remission of debts. The deliverer, the chief of the heavenly beings (literally 'gods', *elohim*), is Melkizedek, identical with the archangel Michael. He will judge and condemn Belial, the Prince of Darkness. The final liberation will come on the Day of Atonement when all the sins of the Sons of Light will be pardoned.

> [*To proclaim liberty to the captives* (Isa. 61.1). Its interpretation is that He] will assign them to the Sons of Heaven and to the inheritance of Melkizedek; f[or He will cast] their [lot] amid the po[rtions of Melkize]dek, who will return them there and will proclaim to them liberty, forgiving them [the wrongdoings] of all their iniquities (2.4–6).

For a preliminary edition see A. S. van der Woude, 'Melchizedek als himmlische Erlösergestalt', *Oudtestamentische Studiën*, Leiden 1965, 354–73. For the *editio princeps*, see A. S. van der Woude, DJD XXIII, 224–30.

109. Words of Consolation (4Q176)

This collection designated *Tanhumim* (Consolations) contains excerpts from Psalm 79.2–3; Isaiah 40.1–5; 41.8–9; 43.1–2, 4–6; 49.7,13–17; 51.22–23; 52.1–3; 54.4–10; 52.1–2 and Zechariah 13.9. The biblical texts are followed by comments, but they are so fragmentary as to be untranslatable.

For the *editio princeps* see J. M. Allegro, *DJD* V, 60–7.

110. Catenae (4Q177, 182, 183)

These Catenae or 'chains' of quotations and interpretations are too damaged for any continuous sense to be made of them, but the following biblical passages can be identified: Deuteronomy 7.15; Ezekiel 20.32; Hosea 5.8; Isaiah 37.30; 32.7; Psalms 11.1; 12.1; Isaiah 22.13; Psalms 12.7; 13.2–3, 5; Ezekiel 25.8; Jeremiah 4.4; 18.18; Psalm 6.2–3; Joel 2.30; Psalm 16.3; Nahum 2.11; Psalm 17.1.

For the *editio princeps* see J. M. Allegro, *DJD* V, 67–74, 80–1.

Miscellaneous compositions

111. 'Horoscopes' or Astrological Physiognomies (4Q186)

This is a curious document written in Hebrew, but from left to right instead of from right to left, incorporating a mixture of archaic and square Hebrew lettering and also Greek letters. It appears to associate physical characteristics with specific spiritual qualities, and to relate both to the position of the planets at the moment of a person's birth. Of the three people mentioned here, one is very bad, with a proportion of Light to Darkness of 1:8; his physique is fat, with thick short toes, hairy fat thighs and uneven teeth. One is middling good, with a ratio of Light to Darkness 6:3; physically he is lean, with long thin toes; his disposition is meek. The third is very good. His Light to Darkness ratio is the reverse of the first man, i.e. 8:1.

> His eyes are black and glowing . . . His voice is gentle. His teeth are fine and well aligned. He is neither tall or short . . . And his fingers are thin and long. And his thighs are smooth . . . [And his toes] are well aligned (4Q186[2] 2,1–6).

For the *editio princeps* see J. M. Allegro, *DJD* V, 42–53.

112. Birth of the Messiah or of Noah (4Q534, 4Q561)

This Aramaic horoscope appears to foretell the physical appearance and the character of the future Prince of the Congregation or royal Messiah, but it is equally possible that it alludes to the miraculous birth of Noah. It prophesies that he will have red hair and a birthmark on his thigh, and will have reached the age of discretion by the time he is two years old.

> Counsel and prudence will be with him, and he will know the secrets of man. His wisdom will reach all the peoples, and he will know the secrets of all the living. And all their designs against him will come to nothing, and (his) rule over all the living will be great. His designs [will succeed] for he is the Elect of God (1.7–10).

For a preliminary edition see J. Starcky, 'Un texte messianique araméen', *Mémorial du Cinquantenaire 1914–1964*, Paris 1964, 51–66.

113. Brontologion (4Q318)

A badly-worn fragment represents a brontologion, or prediction of future events through a combined interpretation of the sound of thunder on given days of the month and the position of the moon in the zodiac.

> Adar. On 1 and on 2 Capricorn; on 3 and on 4 Taurus; on 5 [and on 6 and on 7 Gemini]; on 8 (and) on 9 Can[cer]. (Frg. 2.1–2).

For a preliminary study see J. C. Greenfield et al., 'An Astrological Text from Qumran', *RQ* 16, 1995, 507–25.

114. The Copper Scroll (3Q15)

This list of real or imaginary treasures was found in two parts in Cave 3. As neither section could be unrolled because of the advanced state of oxidization of the material, they were cut into longitudinal strips by H. W. Baker and deciphered by J. T. Milik and J. M. Allegro. Written in the post-biblical (Mishnaic) Hebrew dialect, the Scroll records sixty-four caches of gold, silver, Temple offerings and manuscripts. The total is so enormous that Milik suggests it is fictional; but another theory is that these riches either belonged to the Essene sect, or that they were removed from the Jerusalem Temple by the Zealot defenders of the capital and hidden by them in the Judaean desert.

> At Horebbeh which is in the Vale of Akhor, under the steps that go eastwards, (at) forty cubits: a box of silver totalling 17 talents (1.1–4).

For the *editio princeps* see J. T. Milik, *DJD* III, 199–302.

115. List of false prophets (4Q339)

This is a brief list of false prophets, recorded in Aramaic and palaeo-graphically Herodian in date. The first six names come from the Bible.

> The lying prophets who arose in [Israel: Balaam [son] of Beor (Num. 22–24); [the] elder from Bethel (I Kings 13.11–31); [Zed]ekiah son of

Ke[n]aanah (I Kings 22.11); [Aha]b son of K[o]liah (Jer. 29.21); [Zed]ekiah son of Ma[a]seiah (ibid.) . . .

For the *editio princeps* of 4Q339 see M. Broshi and A. Yardeni, *DJD* XIX, 77–9.

116. List of Netinim (4Q340)

A badly mutilated fragment, dated to the first half of the first century BCE, lists the Temple servants or *netinim* referred to in the biblical books of I Chronicles, Ezra and Nehemiah.

These are the *netin*[*im*] who have been identified by [their] na[mes]: Ithra and . . . To[biah].

For the *editio princeps*, see M. Broshi and A. Yardeni, *DJD* XIX, 81–4.

117. Ostrakon

This inscribed potsherd, found in 1996 at the base of a wall at Qumran, has been deciphered by F. M. Cross and E. Eshel. In their opinion it records the gift of a servant, a house and an orchard by a certain Honi, probably a 'novice', to an official called Eleazar. 1QS 6.18–20 obliges a candidate to hand over all his belongings to the *yahad* or Community. However, Ada Yardeni proposes a completely different reading, with no mention of *yahad*.

In year two of the . . . in Jericho, Honi son of . . . gave Hisday from Holon to Eleazar son of Nahmani .. from this day to perpetuity the boundaries of the house . . . and the fig trees . . . when he fulfilled (his first year) to the Community . . .

For a preliminary edition, see F. M. Cross and E. Eshel, 'Ostracon from Khirbet Qumran', *IEJ* 47, 1997, 17–28. Cf. also A. Yardeni, 'The Draft of a Deed of an Ostracon from Khirbet Qumran', *IEJ* 47, 1997, 233–7.

4

The Community

Since the early 1950s, the information garnered from the Scrolls and from Qumran's archaeological remains has been combined by experts to form a persuasive portrait of the people to which they allude. Yet for all the advances made in knowledge and understanding, the enigma of the sect is by no means definitely solved. After all this time, we are still not certain that we have collated the whole evidence correctly or interpreted it properly. Questions continue to arise in the mind and there is still no way to be sure of the answers.

Our perplexity is mainly due to an absence in the documents, singly or together, of any systematic exposition of the sect's constitution and laws. The Community Rule legislates for a kind of monastic society, the statutes of the Damascus Document for an ordinary lay existence; MMT *(Miqṣat Maʿase ha-Torah,* or Some Precepts of the Law) probably echoes the pre-history or early history of the sect; and the War Scroll and Messianic Rule in their turn, no doubt reflecting to some extent a contemporary state of affairs, plan for a future age.

Taken together, however, it is clear from this literature that the sectaries regarded themselves as the true Israel, the repository of the authentic traditions of the religious body from which they had seceded. Accordingly, they organized their movement so that it corresponded faithfully to that of the Jewish people, dividing it into priests and laity (or Aaron and Israel), the priests being led by the 'sons of Zadok' – Zadok was High Priest in David's time – and the laity grouped after the biblical model into twelve tribes.[1] This structure is described in the War Rule's account of temple worship as it was expected to be at the end of time:

> The twelve chief priests shall minister at the daily sacrifice before God
> . . . Below them shall be the chiefs of the Levites to the number of

twelve, one for each tribe . . . Below them shall be the chiefs of the tribes (1QM 2.1–3).

Still following the biblical pattern, sectarian society (apart from the tribe of Levi) was further distinguished into units of Thousands, Hundreds, Fifties and Tens (1QS 2.21; CD 13.1–2). To what extent these figures are symbolic, we do not know, but it is improbable that 'Thousands' amounted to anything more than a figure of speech. It is not irrelevant, in this connection, to note that the archaeologists have deduced from the fact that the cemetery contained 1100 graves, dug over the course of roughly 200 years, that the population of Qumran, an establishment of undoubted importance, can never have numbered more than 150 to 200 souls at a time. Also, it should be borne in mind that the total membership of the Essene sect at the end of the first century CE only slightly exceeded 'four thousand' (Josephus, *Ant.* 18.21).

To consider now the two types separately, the monastic brotherhood at Qumran alludes to itself in the Community Rule as 'the men of holiness' and 'the men of perfect holiness', and to the sect as 'the Community' and 'Council of the Community' or 'the men of the Law' (4QS^d). The establishment was devoted exclusively to religion. Work must have formed a necessary part of their existence; it is obvious from the remains discovered at Qumran that they farmed, made pots, cured hides and reproduced manuscripts. But no indication of this appears in the documents. It is said only that they were to eat in common, pray in common and deliberate in common' (1QS 6.2–3), living in such a way as to 'seek God with a whole heart and soul' (1QS 1.1–2). Perfectly obedient to each and every one of the laws of Moses and to all that was commanded by the prophets, they were to love one another and to share with one another their 'knowledge, powers and possessions' (1QS 1.11). They were to be scrupulous in their observance of the times appointed for prayer, and for every other event of a liturgical existence conducted apart from the Temple of Jerusalem and its official cult. 'Separate from the habitation of ungodly men' (1QS 8.13), they were to study the Torah in the wilderness and thereby 'atone for the Land' (1QS 8.6, 10) and its wicked men, for whom they were to nourish an 'everlasting hatred' (1QS 9.21), though this went together with a firm conviction that their fate was in God's hands alone. And the poet proclaims in the Hymn with which the Community Rule ends:

I will pay to no man the reward of evil;
I will pursue him with goodness,
For judgment of all the living is with God
And it is He who will render to man his reward.

(1QS 10.17–18)

They were to be truthful, humble, just, upright, charitable and modest. They were to

watch in community for a third of every night of the year, to
read the Book and study the law and to bless together.

(1QS 6.7–8)

These are, as may be seen, mostly the sort of recommendations to be expected of men devoting themselves to contemplation. A point to bear in mind, however, is that the contemplative life is not a regular feature of Judaism. An additional distinctive trait of these sectaries is that another qualification was required of them besides holiness: they were expected to become proficient in the knowledge of the 'two spirits' in which all men 'walk', the spirits of truth and falsehood, and to learn how to discriminate between them. They were taught in the so-called 'Instruction concerning the Two Spirits', the earliest Jewish theological tractate incorporated into the Community Rule, how to recognize a 'son of Light' or potential 'son of Light', and how to distinguish a 'son of Darkness' belonging to the lot of Belial (1QS 3.13–4.25; cf. below pp. 152f.).

The hierarchy at Qumran was strict and formal, from the highest level to the lowest. Every sectary was inscribed in 'the order of his rank' (1QS 6, 22) – the term 'order' recurs constantly – and was obliged to keep to it in all the community meetings and at table. But after democratic beginnings, with the 'Congregation' as such forming the supreme authority (cf. 4QS^{b,d} = 4Q256, 258), the 'sons of Zadok, the priests' came to occupy the leading position. Although nothing to this effect is mentioned specifically in the Community Rule, the superior, the so-called *mebaqqer* or Guardian, was undoubtedly one of their number, as was the Bursar of the Congregation entrusted with handling the material affairs of the Community.[2] In their hands lay the ultimate responsibility for decisions on issues of doctrine, discipline, purity and impurity, and in particular matters pertaining to 'justice and property' (1QS 9.7). It was also a basic rule of the order that a priest was required to be present at any gathering of ten or more meeting for debate, Bible study or prayer. A priest was to recite the grace before the common meals and to pronounce blessings (1QS 6.3–8). He was no doubt the man whose duty it was to study the Law continually (1QS 6.7; 8.11–12). One interesting feature of the priesthood at Qumran is that their precedence was absolute. In Judaism as represented by the Mishnah, the priest is superior to the Levite, the Levite to the Israelite, and the Israelite to the 'bastard' (Horayot 3.8). But the priestly precedence is conditional. If the 'bastard' is a man of learning, we are told, and the High Priest a 'boor', 'the bastard precedes the High Priest'.

The highest office was vested in the person of the Guardian, known also as the 'Master' *(maskil)*. The Community was to be taught by him how to live in conformity with the 'Book of the Community Rule' (1QS 1.1, 4Q255), and to be instructed by him in the doctrine of the 'two spirits'. He was to preside over assemblies, giving leave to speak to those wishing to do so (1QS 6.11–13). He was to assess, in concert with the brethren, the spiritual progress of the men in his charge and rank them accordingly (1QS 6.21–22). And negatively he was not to dispute with 'the men of the Pit' and not to transmit to them the sect's teachings (1QS 9.16–17).

Of the sect's institutions, the most significant appears to have been the Council of the Community, or assembly of the Congregation.[3] From a passage ordering all the members to sit in their correct places – 'The priests shall sit first, and the elders second, and all the rest of the people according to their rank' (1QS 6.8–9) – it would seem to have been a gathering of the whole community, under the priests and men of importance, with the Guardian at the head. But in another text, generally held to be an early section, the rule is as follows:

> In the Council of the Community there shall be twelve men and three Priests, perfectly versed in all that is revealed of the Law, whose works shall be truth, righteousness, justice, loving-kindness and humility. They shall preserve the faith in the Land with steadfastness and meekness and shall atone for sin by the practice of justice and by suffering the sorrows of affliction. They shall walk with all men according to the standard of truth and the rule of the time (1QS 8.1–4).

These three priests and twelve men are also referred to in the hybrid version of the Community Rule and the Damascus Document (4Q265 fr.7). Their presence was obviously essential: both documents state that when 'these are in Israel, the Council of the Community shall be established in truth' (1QS 8.4–5; 4QS 265). But whether they formed the nucleus of the sect as a whole, or the minimum quorum of the sect's leadership symbolizing the twelve tribes and the three Levitical clans, or a special elite within the Council designated elsewhere 'the Foundations of the Community', must be left open to question. The purpose of the meetings is in any case clear. It was to debate the Law, to discuss their current business, to select or reject newcomers under the guidance of the Guardian, to hear charges against offenders, and to conduct a yearly inquiry into the progress of every sectary, promoting or demoting them in rank, again under the Guardian's supervision (1QS 5.23–24; 6.13–23). During their sessions, order and quiet was to prevail: a person wishing to offer his opinion or ask a question was to crave permission in a prescribed way. He was to rise and tell the Guardian and the Congregation, 'I have something to say to the Congregation', and then wait for their consent before going ahead (1QS 6.8–13).

The procedure followed in enquiries into infringements of the Law and the sect's rule has been preserved, and the list of faults with their corresponding sentences tells us more about the mentality of the Dead Sea ascetics than any isolated exposition of their doctrine and principles can do.

Beginning with the blackest sins: any transgression, by commission or omission, of 'one word of the Law of Moses, on any point whatever' earned outright expulsion. No former companion might from then on associate with the sinner in any way at all (1QS 8.21–24).

Expulsion followed, secondly, the pronouncement for any reason whatever of the divine Name:

> If any man has uttered the [Most] Venerable Name, even though frivolously, or as a result of shock, or for any other reason whatever, while reading the Book or praying, he shall be dismissed and shall return no more (1QS 6.27–7.2).

Thirdly, a sectary was expelled for slandering the congregation (1QS 7.16). Fourthly, he was sent away for rebelling against the 'Foundations' of the Community:

Whoever has murmured against the Foundations of the Community shall be expelled and shall not return (1QS 7.17).

Lastly, where a man had been a member of the Council for at least ten years and had then defected to 'walk in the stubbornness of his heart', not only was he to be expelled, but the same judgment was extended to any of his former colleagues who might take pity on him and share with him their food or money (1QS 7.22–23).[4]

The remaining offences are of a kind that might be confessed and censured in any Christian religious order of today, though one cannot perhaps say the same of the penances imposed for them.

In a descending order of gravity: a man who 'betrayed the truth and talked in the stubbornness of his heart' (1QS 7.18–21), or transgressed the Mosaic Law inadvertently (1QS 8.24–9.1), was visited with two years of penance. He was to lose his rank and during the first year be separated from the 'purity' of the Congregation, and during the second year, from its 'drink'. Both notions will be developed presently. He was then to be re-examined by the Congregation and subsequently returned to his place in the order.

Lying in matters of property, in all probability, the partial concealment of personal possessions, earned exclusion from 'purity' for a year and a cut by one quarter in the food ration (1QS 6.25–27). The penal code of the Damascus Document (4Q265), which resembles that of 1QS, prescribes for lying to a companion exclusion for six months and halving of the guilty person's food ration. Disrespect to a companion of higher rank, rudeness and anger towards a priest, slander and deliberate insult, all earned one year of penance and exclusion from 'purity' (1QS 6.25–27; 7.2–5). After this, the sentences decrease to six months, three months, thirty days and ten days of penance.

For lying deliberately and similarly deceiving by word or deed, for bearing malice unjustly, for taking revenge, for murmuring against a companion unjustly, and also for going 'naked before his companion without having been obliged to do so' – a curious proviso – the sectary was to atone for six months. For failing to care for a companion and for speaking foolishly: three months. For falling asleep during a meeting of the council, for leaving the Council while members were standing (in prayer?), for spitting in Council, for 'guffawing foolishly', for being 'so poorly dressed that when drawing his hand from beneath his garment his nakedness was seen': thirty days. The penal code contained in another of the Cave 4 manuscripts of the Damascus Document (4QD^a = 4Q266), also mentions ten days penance in addition to the 30 days' expulsion inflicted on someone who has fallen asleep during a meeting! And for leaving an assembly three times without reason, for interrupting another while speaking, for gesticulating with the left hand: ten days (1QS 7.15). 4Q477 refers to misbehaviour (being short-tempered, leading astray the community spirit) by named sectaries, a Yohanan and two men called Hananiah.

That the common table was of high importance to Qumran daily life is evident from the fact that only the fully professed and the faultless, that is to say those who were 'inscribed . . . for purity' and not subsequently disqualified, were allowed to sit at it. There is no explicit mention of a ritual bath preceding the meals, but from various references to purification by water, as well as the presence of bathing installations at Qumran, it is likely that the sectaries immersed themselves before eating, as did the Essenes according to Josephus *(War* 2.129). But little more is learned of the meal itself from the Community Rule than that when the table had been 'prepared for eating and the new wine for drinking', the priest was to be the first to bless the food and drink (1QS 6.4–5). The implication would be that after him the others did the same, an inference supported by the Messianic Rule, where a similar meal is described attended by two Messiahs (1QSa 2.17–21). Some uncertainty surrounds the meaning of 'new wine', but it would seem from the use in the Scrolls, with the exception of the Temple Scroll, of the alternative Hebrew words for wine – *tirosh* and *yayin* – that the latter often has pejorative connotations. More likely than not, the 'wine' drunk by the sectaries, 'the drink of the Congregation', was unfermented grape-juice.[5]

Another topic to be considered under the heading of communal life and institutions is the crucial one of induction into the sect. And if it should seem strange to place it towards the end rather than at the beginning, the explanation is that with an idea, however sketchy, of what was entailed by adherence to the movement, the process by which it admitted a Jew into its company becomes easier to follow.

According to the regime adopted at Qumran, a person desiring to join the sect remained on probation, certainly for two years and possibly for three or more. His first move was to appear before the Guardian 'at the head of the Congregation', meaning no doubt during a session of the

Congregation, who enquired into his principles to discover if he was a suitable postulant. If they were satisfied, he 'entered the Covenant' (1QS 6.13–15). That is to say, he solemnly swore there and then to adhere to the Torah as the sect interpreted it, vowing

> by a binding oath to return with all his heart and soul to every commandment of the Law of Moses in accordance' with all that has been revealed of it to the sons of Zadok, the Keepers of the Covenant (1QS 5.7–11).

After a further period of unspecified length, during which he received instruction from the Guardian 'in all the rules of the Community', he appeared once more before the Congregation, who confirmed him as a novice or dismissed him. But although he was now accepted into the Council of the Community, he was nevertheless still not admitted to 'purity' for another full year (cf. also 4Q265).

This concept of pure things *(tohorah, taharah* or *tohorot,* literally 'purity' or 'purities') needs some comment. In rabbinic literature, *tohorot* signifies in general ritually pure food (cf. also 4Q274.1) as well as the vessels and utensils in which it is contained or cooked. It also includes garments. The *tohorot,* moreover, are distinguished by the rabbis from *mashqin,* liquids, the latter being considered much more susceptible to contract impurity than solid comestibles. Hence, in ordering the novice not to touch the pure things of the Congregation, the Community forbade him all contact with its pots, plates, bowls, and necessarily the food that they held. He was not, in effect, to attend the common table and had to eat elsewhere. Although the context is very different, a parallel rule figures in the Temple Scroll (63.13–14), prohibiting a Gentile woman married to her Jewish captor to touch his *tohorah* for seven years.

During this first year of the novitiate, the newcomer could not share the sect's property. At a third community inquiry, he was examined for 'his understanding and observance of the Law' and, if his progress was judged to be adequate, he handed over his money and belongings to the 'Bursar of the Congregation', but they were set aside and not yet absorbed into community ownership. During this second year, furthermore, the ban on touching the pure things was relaxed, but he could still not touch liquids, the 'drink of the Congregation' (1QS 6.20–21; 7.20;

cf. also 4Q284ª).[6] Finally, the second year over, the novice had once more to undergo an examination, after which, 'in accordance with the judgment of the Congregation', he was at last inscribed among the brethren in the order of his rank 'for the Law and for justice and for purity'. Also, his property was amalgamated with theirs and he possessed the right from then on to speak his mind in the Council of the Community (1QS 6.13–23).

In sum, this strict and extended curriculum falls into two stages. The postulant is first brought into the Covenant, swearing total fidelity to the Mosaic Law as interpreted by the sect's priesthood, and to 'separate from all the men of falsehood who walk in the way of wickedness' (1QS 5.10–11). He then secondly embarks on a course of training as a preliminary to joining the 'holy Congregation' (1QS 5.20). In other words, entering the Covenant and entering the Community was not one act, but two.[7]

It has long been debated whether the Qumran sectaries were married or celibate.[8] From the image of their life projected so far, few will probably disagree that the idea of the presence of women among them appears incongruous. The impression received is that of a wholly masculine society: indeed, they were actually enjoined 'not to follow a sinful heart and lustful eyes, committing all manner of evil' (1QS 1.6). Moreover, in support of the argument for celibacy, the word *ishah,* woman, occurs nowhere in the Community Rule. Or rather, to be more exact, it is encountered once in the final Hymn, in the cliché 'one born of woman' (1QS 11.21). Moreover, against the Cave 4 Damascus Document regulation (4Q270 fr. 7) which in a community of married members imposes the penalty of expulsion on anyone murmuring against 'the Fathers' but only a ten-day penance for murmuring against 'the Mothers', the Community Rule speaks only of the crime of murmuring against 'the authority of the Community' (1QS 7.17). Silence concerning the presence of women therefore seems deliberate. Yet the fact cannot be overlooked that although in the main graveyard itself the twenty-six tombs so far opened at random (out of eleven hundred) have all contained adult male skeletons, the archaeologists have uncovered on the peripheries of the cemetery the bones of six women and three children too.[9] A more extensive exploration of the cemetery would eliminate most of these uncertainties.

The Damascus Document, 4Q265 and the Temple Scroll, as well as

the Messianic Rule and occasionally the War Rule and MMT, are concerned with a style of religious existence quite at variance from that of
1QS.[10] In the 'towns' or 'camps', as the Damascus Document terms
them (CD 12.19,23), adherents of the sect lived an urban or village life
side by side, yet apart from, their fellow Jews and Gentile neighbours.
Their sexual morality followed stricter rules. One manuscript (4Q270
fr.7) lays down that 'whoever has approached his wife not according to
the rules, (thus) fornicating', will be expelled. The married sectaries
employed servants, engaged in commerce and trade (even with
Gentiles), tended cattle, grew vines and corn in the surrounding fields,
and discharged their duties to the Temple by way of offerings and
sacrifice, but in doing so they were obliged like their brothers in the
desert to show absolute obedience to the Law and to observe the sect's
'appointed times'.[11] There is no indication, however, that the intensive
study of the Torah played any part in their lives. Nor is there any
mention in their regard of instruction in the doctrine of the two spirits
as membership of the group was a birthright and not the outcome of a
process of selection and training.

How many of these people, if any, lived in Jerusalem is not known,
but they must at least have visited the city from time to time, since a
statute forbids them to enter the 'house of worship' in a state of ritual
uncleanness, or to 'lie with a woman in the city of Sanctuary to defile
the city of the Sanctuary with their uncleanness' (CD 1.22; 12.1; TS
45.11–12).[12]

Little is revealed in the Damascus Document of how the lifespan of
the individual progressed in the 'towns', and for this we have to turn to
the Messianic Rule in the hope that it reflects contemporary actuality as
well as the ideal life of an age to come.

According to the latter Rule, members of the Covenant were permitted to marry at the age of twenty, when they were estimated to have
reached adulthood and to 'know [good] and evil' (1QSa 1.9–11).[13] For
the subsequent five years they were then allowed to 'assist' (as opposed
to taking an active part) at hearings and judgments. At twenty-five, they
advanced one grade further and qualified to 'work in the service of the
Congregation' (1QSa 1.12–13). At thirty, they were regarded as at last
fully mature and could 'participate' in the affairs of the tribunals and
assemblies, taking their place among the higher ranks of the sect, the
'chiefs of the thousands of Israel, the Hundreds, the chiefs of the Fifties

and Tens, the judges and the officers of their tribes, in all their families [under the authority] of the sons of [Aa]ron the Priests' (1QSa 1.8–16). As office-holders, they were expected to perform their duties to the best of their ability and were accorded more honour or less in conformity with their 'understanding' and the 'perfection of their 'way'. As they grew older, so their burdens became lighter (1QSa 1.19).

As at Qumran, supreme authority rested in the hands of the priests, and every group of ten or more was to include a priest 'learned in the Book of Meditation' and to be 'ruled by him' (CD 13).[14] The Cave 4 manuscripts of the Damascus Document (4Q266, 269, 272–273) describe at length the diagnosis of the onset and eventual cure of skin disease. Priests with speech defects, those who had been prisoners of war or had settled and been active among Gentiles were disqualified from performing priestly duties or eating 'sacred food' (4Q266 fr. 5). The Cave 4 version of the Damascus Document also legislates on agricultural priestly dues (4Q266 fr. 6; 271 fr. 2).

As in the Community Rule, the head of the 'camp' is designated in the Damascus Document, as well as in 4QDᵃ (4Q266 fr. 5 i) and in the hybrid 4Q265 fr. 1 ii, as the *mebaqqer* or Guardian. He appears, however, not to be supported by a council. In fact, the words 'Council of the Community' are absent from this document apart from the transitional 4Q265 frs. 1 ii and 7 ii, where the use of the term is more general in the first case and represents the ideal nucleus of the sect in the second. There is reference to the 'company of Israel', on the advice of which it would be licit to attack Gentiles (CD 12.8), but this type of war council, mentioned also in the Messianic Rule (1QSa 1.26), can surely have had nothing to do with the assemblies described in the Community Rule. The Guardian of the 'camps', in any case, stands on his own as teacher and helper of his people. He shall love them, writes the author,

> as a father loves his children, and shall carry them in all their distress like a shepherd his sheep. He shall loosen all the fetters that bind them so that in his Congregation there may be none that are oppressed and broken (CD 13.9–10).

The Guardian was to examine newcomers to his congregation, though not, it should be noted, to determine their 'spirit', and was to serve as the deciding authority on the question of their admission (cf. also

4Q265). These offices are of course already familiar to us from the Community Rule. But an additional task of the *mebaqqer* in the towns was to ensure that no friendly contact occurred between his congregation and the 'men of the Pit', i.e. everyone outside the sect. Whatever exchanges took place had to be paid for; and even these transactions were to be subject to his consent (CD 13.14–16).

Instead of dealing with offenders in Community courts of inquiry, the towns had their tribunals for hearing cases, equipped moreover with 'judges'.[15] These were to be ten in number, elected for a specific term and drawn from the tribes of Levi, Aaron and Israel; four priests and Levites, and six laymen (CD 10.4–7). They were to be not younger than twenty-five and not older than sixty – in the Messianic Rule, which also speaks of judges, the age-limits are thirty and sixty years (1QSa 1.13–15) – and were to be expert in biblical law and the 'constitutions of the Covenant'. The arrangement would seem, in fact, to be fairly straightforward. Yet it is not entirely so. For example, it is evident that the Guardian was also implicated in legal matters: he had to determine whether a proper case had been made out against a sectary and whether it should be brought before the court (CD 9.16–20), and in certain cases he appears to have imposed penalties on his own (CD 15.13–14). In 4Q260 fr.7, 'the Priest overseeing the Congregation' appears to perform the same simple judicial function as the Guardian in the case of an inadvertent sin. We are not told whether these ten judges sat together, whether they were all drawn from the locality in which they lived, or whether they travelled on circuit as in the present day. The code of law they were expected to administer, as laid down in the Damascus Document, is in any case totally different in both content and tone from that of the Community Rule: the offences envisaged bear no relation to existence in a quasi-monastic community. Furthermore, although, unlike the Qumran code, a sentence is only rarely prescribed, sometimes it is the death penalty.[16] Thus, instead of recommendations not to spit or guffaw at a meeting of the Council, we have here a sectarian reformulation of scriptural laws regulating Jewish life as such.

The first group of statutes, concerned with vows, opens with the injunction that in order to avoid being put to death for the capital sin of uttering the names of God, the sectary must swear by the Covenant alone. Such an oath would be fully obligatory and might not be cancelled (CD 16.7–8). If he subsequently violated his oath, he would then have only to confess to the priest and make restitution (CD 15.1–5). The sectary is also ordered not to vow to the altar articles acquired unlawfully, or the food of his own house (CD 16.13–15), and not to make any vow 'in the fields' but always before the judges (CD 9.9–10). He is threatened with death if he 'vow another to destruction by the laws of the Gentiles' (CD 9. 1). As for the right conferred by the Bible on fathers and husbands to annul vows made by their daughters or wives, the Damascus Document limits it to the cancellation of oaths which should have never been made (CD 16.1–12; for a somewhat different rule, see TS 53.16–54.5). It is clearly stated that no accusation is valid without prior warnings before witnesses (CD 9.2–3). A fascinating fragment (4Q477) has preserved in writing several cases of warning issued against *named* sectaries: 'Yohanan son of. . .' was 'short-tempered', 'Hananiah Notos' led astray 'the spirit of the Community' and showed favouritism to his kin(?); and another 'Hananiah son of ShM. . .', 'loved' something no doubt prohibited.

A few ordinances follow concerned with witnesses. No one under the age of twenty was to testify before the judges in a capital charge (CD 9.23–10.2). Also, whereas the normal biblical custom is that two or three witnesses are needed before any sentence can be pronounced (Deut. 19.15), a single witness being quite unacceptable, *unus testis nullus testis,* sectarian law allowed the indictment of a man guilty of repeating the same capital offence on the testimony of single witnesses to the separate occasions on which it was committed, providing they reported it to the Guardian at once and that the Guardian recorded it at once in writing (CD 9.17–20).[17] In regard to the capital cases, to which should be added apostasy in a state of demonic possession (CD 12.2–3), the adultery of a betrothed girl (4Q159, frs. 2–4: 10–11), slandering the people of Israel and treason (TS 64.6–13), it is highly unlikely that either the Jewish or the Roman authorities would have granted any rights of execution to the sect. So this is probably part of the sect's vision of the future age, when as Israel *de jure* it would constitute *de facto* the government of the chosen people.

The penal code of the Damascus Document (4Q270) stipulates irrevocable expulsion in the case of a man 'fornicating' with his wife. This may refer to illicit sexual relations with a menstruating woman, or, perhaps even better, with a pregnant woman since, as Josephus clearly states in connection with married Essenes, sex between spouses was licit only if it could result in conception. A section devoted to Sabbath laws displays a marked bias towards severity. In time, rabbinic law developed the Sabbath rules in still greater detail than appears here, but the tendency is already apparent.

The sectary was not only to abstain from labour 'on the sixth day from the moment when the sun's orb is distant by its own fullness from the gate (wherein it sinks)' (CD 10.15–16), he was not even to speak about work. Nothing associated with money or gain was to interrupt his Sabbath of rest (CD 10.18–19). No member of the Covenant of God was to go out of his house on business on the Sabbath. In fact, he was not to go out, for any reason, further than one thousand cubits (about 500 yards), though he could pasture his beast at a distance of two thousand cubits from his town (CD 10, 21; 11.5–6). He could not cook. He could not pick and eat fruit and other edible things 'lying in the fields'. He could not draw water and carry it away, but must drink where he found it (CD 10.22–23). He could not strike his beast or reprimand his servant (CD 11.6, 12). He could not carry a child, wear perfume or sweep up the dust in his house (CD 11.10–11). He could not assist his animals to give birth or help them if they fell into a pit; he could, however, pull a man out of water or fire with the help of a ladder or rope (CD 11.13–14, 16–17). Interpreting the Bible restrictively (Lev. 23.38), the sect's lawmaker (or makers) commanded him to offer nothing on the Sabbath save the Sabbath burnt-offering, and never to send a gift to the Temple by the hand of one 'smitten with any uncleanness permitting him thus to defile the altar' (CD 11.19–20). And as has been said earlier (p. 103), he was also never to have intercourse while in the 'city of the Sanctuary' (CD 12.1–2; TS 45.1–12).

The punishment imposed for profaning the Sabbath and the feasts in any of these ways was not death, as in the Bible (Num. 15.35), nor even expulsion, as in the Community Rule. It was seven years of imprisonment.

> It shall fall to men to keep him in custody. And if he is healed of his error, they shall keep him in custody for seven years and he shall afterwards approach the assembly (CD 12.4–6).

In the last group, the ordinances appear to be only loosely connected, though some of them involve relation with the larger Jewish-Gentile world. One such forbids killing or stealing a non-Jew, 'unless so advised by the company of Israel' (CD 12.6–8). Another proscribes the sale to Gentiles of ritually pure beasts and birds, and the produce of granary and wine-press, in case they should blaspheme by offering them in heathen sacrifice. MMT further prohibits acceptance of offerings by Gentiles (4Q394, frs.3–7). A ban is similarly laid on selling to Gentiles foreign servants converted to the Jewish faith (CD 12.11). But in addition to these regulations affecting contacts with non-Jews, a few are concerned with dietary restrictions. Thus:

> No man shall defile himself by eating any live creature or creeping thing, from the larvae of bees to all creatures which creep in water (CD 12.12–13).

Others deal with the laws of purity (CD 12.16–18), purification (CD 10.10–13) and uncleanness resulting from sexual discharges and childbirth (4Q266 fr.6). MMT (4Q394–395), 4QPurities (4Q274, 276–277, 284) and the Temple Scroll (11QTS 45–51) provide information on purity matters, including the 'red heifer' (MMT 4Q394–395; 4Q276–277).

Two types of meeting are provided for, equally laconically: the 'assembly of the camp', presided over by a priest or a Levite (cf. above, p. 104), and the 'assembly of all the camps' (CD 14.3–6). Presumably the latter was the general convention of the whole sect held on the Feast of the Renewal of the Covenant, the annual great festival alluded to in 4QD (266/270), when both the 'men of holiness' and the 'men of the Covenant' confessed their former errors and committed themselves once more to perfect obedience to the Law and the sect's teachings.[18] According to the available texts, the sectaries were to be mustered and inscribed in their rank by name, the priests first, the Levites second, the Israelites third. A fourth group of proselytes is unique to the 'towns', but as has been observed, these were Gentile slaves converted to Judaism. A further remark that they were in this order to 'be questioned on all matters' leads one to suppose that the allusion must be to the yearly inquiry into the members' spiritual progress mentioned in the Community Rule (CD 14.3–6). Two 4Q Damascus Document manuscripts describe the ceremony of the expulsion of an unfaithful member (4Q266, 270).

Apart from these familiar directions, we learn only that the priest who mustered the gathering was to be between thirty and sixty years old and, needless to say, 'learned in the Book of Meditation'. The 'Guardian of all the camps', in his turn, was to be between thirty and fifty, and to have 'mastered all the secrets of men and the language of all their clans'.[19] He was to decide who was to be admitted, and anything connected with a 'suit or judgment' was to be brought to him (CD 14.7–12).

As for the initiation of new members, the Statutes appear to legislate for young men reaching their majority within the brotherhood and for recruits from outside. This is not entirely clear, but the instruction that an aspirant was not to be informed of the sect's rules until he had stood before the Guardian can hardly have applied to a person brought up within its close circle (CD 15.5–6,10–11).

Of the sect's own young men the Damascus Document writes merely:

And when the children of all those who have entered the Covenant granted to all Israel for ever reach the age of enrolment, they shall swear with an oath of the Covenant (CD 15.5–6).

The Messianic Rule is more discursive. There, enrolment into the sect is represented as the climax of a childhood and youth spent in study. Teaching in the Bible and in the 'precepts of the Covenant' began long before the age of ten, at which age a boy embarked on a further ten years of instruction in the statutes. It was not until after all this that he was finally ready.

From [his] youth they shall instruct him in the Book of Meditation and shall teach him, according to his age, the precepts of the Covenant. He [shall be edu]cated in their statutes for ten years . . . At the age of twenty [he shall be] enrolled, that he may enter upon his allotted duties in the midst of his family [and] be joined to the holy congregation (1QSa 1.6–9).

The newcomer from outside who repented of his 'corrupted way' was to be enrolled 'with the oath of the Covenant' on the day that he spoke to the Guardian, but no sectarian statute was to be divulged to him 'lest when examining him the Guardian be deceived by him' (CD 15.7–11).

Nevertheless, if he broke that oath, 'retribution' would be exacted of him. The text subsequently becomes fragmentary and unreliable, but he is told where to find the liturgical calendar which his oath obliges him to follow.

> As for the exact determination of their times to which Israel turns a blind eye, behold it is strictly defined in the Book of Divisions of the Times into their Jubilees and Weeks (CD 16.2–4).

It should be added here that one big difference between the organization of the brethren in the towns and those of the 'monastic' settlement is that new members were not required to surrender their property. There was none of the voluntary communism found in 1QS. On the other hand, where the desert sectaries practised common ownership, those of the towns contributed to the assistance of their fellows in need. Every man able to do so was ordered to hand over a minimum of two days' wages a month to a charitable fund, and from it the Guardian and the judges distributed help to the orphans, the poor, the old and sick, to unmarried women without support and to prisoners held in foreign hands and in need of redemption (CD 14.12–16).

When the two varieties of sectarian life are compared, numerous similarities appear, especially in the light of 4QD and 4Q265, but some of the differences still remain striking. In the desert of Qumran men lived together in seclusion; in the towns they were grouped in families, surrounded by non-members with whom they were in inevitable though exiguous contact. The desert brotherhood kept apart from the Temple in Jerusalem; that of the towns participated in worship there. The 'Foundations' of the Qumran community had no counterparts in the towns; the judges of the towns had no counterparts at Qumran. The Qumran Guardian was supported by a Council; the town Guardians acted independently. Unfaithful desert sectaries were sentenced to irrevocable excommunication, or to temporary exclusion from the common life, or to suffer lighter penances; offenders from the towns were condemned to death (whether or not the verdict was carried out) or committed to corrective custody. The common table and the 'purity' associated with it played an essential role at Qumran; in connection with the towns the table goes unmentioned and 'purity' in that sense receives attention only once. Furthermore, at Qumran all the new recruits came from outside; in the towns, some were converts but others were the sons of sectaries. The desert novices underwent two years of training and were instructed in the doctrine of the 'two spirits'; the towns' converts were subjected to neither experience. In the desert, property was owned in common; in the towns, it was not. And last but not least, the desert community appears to have practised celibacy, whereas the town sectaries patently did not.

Yet despite the dissimilarities, at the basic level of doctrine, aims and principles, a perceptible bond links the brethren of the desert with those of the towns. They both claim to represent the true Israel. They both are led by priests, Zadokite priests according to 1QS, the Damascus Document and the Messianic Rule, but not 4Q256, 258 and MMT. Both form units of Thousands, Hundreds, Fifties and Tens, both insist on a whole-hearted return to the Mosaic Law in accordance with their own particular interpretation of it. They are both governed by priests (or Levites). The principal, superior, teacher and administrator of both is known by the unusual title of *mebaqqer*. In both cases, initiation into the sect is preceded by entry into the Covenant, sworn by oath. Both groups convene yearly to review the order of precedence of their members after an enquiry into the conduct of each man during the previous twelve months. Above all, both embrace the same 'unorthodox' liturgical calendar that sets them apart from the rest of Jewry.

There can be only one logical conclusion: this was a single religious movement with two branches. It does not, however, answer all our questions. It does not tell us in particular whether the sectaries of desert and towns maintained regular contact among themselves. After all, the history of religions furnishes scores of examples of sister sects which turned into mortal enemies. Did the Qumran desert and town fellowships profess and practise unity? A few vital clues suggest that they did.

One indication of a living relationship between the two groups derives from the Qumran library itself. In it were discovered no less than ten copies of the Damascus Document. It seems hardly likely that it would have been represented in such numbers or have figured so prominently among the Qumran literary treasures if it had been the manual of some rival institution. Besides, there was no trace of any other book in the caves relating to an opposing religious faction. Another pointer towards unity appears in the passage of the Damascus Document outlining the procedure for the 'assembly of all the camps' and prescribing that the members were to be 'inscribed by name' in hierarchical rank. This clause corresponds exactly to the statute in the Community Rule ordaining a yearly ranking of the sectaries (1QS 2.19–23), with a solemn ritual for the Renewal of the Covenant (for an analysis of the rite, see 159–60). This leads us to suppose that the Feast of the Covenant, when the desert brethren held their annual spiritual survey, was also the occasion for that of the towns. Can we go further still and establish that the two ceremonies took place, not only at the same time, but at the same place? In effect, the literary and archaeological evidence tends to support the theory that the 'assembly of all the camps', identical with the yearly assembly of the Qumran branch, gathered at Qumran.

The first clue turns on the qualifications of the *mebaqqer* of the Community Rule and the Damascus Document respectively. As may be remembered, the superior at Qumran was required to be expert in recognizing 'the nature of all the children of men according to the kind of spirit which they possess' (1QS 3.13–14), while the *mebaqqer* of the towns was to be concerned rather more with a man's 'deeds', 'possessions', 'ability', etc., than with his inner spirit. When, however, the Damascus Document describes the attributes needed of the 'Guardian of all the camps', what do we find but a reformulation of those accredited to the superior of the desert community, that he should know 'all the secrets of men and all the languages of their clans'? It would emerge from this, therefore, that the Guardian of all the camps and the Guardian at Qumran were one and the same person.

The next hint comes from the fact that the Damascus Document is directed to both desert and town sectaries. As an example, the passage from the Exhortation advising men to choose whatever is pleasing to God and to reject whatever he hates, 'that you may walk perfectly in all his ways and not follow after thoughts of the guilty inclination and after eyes of lust' (CD 2.14–16), seems to be addressed to celibates. Yet in this very same document we later come upon injunctions aimed explicitly at non-celibates:

And if they live in camps according to the rule of the earth, marrying and begetting children, they shall walk according to the Law and according to the statute concerning binding vows, according to the rule of the Law which says, 'Between a man and his wife and between a father and his son' (Num. 30.17) (CD 7.6–9).

In short, the Exhortation would seem to be a sermon intended for delivery on a certain occasion to married and unmarried members of the sect; and as its theme is perseverance in the Covenant, the appropriate setting would be the Feast of the Renewal of the Covenant, in the third month (4Q266 fr. 19; 270 fr.7), i.e. in the Feast of Weeks or Pentecost, and the venue Qumran.

These literary pointers are supported by two archaeological finds. First, the twenty-six deposits of animal bones buried on the Qumran site – goats, sheep, lambs, calves, cows or oxen – have long intrigued scholars. Can J. T. Milik be correct in identifying them as the remains of meals served to large groups of pilgrims in the Qumran mother-house of the sect?[20] Naturally, he too connects the gathering with the Covenant festival.

The second archaeological clue also is concerned with bones. The skeletons of four women and one child, and possibly of two further female bodies and those of two children, were found in the extension of the Qumran cemetery.[21] Now if the Renewal of the Covenant was attended by sectaries from the towns and their families, this may well account for the presence of dead women and children among the otherwise male skeletons of the graveyard proper.

Drawing the threads of these various arguments together, there would seem to be little doubt that not only were the desert and town sectaries united in doctrine and organization, but that they remained in actual and regular touch with each other, under the ultimate administrative and spiritual authority of the shadowy figure of the Priest, of whom we hear so little, and his dominant partner, the Qumran Guardian, Guardian of all the camps. Qumran, it seems, was the seat of the sect's hierarchy and also the centre to which all those turned who professed the allegiance to the sons of Zadok the Priests, the Keepers of the Covenant.[22]

5

Identification of the Community

During the period with which this study is concerned (140 BCE–70 CE), Palestinian society did not consist of a majority of 'orthodox' Jews interspersed with small minorities of heretics and sectaries. The 'one-party system' which was to prevail in the second century CE did not come into being until after years of hard thinking and argument by the rabbis who survived the unsuccessful revolution of 66–70 CE. Assembled during the final decades of the first century in the little town of Jamnia (Yavneh), about fifteen miles south of Tel Aviv, they set out to re-think and re-shape a Judaism deprived of Temple and sacrifice, and by the end of the first century had reached agreement on all the essentials.[1] The bulk of the Jewish inhabitants of the Holy Land adhered from then on to their teaching, and the minority distinguishable by their lack of 'orthodoxy' were excommunicated and cursed daily in the famous prayer of the synagogue, the Eighteen Benedictions: 'May . . . the heretics perish quickly and may they be erased from the Book of Life!'[2]

Prior to this unification, the situation was very different in that co-hesion within Judaism was the outcome, not of conformity in matters of belief and practice, but of the concrete presence in Israel of legislative and administrative state institutions – supreme among them the Great Sanhedrin – and above all of the universally acknowledged cultic centre, the Temple of Jerusalem. These tangible criteria of unity allowed for a much greater elasticity as long as the central core of Judaism – Bible interpretation, teaching and religious observance – remained intact.

Thus as two first-century CE Jewish writers, Philo and Josephus, and indirectly the New Testament, make abundantly clear, the Jewish population of Palestine was at that period influenced by four parties or sects (in Greek designated as *haireseis*, 'heresies', i.e. divisions, with no pejorative meaning attached to the term). Three of these, the Sadducees, the Pharisees and the Zealots, competed for the leadership of the nation; a fourth, the Essenes, withdrew from the political scene and made their moral and doctrinal impact from outside it. A more recent foundation was that of the Judaeo-Christians, who formed themselves into an autonomous community within Judaism in the thirties of the first century. These were the major religious movements of Palestine and, as might be expected since they display more or less striking similarities with the Qumran Community, each has been suggested as a likely candidate in the search for an identification.

Judaeo-Christianity can be eliminated first; for despite the arguments, more specious than real, of J. L. Teicher of Cambridge, Y. Baer of Jerusalem, the Australian Barbara Thiering and Robert Eisenman of California, equating the Dead Sea sect with the primitive church and the Teacher of Righteousness with Jesus, John the Baptist or James the brother of Jesus, and the Qumran Wicked Priest with St Paul or Jesus (B. Thiering), and despite parallels which undoubtedly exist between the Scrolls and the New Testament, as will be shown in Chapter 8, it will be obvious to most readers, whether experts or not, that the Qumran writings cannot be mistaken for Christian literature.[3] Nor can the persons of Jesus and other New Testament characters be found in the leading figures alluded to in the Dead Sea manuscripts. If this were not enough, proponents of the Christian hypothesis must further explain away the archaeological data, which point to a pre-Christian (second century BCE) origin of the Qumran sect. They must also disregard the confirmation of palaeographical dating by the radiocarbon tests of 1990–91 and 1994. The Judaeo-Christian theory therefore seems untenable, and in consequence we are left with four serious possibilities: Sadducees, Pharisees, Zealots and Essenes. In examining them, we will look for a correspondence of aims and organization rather than of doctrines and beliefs, which could easily have been shared.

The Sadducees

The Sadducees, so called by Josephus and the New Testament, formed the upper tier of Jewish society.[4] They were the select few of highest standing, the party of the wealthy, allied to the high priests and leading sacerdotal families (*Ant.* 13.296, 298; 18.4; 20.199; Acts 5.17, etc.). It is this association with the Zadokite priesthood that is no doubt responsible for their name *ẓadduqim*, or Sadducees. As true aristocrats, they were conservative. Standing firm by the written law, they tended to apply it in its original strictness and severity, resisting the innovations attempted by their opponents in the guise of Bible exegesis (*Ant.* 13.294, 296; 18.16; 20.199). Apart from the short rule of Queen Alexandra Salome or Shelamzion (76–67 BCE), who surrounded herself with Pharisees, the political and religious influence of the Sadducees predominated in the high court and senate of Judaea, the Jerusalem Sanhedrin, from the time when John Hyrcanus I (134–104 BCE) joined their ranks to the outbreak of the first revolution against Rome in CE 66.

A scholarly endeavour to identify the Qumran Community with this group does not seem *a priori* impossible. Both parties flourished during the same period. Both had, or claimed to possess, close bonds with the priesthood, the Sadducees appearing as regular supporters and champions of the pontifical leadership in Jerusalem and the Qumran sectaries subjecting themselves to the supreme authority of the priests, the sons of Zadok, assisted by the lay members of their Covenant. In particular, some of the laws set out in 4QMMT strongly resemble Sadducee practice as opposed to that of the Pharisees.[5]

These resemblances, however, are heavily outweighed by dissimilarities between the two groups. Thus the Sadducees are described in Greek as a *hairesis*, a sect (*Ant.* 13.171; Acts 5.17), but there is no indication whatever of their having had any sectarian organization like that of the Qumran Community. Again, the Qumran Community knew itself as 'the Poor' (1QpHab 12.3, 6), the very opposite of the condition of the Sadducee movement. Also, the Sadducees were nearly always the governing party in Judaea, whereas the Qumran brotherhood considered their existence as spent in exile. Finally, whilst Sadducee High Priests and their associates were the principal figures in the Temple of Jerusalem, one branch of the Dead Sea sect, the Zadokites of the desert, looked on the Sanctuary as contaminated, and on worship offered there as an abomination, and refused to have anything to do with it. Their dream was of the day, in the seventh year of the eschatological war, when all that wicked priesthood would be swept away and replaced by holy priests and a pure divine office. Also angels are everywhere in the Scrolls and the doctrine of resurrection seems attested, while the Sadducees are said to have disbelieved in both (Acts 23.8). It is safe enough therefore to assert that the Qumran sectaries were emphatically not Sadducees.

The Pharisees

According to the popular Jewish view, traceable to an uncritical acceptance of the information contained in rabbinic literature, the Pharisees from the second century BCE onwards were the doctrinal leaders of the nation, occupied as a rule both the presidency and vice-presidency of the Jerusalem Sanhedrin, and exercised absolute and effective control over Palestinian Jewry.[6] The Pharisee, moreover, was a man whose strict observance of the entire Mosaic Law, of the written Bible as well as of the revelation received on Sinai and transmitted by oral tradition, was inspired by deep learning and piety. The Christian popular concept, derived from the polemical exaggerations of Matthew 23, is very different: Pharisaism was an amalgam of hypocrisy, ambition and narrow-mindedness, an overwhelming concern with the minutiae of religion and a consequent neglect of its essence. 'Woe to you, scribes and Pharisees, hypocrites! for you tithe mint and dill and cummin, and have neglected the weightier matters of the law, justice and mercy and faith' (Matt. 23.23). Needless to say, both these portraits, Jewish and Christian, distort historical reality.

Josephus, who himself decided to embrace Pharisaism despite his priestly descent (*Life* 1.12), asserts that at the beginning of the reign of Herod, the Pharisees were a sect, a *hairesis*, numbering hardly more than six thousand members. They were therefore slightly more numerous than the Essene brotherhood with its four thousand adherents. By no stretch of the imagination can they be represented as the bulk of the Jewish nation. Their nickname may also point to their sectarian nature. For although rabbinic sources very seldom employ it, preferring to allude to them as scribes or sages, Josephus and the New Testament regularly use the title Pharisee. This word, *parish* in Aramaic and *parush* in Hebrew, signifies a separated person, and is in all probability intended to convey the meaning of one who keeps himself apart from the common people, from the peasants or *'am ha-arez*. The Pharisees, in short, were a fairly small learned and pious enclave within Jewish society.

Yet though their numbers were restricted, their influence was unquestionably great, above all in the towns and cities (*Ant.* 18.15). In particular, they enjoyed high renown for their expertise in the interpretation of the Bible, and especially of biblical law; when the ancient sources take the trouble to reveal the party allegiance of great teachers such as Pollion and his pupil Samaias, Gamaliel and his son Simeon, each of them turns out to be a Pharisee (*Ant.* 15.3, 370; *Life* 191; Acts 5.34).

Josephus also discloses that the Pharisees were popular (*Ant.* 12.294) and that they were liked by devout women (17.41). In matters of worship their teaching was regularly followed (18.15), and in public functions even the Sadducees adopted their rulings 'since otherwise the masses would not tolerate them' (18.17). But Pharisee piety was extra zealous in matters pertaining to dietary laws, tithing and ritual purity, all of which necessitated continuous attention to petty details. It had nevertheless not been the intention of the creators of Pharisaism, noble characters such as Antigonus of Sokho, Hillel, or Gamaliel the Elder, to lose sight of the essence of religion. Rather was it the reverse; the status of every Pharisee was ideally to be raised to the dignity of a Temple priest, and his table to the holiness of God's table in Jerusalem.

To pursue these aims, some Pharisees formed themselves into closed fellowships or *haburoth* to which new members were admitted after a trial period varying from thirty days to a year, though where candidates were familiar with the rules of the *haburah* and accustomed to practising them, they could be admitted immediately.[7] Once accepted, a man could be either a *ne'eman*, a 'trustworthy man', or a *haber*, a fellow. A *ne'eman* was obliged merely to tithe everything bought, sold and eaten by him, and to refrain from staying in the house of a non-initiate. A *haber* was required to submit in his daily life to the stringent rules of levitical purity to which the priests were subject when partaking of their sacred meals.

Membership of the *haburah* was thought to be incompatible with certain professions considered dishonourable. If a *haber* became a tax-collector, he was expelled. If, on the other hand, he resigned from this detested calling, he could re-enter as a 'trustworthy man', though not as a fellow.

These fragments of information provide no more than an outline of the complex reality of Pharisaism, but they show parallels with the

Qumran sect. The Pharisees and the people at Qumran were devout, consecrated to the study and practice of biblical religion; both parties aimed at purity and holiness and kept themselves apart in order to attain to it. In connection with the initiation of new members and the rejection of the unworthy, other similarities are evident, more general than distinctive. Yet, although these coincidences reveal common aspirations and possibly a common origin, the most important Qumran features are lacking in documents relating to the Pharisees.

One of these is the placing of ultimate authority at Qumran in the hands of the priests: the Pharisees were essentially a lay organization. Some Pharisees belonged to priestly families – Josephus was one of them – but this appears to have been the exception rather than the rule. Another difference is that whereas the Qumran sectaries and the Pharisees set themselves apart from the common people, the Pharisees continued to be involved with them and to teach them, while the Dead Sea brotherhood reserved the treasures of their doctrine for initiates alone. Also, although admission to the Pharisee *ḥaburah* proceeded by stages, they were more elastic than their Qumran counterparts; the Pharisee could, for instance, enter without undergoing a period of formal training or 'noviciate'. And again, there is no hint in accounts of the Pharisees of the common ownership of property so emphatically stressed in the Community Rule as a precondition to membership.

Last but not least, celibacy at Qumran cannot be ruled out and remains indeed highly probable. Among the Pharisees such a custom not only did not exist but was disapproved of in principle – if, that is to say, we are allowed to see in them the source of the firmly established and strongly held view of their rabbinic successors that procreation is a religious duty. 'Be fruitful and multiply,' they taught, is the first commandment proclaimed by God, and voluntary abstention from it is tantamount for murder.[8]

Were the Qumran sectaries Pharisees? The answer is no.

The Zealots

The theory claiming that the Qumran sectaries were Zealots, i.e. members of the revolutionary movement initiated at the beginning of the Christian era by Judas the Galilean, was advanced in Oxford from the end of the 1950s by the late Sir Godfrey Driver and the late Cecil Roth and more recently revived with an odd Christian twist by Robert Eisenman in California.

A proper assessment of this idea is made the more difficult in that academic opinion concerning the Zealots is confused.[9] There are two principal reasons for this. First, the evidence of the main source, Josephus, is tendentious. He hated the Zealots and held them fully responsible for the disaster of 70 CE. For him they were nothing but brigands and murderers. Secondly, the title 'Zealot' is an umbrella notion under which all sorts of revolutionaries sheltered. Recently matters have become even more chaotic as a result of attempts to supplement Josephus's meagre information on Zealot teaching with a concatenation of data borrowed from later rabbinic sources. On the other hand, while admitting the fluidity of both the terminology and the historical realities, enough essential information undoubtedly exists for a basic outline of the 'philosophical school', or religious party, of the Zealots to be reconstructed.

Josephus writes that in 6 CE, after complaints lodged against him by Jewish and Samaritan dignitaries had resulted in the banishment of Herod Archelaus, ethnarch of the Jews, Judaea was converted into a Roman province. This administrative change was preceded by a registration or census for purposes of taxation ordered and executed by the legate of Syria, Publius Sulpicius Quirinius. (The Gospel of Luke wrongly places this event in the reign of Herod the Great, who died ten years earlier.) To Judas the Galilean and to a Pharisee called Zadok, such a census appeared intolerable, and they advocated rebellion and launched a patriotic movement. Their manifesto was short: God is the one Lord, therefore no tribute must be paid to anyone else, including the emperor of Rome. Apart from these two dogmatic points, one positive and the other negative, Josephus has little to add to their Zealot 'philosophy', and even that seems to be contradictory. As an illustration, in his earlier account (*War* 2.118) he asserts that the Zealots are unlike anything else in Judaism; then some twenty years later (*Ant.* 15.23) he represents them as a group indistinguishable from the Pharisees except for their burning passion for freedom. He does not give a name to the movement started by Judas, but makes it clear in sundry references that Judas's rebellious spirit was shared by other members of his family. Judas himself was killed (Acts 5.37); two of his sons, Jacob and Simon,

were crucified by Tiberius Julius Alexander, procurator of Judaea
(46–48 CE); more relations took part in the first war against the
Romans, as will be indicated presently. The title 'Zealot' definitely
existed earlier in the first century; one of the apostles of Jesus was called
Simon the Zealot (Luke 6.15; Acts 1.13), or *Kananaios* (Matt. 10.4, a
garbled Greek transliteration of the Aramaic *qannai* = Zealot) – but
positive evidence for its use by the revolutionaries dates only to the time
of the war of 66–70 CE (*War* 4.160). A few years earlier, a faction
associated with the family of Judas the Galilean had been active, known
as *Sicarii*, men armed with a *sica*, a curved dagger (*War* 2.254). These
had supported Menahem, the last surviving son of Judas the Galilean,
in his attempt to seize the leadership of the uprising. When he was
murdered in Jerusalem (*War* 2.433–48), they established themselves in
the fortress of Masada under the command of Eleazar the son of Jairus,
probably a grandson of Judas, and from there carried on the fight with
the Romans until 74 CE.[10]

A few arguments can be adduced in favour of identifying the Qumran
sect as Zealots.[11] The final adversaries mentioned in the War Scroll are
Kittim/Romans led by a 'king'. More support comes from the discovery
of a Qumran sectarian writing (Songs for the Holocaust of the Sabbath),
first attested in Cave 4, in the ruins of the Zealot stronghold of Masada.
But as proofs they are hardly convincing. Archaeological evidence
shows in any case that the Qumran establishment was occupied from
about 140 BCE while the Zealot party did not come into being until 6
CE. If it were identical with the Community of the Scrolls, there would
have been visible changes at one point in the Qumran settlement which
the excavations have not in fact confirmed. Besides, the general description of the Community as it emerges from its literature has nothing in
common with the Zealots and their aims and aspirations, though no
real comparison can be made because nothing is known of the Zealot
organization, the reason perhaps being that as an underground movement they could not afford to possess an identifiable structure.

As for the discovery of a Qumran writing at Masada, it does not *ipso
facto* equate the inhabitants of the Dead Sea establishment with the
garrison of Masada. It is more likely to mean either that some of the
Qumran sectaries made common cause with the revolution during the
last stage of the Community's history and brought their manuscripts to
Masada with them, or that the Masada rebels considered the Qumran

Community politically unreliable and seized its settlement as the Romans advanced towards the Dead Sea.

In short, identification of the Qumran sectaries as Zealots is without any solid basis, and the attempt made by Driver and Roth to expound various cryptic historical allusions in the Scrolls as pointing to events that took place during the first Jewish revolution is without recognizable substance. The fresh venture by Robert Eisenman is unlikely to be any more successful.

The Essenes

The Essenes, who are not mentioned in the New Testament, are extensively described by Josephus and his older contemporary, the Jewish philosopher Philo of Alexandria. Another first-century author, the Roman geographer and naturalist Pliny the Elder, devotes only one paragraph to them, but those few lines include information of inestimable value.[12]

Unlike the three other religious parties discussed here, the Essenes formed a sect proper. They lived on the fringes of Jewish society as an esoteric community and imposed a lengthy initiation on aspiring candidates. Chronologically, Josephus first introduces them as one of three groups – the other two being the Pharisees and the Sadducees – in the middle of the second century BCE under Jonathan Maccabaeus (*Ant.* 13.171), and continues to attest their existence until his own time. Indeed, he himself experimented with the Essene way of life when he was sixteen years old, i.e. *circa* 53–54 CE (*Life* 10–11). Josephus and Philo locate the sect in Palestine (*War* 2.114; *Probus* 75–6; *Hypothetica* 11.1), and both estimate that it numbered over four thousand souls (*Ant.* 18.21; *Probus* 75). Pliny places the Essenes by the Dead Sea on the western shore between Jericho and Engedi (*Natural History* 5.73).

The sect was rigorously organized. Its superiors were elected. Reception into its ranks proceeded by degrees; every novice had to undergo a year of probation before being permitted to take part in the ritual ablutions and, following this, a further two years of training. He had then to make his vows as a full member and was accepted at the common table. If he subsequently offended against the rule in grave matters, he was excommunicated by a community tribunal composed of one hundred judges.

The Essenes practised a kind of communism. The fully professed members were required to hand over their belongings and earnings to stewards, and all their needs were met. Buying and selling was thereby exduded among themselves, and if Philo is to be believed, even with outsiders. Pliny also asserts that the Essenes lived *sine pecunia*, without money.

All three ancient witnesses are unanimous in their testimony that the Essenes shunned marriage and chose celibacy. In Pliny's words, they lived *sine venere*, without sex. Josephus, however, adds that there was in addition a branch of married Essenes.

Another Essene feature was their critical attitude to the Temple. Philo alludes to their rejection of animal sacrifice. Josephus is more equivocal; on the one hand he reports that they sent offerings to the sanctuary, but in the next sentence we are told that they kept away from its precincts and substituted their own worship for that in Jerusalem. Also, instead of the ritual washing of hands, they took purificatory baths before eating like the priests in the Temple. Their meals, according to Josephus, were special and solemn, and were eaten in refectories open, like sanctuaries, to initiates only. Sacred white garments were worn, and priests – who also prepared the simple food – recited grace before and after the meal.

The Essenes were opposed to slavery. They were also against taking vows, except of course the formidable oath sworn on reception into the sect by which they undertook, among other obligations, not to divulge their peculiar doctrines to non-members. They observed the Sabbath and obeyed the laws of purity more punctiliously than the rest of Jewry. Another of their specialities, one that would appear to argue the derivation of their Greek name *Essaioi* from the Aramaic *asayya*, 'healers',[13] was an interest in healing implied by Josephus's reference to their expert knowledge of the medicinal properties of roots and stones.

In view of the undeniable similarities and overlaps between the sect of the Scrolls and the Essenism of the classical accounts, it is not surprising that ever since the early days of Qumran a strong school of thought has regarded the two as identical.[14] Its case is as follows:

Josephus's testimony concerning the Essenes, and the archaeological finds made at Qumran, point to the same chronological context: from the middle of the second century BCE to the first Jewish war (66–70 CE).

Likewise, Pliny's location of the Essene village appears to correspond to the Qumran site; but here some explanation is called for. Pliny first mentions Jericho, then the Essenes by the Dead Sea, then Engedi 'below them' (*infra hos Engada*), a town situated twenty-eight miles south of Jericho; and finally Masada, south of Engedi. The general direction of his description is therefore from north to south. But what does the phrase 'below them' mean? It may be interpreted in two senses. Literally, it could indicate that the Essenes lived in the vicinity of Engedi, on some place high above the town. If so, the Qumran site is excluded, since it lies twenty miles north of Engedi. But the likelihood of an Essene establishment near Engedi is in any case slender. A thorough exploration of the area by Benjamin Mazar and his team of Israeli archaeologists in the early 1960s revealed no ruins remotely connected with Pliny's account. On the other hand, if 'below them' means 'south of them', or 'further down', or 'downstream', in the context of Pliny's journey southward, then Qumran fits perfectly: travelling eight miles south of Jericho we come to Qumran; twenty miles south of Qumran, to Engedi; and eleven miles south of Engedi, to Masada. In view of the importance of the Qumran archaeological site, Pliny's evidence offers a powerful argument in favour of the Essene thesis.[15]

Then there is the information contained in the Scrolls themselves, which on many points coincides with the Greek and Latin reports on the Essenes; though there are also differences. Thus Essenes and Qumran desert sectaries both favoured the common ownership of property, both refused to participate in Temple worship, both had purificatory baths, both partook of a sacred meal blessed by a priest. Both furthermore were opposed to taking vows apart from the vow of entry, and both appear to have been interested in healing (in the Scrolls it figures at the head of the spiritual blessings). As for celibacy, although it is not positively referred to in the Qumran Community Rule, its probability in the brotherhood has been shown to be great.[16]

Geography, chronology, and especially organization and customs, therefore militate in favour of a close relationship between Essenism and Qumran: at the very least they both belong to the same general movement. But before suggesting that we have here something more, the conflicting evidence must also be confronted honestly.

Some of the difficulties arise from internal contradictions. For instance, the Community Rule envisages common ownership, but the Damascus Document also legislates in matters of private property. Or while Pliny, Philo and Josephus emphasize that the Essenes were celibate, Josephus admits elsewhere that there were also married sectaries. Again, Philo, and Josephus in his later work (*Antiquities*), state that the Essenes were opposed to slavery; but Josephus in his earlier and much more detailed account (*War*) says nothing of this. The Damascus Document, on the other hand, implies, by its ban on the sale to a Gentile of a slave converted to Judaism, that such slaves may have been owned by members of the Dead Sea sect.

Other points of difference exist between the Scrolls and the Graeco-Latin documents. In the latter, the sectaries are called Essenes, a title completely absent from the Hebrew-Aramaic sources. At Qumran, the oath is the first act in the initiation procedure; among the Essenes of Josephus it is the last.

Apart from the possibility that some of the discrepancies may represent various stages of development, this lack of conformity between the classical evidence and the Scrolls may be attributed to two causes: the varying reliability of the witnesses and the diversity of the readership addressed.

Pliny, Philo and Josephus are not fully trustworthy. This is not to say that they deceive deliberately, though Philo in particular is apt to force his story so that it illustrates some cherished philosophical principle. For example, he mentions in *Probus* 76 that the Essenes avoided the cities, a habit of which he approved. Yet in *Hypothetica* 11.1 he writes that they lived 'in many towns of Judaea'. But even if all three had intended to tell the whole unadulterated truth, it would not have been in their power. Neither of them was a full member of the Essene sect, so neither was privy to its secret teachings. Nor as non-initiates would they have understood in any depth the Essene customs with which they were superficially familiar.

As far as the readership of the two types of literature is concerned, the fact that the Scrolls were directed to internal use among the sectaries themselves, whereas Philo, Josephus and Pliny wrote for non-Essenes and even largely for non-Jews, is bound to have affected the presentation of their material. Thus Josephus reports on the Essene abstinence from vows (though he knows of the vow taken on admission), and from animal sacrifice, and also on their frequent purificatory baths, with a view to presenting the sectaries as Jewish equivalents to the Pythagoreans, a much admired Hellenistic philosophico-religious group renowned for such practices. That this is not speculation, and that Josephus actually intended to portray his Jewish 'philosophies' as comparable to Greek schools of thought, is patent to anyone familiar with his description of the Pharisees as quasi-Stoics (*Life* 12), and of the Essenes as 'a group which follows a way of life taught to the Greeks by Pythagoras' (*Ant.* 15.371).

When these observations are borne in mind, most of the conflicts can be solved without difficulty. The contradictions between celibacy and marriage (Josephus testifies unwillingly, as it were, to the same duality of practice) and between communism and private ownership are to be seen in the context of the difference between the strict discipline of the members who lived at Qumran and the less demanding regulations followed by the other adepts of the Covenant. The discrepant information about when the oath was sworn may be due to Josephus's desire to emphasize the secret character of the Essene association. Similarly, the Scrolls impart a new meaning to the confused classical information in that the War Scroll makes it plain that, where it existed, the ban on Temple worship was not absolute but temporary, and valid only while the Temple was in the hands of the wicked priests.

As for the absence of the word 'Essene' from the Scrolls, the title 'Pharisee' is likewise generally avoided in rabbinic sources. Both names appear to have been coined and used by outsiders. So the non-employment of the Hebrew/Aramaic word for 'Essene' cannot be used as an argument against the Essene thesis.[17]

The final verdict must therefore be that of the proposed solutions, the Essene theory, despite recent efforts to discredit it, remains relatively the soundest. It is even safe to say that it possesses a high degree of intrinsic probability. The only remaining alternative is that the archaeologists have uncovered relics of a hitherto totally unknown Jewish sect almost identical to the Essenes; which reminds one of the story of the Old Testament scholar who would not accept that Joshua led the Israelites in the conquest of Canaan and argued that the real leader was a cousin who happened to bear the same name.[18]

6

The History of the Community

The absence from the Dead Sea Scrolls of historical texts proper should not surprise us. Neither in the inter-testamental period, nor in earlier biblical times, was the recording of history as we understand it a strong point among the Jews. Chroniclers are concerned not with factual information about bygone events, but with their religious significance. In scripture, the 'secular' past is viewed and interpreted by the prophets as revealing God's pleasure or displeasure. Victory or defeat in war, peace or social unrest, abundance of harvest or famine, serve to demonstrate the virtue or sinfulness of the nation and to forecast its future destiny. And when prophecy declined in the fifth century BCE, it was still not succeeded by a growth of historiography: only the memoirs of Ezra and Nehemiah and the retelling of the age-old stories of the kings of Israel and Judah in the Books of Chronicles belong to the historical *genre*. It was followed instead by eschatological speculation, by apocalyptic visions of the end of time, with its awe-inspiring beasts and battles, and by announcements of the ultimate triumph of truth and justice in a future kingdom of God.

In the Scrolls, the apocalyptic compositions form part of this later tradition. On the other hand, most of the knowledge we possess of the sect's history is inserted into works of Bible interpretation. The Qumran writers, while meditating on the words of the Old Testament prophets, sought to discover in them allusions to their own past, present and future. Convinced that they were living in the last days, they read the happenings of their times as the fulfilment of biblical predictions. Further scraps of historical references have survived in liturgical calendars (4Q322, 324) and in a poetic prayer (4Q448).

Yet all that these non-historical sources provide are fragments. Even with the help of the archaeological data from Qumran they cannot be made into a consistent and continuous narrative. For an understanding

of the sect's past as it developed within the larger framework of inter-
testamental Jewish history, we have to rely principally on Flavius
Josephus, the Palestinian Jew who became a Greek man of letters, and
on other Jewish Hellenists, such as the authors of the Books of the
Maccahees, and Philo of Alexandria, all of whom inherited the Greek
predilection for recording and interpreting the past and set out to depict
the life of the Jews of Palestine in itself, and as part of the Graeco-
Roman world, from the early second century BCE to the first anti-
Roman war in 66–70 CE. It is only with the help of the wider canvas
painted by these ancient scholars that places can be found for the often
cryptic historical indications contained in the Scrolls.

Inter-testamental Jewish history: 200 BCE–70 CE

At the beginning of the second century BCE, Palestinian Jewry passed
through a state of crisis.[1] Alexander the Great had conquered the Holy
Land in 332 BCE, and after the early uncertainties which followed his
death, it became part of the empire of the Greeks of Egypt, the
Ptolemies. During the third century, the Ptolemies avoided, as much as
possible, interfering with the internal life of the Jewish nation and, while
taxes were required to be paid, it remained under the rule of the High
Priest and his council. Important changes in the patterns of population
nevertheless took place during this time. Hellenistic cities were built
along the Mediterranean coast, such as Gaza, Ascalon (Ashkelon),
Joppa (Jaffa), Dor, and Acco, renamed Ptolemais. Inland also, to the
south of the Lake of Tiberias, the ancient town of Beth Shean was
reborn as the Greek city of Scythopolis; Samaria, the capital city of the
Samaritans, was Hellenized as Sebaste; and in Transjordan, Rabbath-
Ammon (Amman) was re-founded as Philadelphia. In other words,
Greeks, Macedonians and Hellenized Phoenicians took up permanent
residence on Palestinian soil and the further spread of Greek civlization
and culture was merely a matter of time.

With the conquest of the Holy Land by the Seleucids, or Syrian
Greeks, in 200 BCE, the first signs appeared of Jews succumbing to a
foreign cultural influence. In the apocryphal Book of Ecclesiasticus
dated to the beginning of the second century BCE, its author, Jesus ben
Sira, a sage from Jerusalem, rages against those 'ungodly men' who have

'forsaken the Law of the Most High God' (41.8). But the real trouble started when Antiochus IV Epiphanes (175–164 BCE) officially promoted a Hellenizing programme in Judaea that was embraced with eagerness by the Jewish elite. The leader of the modernist faction was the brother of the High Priest Onias III. Known as Jesus among his compatriots, he adopted the Greek name of Jason, and set about transforming Jerusalem into a Hellenistic city, building a gymnasium there and persuading the Jewish youth to participate in athletic games. As II Maccabees describes the situation:

> So Hellenism reached a high point with the introduction of foreign customs through the boundless wickedness of the impious Jason, no true High Priest. As a result, the priests no longer had any enthusiasm for their duties at the altar, but despised the temple and neglected the sacrifices; and in defiance of the law they eagerly contributed to the expenses of the wrestling-school whenever the opening gong called them. They placed no value on their hereditary dignities, but cared above everything for Hellenic honours (II Macc. 4.13–15).

Jason was succeeded by two other High Priests with the same Greek sympathies, Menelaus and Alcimus. In 169 BCE Antiochus IV visited Jerusalem and looted the Temple. But when in 167 he actually prohibited the practice of Judaism under pain of death and re-dedicated the Jerusalem Sanctuary to Olympian Zeus, the 'abomination of desolation', the opponents of the Hellenizers finally rose up in violent resistance. An armed revolt was instigated by the priest Mattathias and his sons the Maccabee brothers, supported by all the traditionalist Jews, and in particular by the company of the Pious, the Asidaeans or Hasidim, 'stalwarts of Israel, every one of them a volunteer in the cause of the Law' (I Macc. 2.42–43). Led by Judas Maccabaeus and, after his death on the battlefield, by his brothers Jonathan and Simon, the fierce defenders of Judaism were able not only to restore Jewish worship in Jerusalem, but against all expectations even managed to eject the ruling Seleucids and to liberate Judaea.

The Maccabaean triumph was not, however, simply a straightforward victory of godliness and justice over idolatry and tyranny; it was accompanied by serious social and religious upheavals. There was first a change in the pontifical succession. With the murder in 171 BCE of

Onias III and the deposition of the usurper, his brother Jason, the Zadokite family, from which the incumbents of the High Priest's office traditionally came, lost the monopoly which it had held for centuries. Furthermore, when Onias IV, the son of Onias III, was prevented from taking over the High Priesthood from Menelaus, he emigrated to Egypt and in direct breach of biblical law, authorizing only a single sanctuary in Jerusalem, erected a Jewish temple in Leontopolis with the blessing of King Ptolemy Philometor (182–146 BCE). His inauguration of Israelite worship outside Zion, with the connivance of some priests and Levites, must have scandalized every Palestinian conservative, even those priests who belonged, or were allied, to the Zadokite dynasty.

There was trouble also within the ranks of the Maccabaean party. The Hasidim – or part of their group – defected when Alcimus whom they trusted was appointed High Priest in 162 BCE. This move on their part turned out to be naive; Alcimus's Syrian allies massacred sixty of them in one day (I Macc. 7.12–20).

Lastly, a major political change came about when Jonathan Maccabaeus, himself a priest but not a Zadokite, in 153–2 BCE accepted pontifical office from Alexander Balas, a usurper of the Seleucid throne. Alexander was anxious for Jewish support and was not mistaken in thinking that an offer of the High Priesthood would be irresistible. For the conservatives this was an illegal seizure of power. But they were even more scandalized by the appointment in 140 BCE, following Jonathan's execution in 143–2 by the Syrian general Tryphon, of Simon Maccabaeus as High Priest and hereditary leader of the people by means of a decree passed by a Jewish national assembly.

From then on, until Pompey's transformation of the independent Jewish state into a Roman province in 63 BCE, Judaea was ruled by a new dynasty of high priests, later priest-kings, known as the Hasmonaeans after the grandfather of the Maccabees, Hasmon, or Asamonaeus according to Josephus, *War* 1.36. During the intervening years, all Simon's successors, but especially John Hyrcanus I (134–104 BCE) and Alexander Jannaeus (103–76 BCE), for whom their political role took precedence over their office of High Priest, occupied one by one the Hellenistic cities of Palestine and conquered the neighbouring territories of Idumaea in the south, Samaria in the centre and Ituraea in the north.

Throughout this period of territorial expansion, the Hasmonaean rulers enjoyed the support of the Sadducees, one of the three religious parties first mentioned under Jonathan Maccabaeus (cf. Josephus, *Ant.* 13.171) and regular allies of the government. They were opposed by the Pharisees, an essentially lay group formed from one of the branches of the Hasidim of the Maccabaean age. Already in the days of John Hyrcanus I there was Pharisaic objection to his usurpation of the high priesthood, though they were willing to recognize him as national leader *(Ant.* 13.288–98), but on one other occasion, at least, their opposition was overcome by force. Accused of plotting against Alexander Jannaeus in 88 BCE in collusion with the Syrian Seleucid king Demetrius III Eucaerus, eight hundred Pharisees were condemned by Jannaeus to die on the cross (*Ant.* 13.380–3; *War* 1.96–8).

After Pompey's seizure of Jerusalem, the Hasmonaean High Priesthood continued for another three decades, but the political power formerly belonging to them passed to the Judaized Idumaean, Herod the Great, when he was promoted to the throne of Jerusalem by Rome in 37 BCE. It is to the last year or two of his reign – he died in 4 BCE – that the Gospels of Matthew and Luke date the birth of Jesus of Nazareth (Matt. 2.1; Luke 1.15).

After the ephemeral rule of the successor to Herod the Great, Herod Archelaus (4 BCE–6 CE), who was deposed by Augustus for his mis-government of Jews and Samaritans alike, Galilee continued in semi-autonomy under the Herodian princes Antipas (4 BCE–39 CE) and Agrippa (39–41 CE), but Judaea was placed under the direct adminis-tration of Roman authority. In 6 CE, Coponius, the first Roman prefect of Judaea, arrived to take up his duties there. This prefectorial regime, whose most notorious representative was Pontius Pilate (26–36 CE), lasted for thirty-five years until 41, when the emperor Claudius appointed Agrippa I as king. He died, however, three years later, and in 44 CE the government of the province once more reverted to Roman officials, this time with the title of procurator. Their corrupt and unwise handling of Jewish affairs was one of the chief causes of the war of 66 which led to the destruction of Jerusalem in 70 CE, and to the subsequent decline of the Sadducees, the extinction of the Zealots in Masada in 74, the disappearance of the Essenes, and the survival and uncontested domination of the Pharisees and their rabbinic succes-sors.

It is into this general course of events that the history of Qumran has to be inserted. Document by document the Scrolls will be scrutinized and the literary information combined both with the findings of Qumran archaeology and with the incidental reports provided by Josephus. In the end it is hoped that the history of the Essene sect will begin to fall reliably into place.

The history of the Essenes[2]

1. *Concealed references in the Scrolls*

The search for clues to the origins and story of the movement begins with the Damascus Document, because it is a document particularly rich in such hints. Here, the birth of the Community is said to have occurred in the 'age of wrath', 390 years after the destruction of Jerusalem by Nebuchadnezzar, king of Babylon.[3] At that time, a 'root' sprung 'from Israel and Aaron', i.e. a group of pious Jews, laymen and priests, came into being in a situation of general ungodliness. These people 'groped for the way' for twenty years, and then God sent them a 'Teacher of Righteousness' to guide them 'in the way of His heart' (1.5–11). The Teacher did not meet with unanimous approval within the congregation, and a faction described as 'seekers of smooth things', 'removers of the bounds' and 'builders of the wall', all metaphors seeming to point to religious laxity and infidelity, turned against him and his followers. The leader of the breakaway party, though accorded a number of unflattering sobriquets, such as 'Scoffer', 'Liar' or 'Spouter of Lies', seems to be one and the same person. His associates erred in matters of ritual cleanness, justice, chastity, the dates of festivals and Temple worship; they were lovers of money and enemies of peace. In the ensuing fratricidal struggle, the Teacher and those who remained faithful to him went into exile in the 'land of Damascus' where they entered into a 'new Covenant'. There, the Teacher of Righteousness was 'gathered in', meaning that he died. In the meantime, the wicked dominated over Jerusalem and the Temple, though not without experiencing God's vengeance at the hands of the 'Chief of the Kings of Greece'.

A similar picture emerges from the Habakkuk Commentary with its explicit reference to desertion by disciples of the Teacher of Righteousness to the Liar, but also by members unfaithful to the 'new Covenant'. The allusions to the protagonists of the conflict are sharper in this document than in the Damascus Document. We learn that the villain, known in this Scroll as the 'Wicked Priest' as well as the 'Liar' and 'Spouter of Lies', was 'called by the name of truth' before he became Israel's ruler and was corrupted by wealth and power (8.8–11) – the implication being that for a time he had met with the sect's approval. Subsequently, however, he defiled Jerusalem and the Temple. He also sinned against the Teacher of Righteousness and his disciples, chastizing him while the 'House of Absalom' looked silently on (5.9–12), and confronting him in his place of exile on the sect's Day of Atonement (11.6–8). He 'vilified and outraged the elect of God', 'plotted to destroy the Poor', i.e. the Community, and stole their riches. As a punishment, God delivered him 'into the hand of his enemies', who 'took vengeance on his body of flesh' (9.2). At the last judgment, predicts the Commentary, the Wicked Priest will empty 'the cup of wrath of God'. His successors, the 'last Priests of Jerusalem', are also charged with amassing 'money and wealth by plundering the peoples', i.e. foreigners. But, so the commentator asserts, all their riches and booty will be snatched from them by the Kittim, the conquerors of the world commissioned by God to pay them their just deserts.

Because of lacunae, one cannot be quite sure from the Habakkuk Commentary that the Teacher was a priest. The Commentary on Psalm 37 (4Q171,173), by contrast, makes this plain. Interpreting verses 23–4, it reads: 'this concerns the Priest, the Teacher of [Righteousness]'. It further supplies a significant detail by assigning to 'the violent of the nations', that is to say to the Gentiles as opposed to the Jews, the execution of judgment on the Wicked Priest. Another point of interest is that the enemies of the sect are alluded to as 'the wicked of Ephraim and Manasseh', i.e. as of two distinct factions. They also appear in the Commentary on Nahum.

In the Messianic Anthology or Testimonia (4Q175), references appear in the final section, borrowed from a Joshua Apocryphon, to two 'instruments of violence' who ruled Jerusalem. They are cursed for making the city a 'stronghold of ungodliness' and for committing 'an abomination' in the land. They are also said to have shed blood 'like water on the ramparts of the daughter of Zion'. The relationship of the two tyrants to one another cannot be established with certainty because of the fragmentary nature of the manuscript. They could be father and son. On the other hand, the expression 'instruments of violence' depends on Genesis 49, where it describes the brother murderers Simeon and Levi, the destroyers of Shechem.

The Nahum Commentary moves on to an age following that of the Teacher of Righteousness and the Wicked Priest, as neither of them is mentioned. The principal character here is the 'furious young lion', a Jewish ruler of Jerusalem. He is said to have taken revenge on the 'seekers of smooth things', whom he reproached for having invited 'Demetrius' the king of Greece to Jerusalem. The attempt failed; no foreigner entered the city 'from the time of Antiochus until the coming of the rulers of the Kittim'. The enemies of the 'furious young lion' were 'hanged alive on the tree', a familiar Hebrew circumlocution for crucifixion. As in the Commentary on Psalm 37, the sobriquets 'Ephraim' and 'Manasseh' are attached to the Community's opponents. 'Ephraim' is said to 'walk in lies and falsehood', but because of gaps in the manuscript, the description of 'Manasseh' is less clear. It seems nevertheless that this party included 'great men', 'mighty men', 'men of dignity'.

The Nahum Commentary was the first of the Qumran Scrolls to disclose historical names: those of two Seleucid kings, Antiochus and Demetrius. But their identity has still to be determined, because nine monarchs in all bore the first name, and three the second. Additional names figure in various Cave 4 manuscripts of a liturgical calendar (4Q322, 324a–b): 'Shelamzion', the Hebrew name of Queen Alexandra-Salome, widow of Alexander Jannaeus, who reigned from 76 to 67 BCE, 'Hyrcanus' and 'John', probably John Hyrcanus II, son of Alexandra and High Priest from 76 to 67 and again from 63 to 40; and 'Emilius', no doubt M. Aemilius Scaurus, the first Roman governor of Syria from 65 to 62 BCE, who is charged with killing people. Note also that the Balakros of 4Q343 may be Alexander Balas.

A remarkable piece of prayer-poetry (4Q448) refers to 'King Jonathan' in connection with Jerusalem and Diaspora Jewry. A good case has been made out by E. and H. Eshel for identifying him with Alexander Jannaeus, but in my opinion an even stronger argument points towards Jonathan Maccabaeus as 'King Jonathan'.[4] In the Commentaries on Habakkuk and Nahum, the Kittim are represented as instruments appointed by God to punish the ungodly priests of Jerusalem. The War Scroll, however, testifies to a changed attitude towards them on the part of the sect by making the Kittim appear as the chief allies of Satan and the final foe to be subjugated by the hosts of the sons of Light. The Book of War (4Q285), although very fragmentary, appears to point in the same direction.

Several Qumran Hymns reflect the career and sentiments of a teacher, possibly of the Teacher of Righteousness himself. According to them, he was opposed by 'interpreters of error', 'traitors', 'deceivers', by 'those who seek smooth things', all of whom were formerly his 'friends' and 'members of (his) Covenant', bearers of the 'yoke of (his) testimony'. In one of them, the reference to a 'devilish scheme' is reminiscent of the allusion in the Habakkuk Commentary to the visit of the Wicked Priest to the Community's place of exile in order to cause them 'to stumble':

Teachers of lies [have smoothed] Thy people with words
    and false prophets have led them astray . . .
They have banished me from my land
    like a bird from its nest . . .
    And they, teachers of lies and seers of falsehood,
    have schemed against me a devilish scheme,
to exchange the Law engraved on my heart by Thee
    for the smooth things [which thy speak] to Thy people.
And they withhold from the thirsty the drink of knowledge,
    and assuage their thirst with vinegar,
that they may gaze on their straying,
    on their folly concerning their feast-days
    on their fall into the snares.

                      (1QH 4 [12].7–12)

Another Hymn appears to hint at the Teacher's withdrawal from society and to announce with confidence his eventual glorious justification:

For Thou, O God, hast sheltered me
    from the children of men,
and hast hidden Thy Law within me
    against the time when Thou shouldst reveal
    Thy salvation to me.

                      (1QH 5. [13].11–12)

Some scholars consider these poems autobiographical, i.e., written by the Teacher, but this is mere speculation.

It would be unrealistic, taking into account the vagueness of all these statements, the cryptic nature of the symbolism and the entire lack of any systematic exposition of the sect's history, to expect every detail to be identified. We can, however, attempt to define the chronological framework of the historical references and thus be in a position to place at least some of the key events and principal personalities within the context of Jewish history as we know it.

2. *The chronological framework*

The chronological setting of Qumran history may be reconstructed from archaeological and literary evidence. The excavations of 1951–6 date the beginning, the *terminus a quo,* of the sectarian establishment to 150–140 BCE and its end, the *terminus ad quem,* to the middle of the first war against Rome, 68 CE. The literary allusions, particularly the identifiable historical names, confirm this general finding. It goes without saying, however, that the initial phases of the Community's existence must have preceded the actual establishment of the sect at Qumran by some years or decades. The first task, therefore, is to examine the Scrolls for indications of its origins. The Nahum Commentary implies that a king by the name of Antiochus was alive at the beginning of the period with which the documents are concerned. This Antiochus, although one among several so called, can only have been Antiochus IV Epiphanes, notorious for his looting of Jerusalem and the profanation of the Temple in 169–168 BCE.

More significant as a chronological pointer is the dating, in the Damascus Document, of the sect's beginnings to the 'age of wrath', 390 years after the conquest of Jerusalem by Nebuchadnezzar in 586 BCE. This should bring us to 196 BCE, but, as is well known, Jewish historians are not very reliable in their time-reckoning for the post-exilic era. They do not seem to have had a clear idea of the length of the Persian domination, and in addition they were not free of the theological influence of the Book of Daniel, where a period of seventy weeks of years, i.e. 490 years, is given as separating the epoch of Nebuchadnezzar from that of the Messiah. As it happens, if to this figure of 390 years is added, first twenty (during which the ancestors of the Community 'groped' for their way until the entry on the scene of the Teacher of Righteousness), then another forty (the time span between the death of the Teacher and the dawn of the messianic epoch), the total stretch of years arrived at is 450. And if to this total is added the duration of the Teacher's ministry of, say, forty years – a customary round figure – the final result is the classic seventy times seven years.

Yet even if the literal figure of 390 is rejected, there are still compelling reasons for placing the 'age of wrath' in the opening decades of the second pre-Christian century. Only the Hellenistic crisis which occured at that time, and which is recalled in various Jewish literary sources from the last two centuries BCE, provides a fitting context for the historical allusions made in the sectarian writings (cf. Daniel 9–11; Enoch 90.6–7; Jubilees 23.14–19; Testament of Levi 17; Assumption of Moses 4–5). Also, it is the Hasidim of the pre-Maccabaean and early Maccabaean era who best correspond to the earlier but unorganized group as it is described there (cf. pp. 129–30).

As for the *terminus ad quem* of Qumran history, since this is linked to the appearance of the Kittim, we have to determine who these people were. In its primitive sense, the word 'Kittim' described the inhabitants of Kition, a Phoenician colony in Cyprus. Later the name tended to be applied indiscriminately to those living in 'all islands and most maritime countries' (Josephus, *Ant.* 1.128). But from the second century BCE, Jewish writers also used 'Kittim' more precisely to denote the greatest world power of the day. In I Maccabees (1.1; 8.5) they are Greeks: Alexander the Great and Perseus are called kings of the 'Kittim'. In Daniel 11.30, on the other hand, the 'Kittim' are Romans: it was the ambassador of the Roman senate, Poppilius Laenas, brought to Alexandria by 'ships of Kittim', who instructed the 'king of the North', the Seleucid monarch Antiochus Epiphanes, to withdraw at once from Egypt. The term 'Romans' is substituted for 'Kittim' already in the old Greek or Septuagint version of Daniel 11.30. None of these texts is critical of the 'Kittim'. They are seen as the ruling force of the time, but not as hostile to Israel. In fact, in Daniel they humiliate the enemy of the Jews. It is not till a later stage, especially after 70 CE, that they come to symbolize oppression and tyranny.

In the Habakkuk Commentary, the portrait of the Kittim is neutral, as in Maccabees and Daniel. (In the Damascus Document they play no part; the alien adversary there is the 'Chief of the Kings of Greece'.)

Feared and admired by all, they are seen to be on the point of defeating the 'last Priests of Jerusalem' and confiscating their wealth, as they have done to many others before. Such a representation of a victorious and advancing might would hardly apply to the Greek Seleucids of Syria, who by the second half of the second century BCE were in grave decline. But it does correspond to the Romans, whose thrust to the east in the first century BCE resulted in their triumphs over Pontus, Armenia and Seleucid Syria, and finally, with the arrival of Pompey in Jerusalem in 63 BCE in the transformation of the Hasmonaean state into Judaea, a province of the Roman republic.

Since the identification of the 'Kittim' as Romans is nowadays generally accepted,[5] it will suffice to cite a single, but very striking, feature in the Habakkuk Commentary to support it. Interpreting Hab.1.14–16 as referring to the 'Kittim', the commentator writes: 'This means that they sacrifice to their standards and worship their weapons of war' (1QpHab. 6.3–5). Now this custom of worshipping the *signa* was a characteristic of the religion of the Roman armies both in republican and in imperial times, as Josephus testifies in his report of the capture of the Temple of Jerusalem by the legionaries of Titus in 70.

> The Romans, now that the rebels had fled to the city, and the Sanctuary itself and all around it were in flames, carried their standards into the Temple court, and setting them up opposite the eastern gate, there sacrificed to them (*War* 6.316).

It is also worth noting that the 'Kittim' of the War Scroll, the final opponents of the eschatological Israel, are subject to a king or emperor *(melekh)*. Previously, in the Commentaries on Habukkuk and Nahum, they are said to have been governed by rulers *(moshelim)*.

In brief, the time-limits of the sect's history appear to be at one extreme the beginning of the second century BCE, and at the other some moment during the Roman imperial epoch, i.e. after 27 BCE. And this latter date is determined by Qumran archaeology as coinciding with the first Jewish war, and even more precisely, with the arrival of the armies of Vespasian and Titus in the neighbourhood of the Dead Sea in June 68 CE.

3. Decipherment of particular allusions

The 'age of wrath' having been identified as that of the Hellenistic crisis of the beginning of the second century BCE, the 'root' as the Hasidim of the pre-Maccabaean age, and the 'Kittim' as the Romans, the next major problem is to discover who was, or were, the principal Jewish enemy or enemies of the sect at the time of the ministry of the Teacher of Righteousness variously known as 'the Scoffer', 'the Liar', 'the Spouter of Lies' and 'the Wicked Priest' (1QpHab, 4QPs^a, CD).

It is not unreasonable to conclude that all these insults are directed at the same individual. It would appear from the Damascus Document that the 'Scoffer' and the 'Liar' (cf. also 4QPs^a [37]) were one and the same ('when the Scoffer arose who shed over Israel the waters of lies', CD 1.14). And we read of the 'Wicked Priest' that he was called 'by the name of truth' (1QpHab 8.8–9) at the outset of his career, the inference being that later he changed into a 'Liar'.

Another basic premise must be that the person intended by the fragments of information contained in the Scrolls became the head, the national leader, of the Jewish people. For although biblical names are often used symbolically, including that of 'Israel', the actions attributed to the 'Wicked Priest' make little sense if the person in question did not exercise both pontifical and secular power. He 'ruled over Israel'. He 'robbed . . . the riches of the men of violence who rebelled against God', probably Jewish apostates, as well as 'the wealth of the peoples', i.e. the Gentiles. He built 'his city of vanity with blood', committed 'abominable deeds in Jerusalem and defiled the Temple of God' (1QpHab). Taken separately, these observations might be understood allegorically, but considered together, they constitute a strong argument for recognizing the 'Wicked Priest' as a ruling High Priest in Jerusalem.

The 'Wicked Priest', then, was a Pontiff who enjoyed good repute before he assumed office. He was victorious over his adversaries at home and abroad. He rebuilt Jerusalem (cf. 1QpHab 8.8–11; 4Q448). And he was eventually captured and put to death by a foreign rival.

The chronological guide-lines established in the preceding section locate the period in which this individual flourished between the reign of Antiochus Epiphanes (175–164 BCE) and the probable date of the foundation at Qumran (150–140 BCE). During that time, five men held the office of High Priest. Three of them were pro-Greek: Jason,

Menelaus and Alcimus. The remaining two were the Maccabee brothers, Jonathan and Simon. All the Hellenizers can be eliminated as candidates for the role of 'Wicked Priest' since none can be said to have enjoyed anything like good repute at the beginning of their ministry. Jason and Alcimus also fail because neither was killed by an enemy as implied in 1QpHab 8–9. Jason died in exile (II Macc. 5.7–9) and Alcimus in office (I Macc. 9.54–56). The Maccabee brothers, by contrast, meet all the conditions. The careers of both men fall easily into two stages marked, in the case of Jonathan, by his acceptance of the high priesthood from Alexander Balas, and in the case of Simon, by his willingness to become a hereditary high priest. Both were also 'instruments of violence' and both died by violence. Jonathan is nevertheless to be chosen rather than Simon because he alone suffered the vengeance of the 'Chief of the Kings of Greece' and died at the hands of the 'violent of the nations', whereas Simon was murdered by his son-in-law (I Macc.16.14–16). A gallant defender of Jewish religion and independence, Jonathan succeeded the heroic Judas in 161 BCE when the latter fell in battle. But he qualified for the epithet 'Wicked Priest' when he accepted in 153–2 BCE from Alexander Balas, a heathen usurper of the Seleucid throne who had no right to grant them, the pontifical vestments which Jonathan was not entitled to wear. Captured later by a former general of Alexander Balas, Tryphon, he was killed at Bascama in Transjordan (I Macc. 13.23).

Concerning the identity of the 'last Priests of Jerusalem',[6] the passion for conquest, wealth and plunder for which they are reproached points to the Hasmonaean priestly rulers, from Simon's son, John Hyrcanus I (134–104 BCE), to Judas Aristobulus II (67–63 BCE). In particular there can be little doubt that the 'furious young lion', also designated 'the last Priest' in a badly damaged Commentary on Hosea (4QpHos 2.2–3), was one of them, namely Alexander Jannaeus. The application to him of the words of Nahum, 'who chokes prey for its lionesses', and the report that the 'young lion' executed the 'seekers of smooth things' by 'hanging men alive', accord perfectly with the known story that Jannaeus crucified eight hundred Pharisees whilst feasting with his concubines (cf. above, 131).

From this it follows that 'Ephraim', equated in the Commentary on Nahum with the 'seekers of smooth things', symbolizes the Pharisees, and that if so, 'Manasseh' and his dignitaries must refer to the

Sadducees. In other words, the political and doctrinal opponents of the Essene community, itself not without proto-Sadducaean links on account of its priestly leadership, were the Sadducees and the Pharisees.

This division of Jewish society into three opposing groups corresponds to the conformation described by Josephus as existing from the time of Jonathan Maccabaeus *(Ant.* 13.171), but the new insight provided by the Scrolls suggests that the united resistance to Hellenism first fell apart when the Maccabees, and more precisely Jonathan, refused to acknowledge the spiritual leadership of the Teacher of Righteousness, the priestly head of the Hasidim. From then on, the sect saw its defectors as 'Ephraim' and 'Manasseh', these being the names of the sons of Joseph, associated in biblical history with the apostate North of the kingdom, and referred to itself as the 'House of Judah', the faithful South.

Unfortunately, on the most vital topic of all, the question of the identity of the Teacher of Righteousness, we can be nothing like as clear. If the 'Wicked Priest' was Jonathan Maccabaeus, the Teacher would, of course, have been one of his contemporaries. Yet all we know of him is that he was a priest (1QpHab 2.8; 4Qp Ps^a [xxxvii II,15), though obviously opposed to Onias IV, since he did not follow him to Egypt and to his unlawful temple in Leontopolis.[7] He founded or refounded the Community. He transmitted to them his own distinctive interpretation of the Prophets and, if we can rely at least indirectly on the Hymns, of the laws relating to the celebration of festivals. The 'Liar' and his sympathizers in the congregation of the Hasidim disagreed with him, and after a violent confrontation between the two factions in which the 'Liar' gained the upper hand, the Teacher and his remaining followers fled to a place of refuge called 'the land of Damascus': it has been suggested that this is a cryptic designation of Babylonia, the original birth place of the group, or that 'Damascus' is a symbolic name for Qumran.[8] The 'House of Absalom' gave the Teacher of Righteousness no help against the 'Liar', writes the Habakkuk commentator (1QpHab 5.9–12), the implication being that this was support on which he might have relied. If 'Absalom' is also a symbol, it doubtless recalls the rebellion of Absalom against his father David, and thus points to the perfidy of a close relation or intimate friend of the Teacher. On the other hand, since the 'House of Absalom' is accused not of an actual attack but simply of remaining silent during the Teacher's 'chastisement', this allegorical solution may not be convincing. The allusion may then be a straightforward one. A certain Absalom was an ambassador of Judas Maccabaeus (II Macc. 11.17), and his son Mattathias was one of Jonathan's gallant officers (I Macc. 11.70). Another of his sons, Jonathan, commanded Simon's army which captured Joppa (I Macc. 13.11).

Meanwhile, even in his 'place of exile' the Teacher continued to be harassed and persecuted by the Wicked Priest. In this connection, the most important and painful episode appears to have been the Priest's pursuit of the Teacher to his settlement with the purpose of confusing him 'with his venomous fury'. Appearing before the sectaries on 'their sabbath of repose', at the 'time appointed for rest, for the Day of Atonement', his intention was to cause them 'to stumble on the Day of Fasting'. It is impossible to say, from the evidence so far available, precisely what happened on this portentous occasion, or whether it was then or later that the Wicked Priest 'laid hands' on the Teacher 'that he might put him to death'. The wording is equivocal. For example, the verb in 1QpHab 11.5,7 translated 'to confuse' can also mean 'to swallow up', and some scholars have chosen to understand that the Teacher was killed by the Wicked Priest at the time of the visit. On the other hand, we find recounted in the imperfect tense (which can be rendered in English into either the future or the present tense): 'The wicked of Ephraim and Manasseh . . . seek/will seek to lay hands on the Priest and the men of his Council . . . but God redeems/will redeem them from out of their hand' (4QpPs^a [37 2.17–19]). In other words, we neither know who the founder of the Essenes was, nor how, nor where, nor when he died.'[9]

It has been argued that this inability to identify the Teacher of Righteousness in the context of the Maccabaean period undermines the credibility of the reconstruction as a whole. Is it conceivable, it is asked, that a figure of the stature of the Teacher should have left no trace in the literature relating to that time? The answer to this objection is that such writings are to all intents and purposes restricted to the Books of the Maccabees, sources politically biassed in favour of their heroes and virtually oblivious of the very existence of opposition movements. Josephus himself relies largely on I Maccabees and cannot therefore be regarded as an independent witness. But even were this not so, and he had additonal material at his disposition, his silence *vis-à-vis* the

Teacher of Righteousness would still not call for particular comment, since he makes no mention of the founders of the Pharisees and Sadducees either. And incidentally, not a few historians hold that he has nothing to say of Jesus of Nazareth. The so-called Testimonium Flavianum *(Ant.* 18.63–64), they maintain, is a Christian interpolation into the genuine text of *Antiquities* (though others, myself included, think that part of the text is authentic).[10] Be this as it may, not a word is breathed by him about Hillel, the greatest of the Pharisee masters, or about Yohanan ben Zakkai, who re-organized Judaism after the destruction of the Temple, although both of these men lived in Josephus's own century and Yohanan was definitely his contemporary.

Admittedly, the various fragments of information gleaned from the Dead Sea Scrolls result in an unavoidably patchy story, but it is fundamentally sound, and the continuing anonymity of the Teacher does nothing to impair it. For the present synthesis to be complete it remains now to turn to Josephus for his occasional historical references to individual Essenes and to Essenism.[11]

To begin with, it should be pointed out that four members of the Community are actually mentioned by the Jewish historian, three of them associated with prophecy, one of the distinctive interests of the Teacher of Righteousness himself. The first, called Judas, is encountered in Jerusalem surrounded by a group of pupils taking instructions in 'foretelling the future', which probably means, in how to identify prophetic pointers to future events. Josephus writes of him that he had 'never been known to speak falsely in his prophecies', and that he predicted the death of Antigonus, the brother of Aristobulus I (104–103 BCE) *(Ant.* 13.311–13). A second Essene prophet, Menahem, apparently foretold that Herod would rule over the Jews (15.373–8). Herod showed his gratitude to him by dispensing the Essenes, who were opposed to all oaths except their own oath of the Covenant, from taking the vow of loyalty imposed on all his Jewish subjects. A third Essene named Simon interpreted a dream of Archelaus, ethnarch of Judaea (4 BCE–6CE), in 4 BCE to mean that his rule would last for ten years (17.345–8). John the Essene, the last sectary to be referred to by Josephus, was not a prophet, but the commander or *strategos* of the district of Thamna in north-western Judaea, and of the cities of Lydda (Lod), Joppa/Jaffa and Emmaus at the beginning of the first revolution

(War 2.567). A man of 'first-rate prowess and ability', he fell in battle at Ascalon (3.11, 19).[12]

Finally, Josephus depicts in vivid language the bravery of the Essenes subjected to torture by the Romans.

> The war with the Romans tried their souls through and through by every variety of test. Racked and twisted, burned and broken, and made to pass through every instrument of torture in order to induce them to blaspheme their lawgiver or to eat some forbidden thing, they refused to yield to either demand, nor ever once did they cringe to their persecutors or shed a rear. Smiling in their agonies and mildly deriding their tormentors, they cheerfully resigned their souls, confident that they would receive them back again *(War* 2.152–3).

Since it would appear from this passage that the Romans were persecuting not individuals, but a group, it is tempting, bearing in mind the archaeologists' claim that the Qumran settlement was destroyed by the Romans, to associate it with the story of Essenes captured by the Dead Sea. If such a surmise is correct, the sect's disappearance from history may well have been brought about in the lethal blow suffered by its central establishment during the fateful summer of 68 CE. The fact that no attempt was made to recover the many hundreds of manuscripts from the caves appears to confirm that the end of Qumran and Essenism was abrupt and quasi-instantaneous.[13]

7

The Religious Ideas of the Community

The first essays in the 1950s on the religious outlook of the Qumran sect all suffered from a serious defect in that scholars in those days tended to envisage the Scrolls as self-contained and entitled to independent treatment. Today, with the hindsight of more than four decades of research and a considerably increased documentation, it is easier to conceive of the theology of the Community as part of the general doctrinal evolution of ancient Judaism.

On the other hand, it is no simple task to follow that development itself, the reason being that the systematic exposition of beliefs and customs is not a traditional Jewish discipline. In a sense, the Instruction on the Two Spirits, incorporated in the Community Rule, alluded to earlier (p. 96), is an exception, forming the one and only doctrinal treatise among ancient Hebrew writings. The theology of Judaism, biblical, inter-testamental, mediaeval or modern, even when written by contemporary Jewish authors, is often modelled consciously or unconsciously on Christian dogmatic structures: God, creation, human destiny, messianic redemption, judgment, resurrection, heaven and hell. Such structures may and sometimes do distort the religious concepts of Judaism. For example, the interest of the church in the messianic role of Jesus is apt to assign a greater importance to Messianism in Jewish religion than the historical evidence justifies, and Paul's hostility to the 'legalism' of Israel obscures the Jewish recognition of the humble realities of everyday life prescribed by the law as no mere 'works', but as a path to holiness walked in obedience to God's commandments.[1]

The Covenant

Since the key to any understanding of Judaism must be the notion of the Covenant, it may safely be taken as an introduction to Essene religious thought.² The history of mankind and of the Jewish people has seen a series of such covenants. God undertook never to destroy mankind again by a flood; in exchange, Noah and his descendants were required to abstain from shedding human blood and, on the ritual level, from eating animal 'flesh with the life, which is the blood, still in it' (Gen. 9.1–17). To Abraham, who was childless and landless, God offered posterity and country provided he led a perfect life and marked his body and that of all his male progeny with a visible reminder of the Covenant between himself and heaven, circumcision (Gen. 17.1–14). Again, in the days of Moses the Israelites were declared 'a kingdom of priests, and a holy nation' (Ex. 19.5), God's special possession, on condition that they obeyed the Torah, the divine Teaching of the religious, moral, social and ritual precepts recorded in the Pentateuch from Exodus 20 and repeated in the farewell discourse addressed by Moses to his people in the Book of Deuteronomy.

After the conquest of Canaan and the distribution of the land to the tribes, the fulfilment of God's promise to Abraham, the Covenant was renewed by Joshua and the Israelites reasserted their commitment to their heavenly Helper (Josh. 24). From then on, the biblical story is one of continuous unfaithfulness to the Covenant. But God was not to be thwarted by human unworthiness and ingratitude, and for the sake of the handful of just men appearing in every generation he allowed the validity of the Covenant to endure. Though he punished the sinful and the rebellious, he spared the 'remnant' because of their fidelity to it.

From time to time, saintly leaders of the Jewish people, King David and King Josiah before the Babylonian exile (II Sam. 7; II Kings 23.1–3) and Ezra the Priest after the return from Mesopotamia (Neh. 8–10), persuaded them to remember their Covenant with God with solemn vows of repentance and national re-dedication but the promises were usually short-lived. This would no doubt account for the development of an idea in the sixth century BCE of a 'new Covenant' founded not so much on undertakings entered into by the community as on the inner transformation of every individual Jew, for whom the will of God was to become, as it were, second nature.

The time is coming . . . when I will make a new Covenant with Israel
. . . This is the new Covenant which I will make with Israel in those
days . . . I will set my law within them and write it on their hearts
. . . (Jer. 31.31–33; Isa. 54.13).

It was this same Covenant ideology that served as the foundation of
the Qumran Community's basic beliefs. The Essenes considered themselves to be not only the 'remnant' of their time, but the 'remnant' of all
time, the final 'remnant'. In the 'age of wrath', while God was making
ready to annihilate the wicked, their founders had repented. They had
become 'the Converts of Israel' (cf. CD 4.2; 4Q266 fr.5). As a reward
for their conversion, the Teacher of Righteousness had been sent to
establish for them a 'new Covenant', which was to be the sole valid
form of the eternal alliance between God and Israel. Consequently, their
paramount aim was to pledge themselves to observe its precepts with
absolute faithfulness. Convinced that they belonged to a Community
which alone interpreted the Holy Scriptures correctly, theirs was 'the
last interpretation of the Law' (4Q266 fr.11; 270 fr.7), and they devoted their exile in the wilderness to the study of the Bible.[3] Their intention was to do according to all that had been 'revealed from age to age,
and as the Prophets had revealed by His Holy Spirit' (1QS 8.14–16; cf.
4Q265 fr.7).

Without an authentic interpretation it was not possible properly to
understand the Torah. All the Jews of the intertestamental era, the
Essenes as well as their rivals, agreed that true piety entails obedience to
the Law, but although its guidance reaches into so many corners of life
– into business and prayer, law court and kitchen, marriage-bed and
Temple – the 613 positive and negative commandments of which it consists still do not provide for all the problems encountered, especially
those which arose in the centuries following the enactment of biblical
legislation. To give but one example, the Diaspora situation was not
envisaged by the jurists of an autonomous Jewish society.

Torah interpretation was entrusted to the priests and Levites during
the first two or three centuries following the Babylonian exile. Ezra and
his colleagues, the ancient scribes of Israel, 'read from the book of the
Law . . . made its sense plain and gave instruction in what was read'. In
this passage from the Book of Nehemiah 8.8, Jewish tradition acknowledges the institution of a regular paraphrase of scripture known as

Targum, or translation into the vernacular of the members of the congregation. When the parties of the Pharisees, Sadducees, Essenes, etc., came into being with their different convictions, they justified them by interpretations suited to their needs.

A classic example in the Scrolls of idiosyncratic Bible interpretation concerns a law on marriage. Since no directly relevant ruling is given in the Pentateuch on whether a niece may marry her uncle, Pharisaic and rabbinic Judaism understands this scriptural silence to mean that such a union is licit. When the Bible wishes to declare a degree of kinship unlawful, it does so: thus we read apropos of marriage between nephew and aunt, 'You shall not approach your mother's sister' (Lev. 18.13). So a tradition surviving in the Babylonian Talmud is able to go so far as even to praise marriage with a 'sister's daughter' and to proclaim it as a particularly saintly and generous act comparable to the loving kindness shown to the poor and needy (Yebamot 62b). The Qumran Essenes did not adopt this attitude at all. On the contrary, they regarded an uncle/niece union as straightforward 'fornication'. Interpreted correctly, they maintained, the Leviticus precept signifies the very opposite of the meaning accepted by their opponents; the truth is that whatever applies to men in this respect applies also to women.

> Moses said, 'You shall not approach your mother's sister (i.e. your aunt); she is your mother's near kin' (Lev. 18.13). But although the laws against incest are written for men, they also apply to women. When therefore a brother's daughter uncovers the nakedness of her father's brother, she is (also his) near kin' (CD 5.7–9).

The Temple Scroll (66.16–17) proclaims this prohibition clearly in proper legal terms.

> A man shall not take the daughter of his brother or the daughter of his sister, for this is abominable.

Again, according to the strict views of the sectaries, fidelity to the Covenant demanded not only obedience to the Law, to all that God has 'commanded by the hand of Moses', but also adherence to the teaching of 'all his servants, the Prophets' (1QS 1.2–3). Although not expressly stated, this special attention to the Prophets implies, first, that the

Essenes subscribed to the principle incorporated into the opening paragraph of the Sayings of the Fathers in the Mishnah that the Prophets served as an essential link in the transmission of the Law from Moses to the rabbis.

> Moses received the Torah from (God on) Sinai and passed it on to Joshua; Joshua to the Elders (= Judges); the Elders to the Prophets; and the Prophets passed it on to the members of the Great Assembly (= the leaders of Israel in the post-exilic age) (Abot 1.1).

The second inference to be drawn is that the sect believed the Prophets to be not only teachers of morality, but also guides in the domain of the final eschatological realities. But as in the case of the Law, their writings were considered to contain pitfalls for the ignorant and the misinformed, and only the Community's sages knew how to expound them correctly. Properly understood, the books of Isaiah, Hosea and the rest indicate the right path to be followed in the terrible cataclysms of the last days. A simple reading can convey only their superficial meaning, but not their profounder significance. The Book of Daniel sets the biblical example here when it announces that Jeremiah's prediction that the Babylonian domination would last for seventy years is not to be taken literally; the real and final message is that seventy times seven years would separate Nebuchadnezzar from the coming of the Messiah (Dan. 9.21–24). But the Qumran sectaries went even further than Daniel. They argued that it is quite impossible to discover the meaning without an inspired interpreter because the Prophets themselves were ignorant of the full import of what they wrote. Habakkuk, for instance, was commanded to recount the history of the 'final generation', but he did so without having any clear idea of how far ahead the eschatological age lay. God 'did not make known to him when time would come to an end'. Knowledge of the authentic teaching of the Prophets was the supreme talent of the Teacher of Righteousness. The surviving Bible commentaries are also all concerned with predictions concerning the ultimate destiny of the righteous and the wicked, the tribulations and final triumph of the 'House of Judah' and the concomitant annihilation of those who had rebelled against God.

But in addition to this general evidence of the subject-matter, the

Scrolls directly impute to the Teacher a particular God-given insight into the hidden significance of prophecy. He was 'the Teacher of Righteousness to whom God made known all the mysteries of His servants the Prophets' (1QpHab. 7.1–5). He was 'the Priest (in whose heart) God set (understanding) that he might interpret all the words of his servants the Prophets, through whom he foretold all that would happen to His people' (1QpHab. 2.8–10). He was the Teacher who 'made known to the latter generations that which God would do to the last generation, the congregation of traitors, those who depart from the way' (CD 1.12–13). The Teacher's interpretation alone, propagated by his disciples, offered true enlightenment and guidance.

Supported in this way by the infallible teaching of the Community, the sectary believed himself to be living in the true city of God, the city of the Covenant built on the Law and the Prophets (cf. CD 7.13–18).

Again and again, the architectural metaphors used in the Scrolls suggest security and protection. The sect is a 'House of Holiness', a 'House of Perfection and Truth', (1QS 8.5, 9), a 'House of the Law' (CD 9. [B2]: 10, 13); it is a 'sure House' (CD 3.19) constructed on solid foundations. Indeed the language used is reminiscent of Isaiah 28.16, and of Jesus' simile about the church built not on sand but on rock (Matt. 7.24–27; 16.18):

> But I shall be as one who enters *a fortified city*,
> as one who seeks refuge behind a *high wall* . . .
> I will [lean on] Thy truth, O my God.
> For Thou wilt set the *foundation* on *rock*
> and the *framework* by the *measuring cord* of justice;
> and the tried *stones* [Thou wilt lay]
> by the *plumb-line* [of the truth],
> to [build] a mighty [wall] which shall not sway;
> and no man entering there shall stagger.
>
> (1QH 6 [14]. 24–27)

Fortified by his membership of the brotherhood, the sectary could even carry his notions of solidity and firmness over into his own self so that he too became a 'strong tower':

Thou hast strengthened me
before the battles of wickedness . . .
Thou hast made me like a *strong tower*, a *high wall*,
and hast established my *edifice* upon the rock;
eternal foundations serve for my ground,
and all my *ramparts* are a *tried wall* which shall not sway.

(1QH7 [15].7–9).

Election and holy life in the Community of the Covenant

In the ideology of the Old Testament, to be a member of the chosen people is synonymous with being party to the Covenant. Israel willingly accepts the yoke of the Law given on Sinai, and God in his turn acknowledges her as his 'special possession' (Ex. 19.5):

> For you are a people holy to the Lord your God; the Lord your God has chosen you to be a people for his own possession, out of all the peoples that are on the face of the earth.
>
> You shall therefore be careful to do the commandment, and the statutes, and the ordinances which I command you this day (Deut. 7.6, 11).

Theoretically, there is no distinction between election *de jure* and election *de facto*: every Jew is chosen. But already in biblical times a deep gulf is in fact seen to divide righteous observers of the Covenant from the wicked of Israel. Though not deprived of their birthright, the unfaithful are viewed as burdened with guilt and as such excluded, provisionally at least, from the congregation of the children of God. The fully developed concept of election is summarized in the Palestinian Talmud by the third century CE Galilean Rabbi Lazar. Expounding the words of Deuteronomy quoted above, he comments:

> When the Israelites do the will of the Holy One, blessed by He, they are called sons: but if they do not do His will, they are not called sons (Kiddushin 61c).

Inevitably, for the Qumran Essenes such a notion of Covenant membership was far too elastic. Consistent with their approach to legal matters, their attitude in regard to the Covenant was that only the initiates of their own 'new Covenant' were to be reckoned among God's elect and, as such, united already on earth with the angels of heaven.

> [God] has caused [His chosen ones] to inherit
> the lot of the Holy Ones.
> He has joined their assembly
> to the Sons of Heaven,
> to be a Council of the Community,
> a foundation of the Building of Holiness,
> an eternal Plantation throughout all ages to come.
>
> (1QS 11.7–9).

They insisted, moreover, on the individual election of each sectary. The ordinary Jew envisaged entry into the congregation of the chosen primarily through birth, and secondly through the symbolical initiation of an eight-day-old male infant submitted to circumcision. An Essene became a member of his sect by virtue of the deliberate and personal adult commitment of himself. For this reason, as will be remembered, even children born to married members and brought up in their schools had to wait until their twentieth birthday before they were allowed to make their solemn vows of entry into the Covenant. Also, believing in divine foreknowledge, they considered their adherence to the 'lot of God' as the effect of grace, as having been planned for each of them in heaven from all eternity. They, the elect, were guided by the spirit of truth in the ways of light, while the unprivileged, Jew and Gentile alike, were doomed to wander along paths of darkness. The section of the Community Rule known as the Instruction on the Two Spirits gives a fascinating description of these two human groups, the chosen and the unchosen.

> The Master shall instruct all the sons of light and shall teach them the nature of all the children of men according to the kind of spirit which they possess . . .
> From the God of Knowledge comes all that is and shall be. Before ever they existed He established their whole design, and when, as ordained for them, they come into being, it is in accord with His glorious design that they accomplish their task without change . . .

He has created man to govern the world, and has appointed for him two spirits in which to walk until the time of His visitation: the spirits of truth and injustice.

Those born of truth spring from a fountain of light, but those born of injustice spring from a source of darkness. All the children of righteousness are ruled by the Prince of Light and walk in the ways of light, but all the children of injustice are ruled by the Angel of Darkness and walk in the ways of darkness.

The Angel of Darkness leads all the children of righteousness astray, and until his end, all their sins, iniquities, wickednesses, and all their unlawful deeds are caused by his dominion in accordance with the mysteries of God.

But the God of Israel and His Angel of Truth will succour all the sons of light. For it is He who created the spirits of Light and Darkness and founded every action upon them and established every deed (upon) their (ways).

And He loves the one everlastingly and delights in its works for ever; but the counsel of the other He loathes and for ever hates its ways (1QS 3.13–4.1).[4]

Convictions of this kind, with their theories of individual election and predestination, coupled with a precise knowledge of the boundary dividing right from wrong, can lead to self-righteousness and arrogant intolerance of the masses thought to be rejected by God. The Essenes, however, appear to have concentrated more on the blessedness of the chosen than on the damnation of the unpredestined. Besides, they could always argue that Jews who refused to repent and remained outside the new Covenant were responsible for their own doom.

But the spiritual masters of the Community were doubtless aware of the danger of the sin of pride to which their less enlightened brothers were exposed and attacked it on three fronts. The Qumran Hymns, unlike certain biblical Psalms (e.g. Psalm 26) which testify to an acute form of sanctimoniousness, never cease to emphasize the sectary's frailty, unworthiness and total dependence on God.

Clay and dust that I am,
what can I devise unless Thou will it,
and what contrive unless Thou desire it?

What strength shall I have
unless Thou keep me upright
and how shall I understand
unless by (the spirit) which Thou hast shaped for me?

(1QH 10 [18].5–7)

Not only is election itself owed to God's grace, but perseverance in the way of holiness cannot be counted on unless he offers his continuous help and support.

When the wicked rose against Thy Covenant
and the damned against Thy word,
I said in my sinfulness,
'I have been forsaken by Thy Covenant.'
But calling to mind the might of Thy hand
and the greatness of Thy compassion,
I rose and stood.
I lean on Thy grace and on the multitude of Thy mercies.

(1QH 4 [12].34–37)

Another theme constantly stressed in Essene teaching is that not only is God's assistance necessary in order to remain faithful to his Law; the very knowledge of that Law is a gift from heaven. All their special understanding and wisdom comes from God.

From the source of His righteousness
is my justification,
and from His marvellous mysteries
is the light in my heart.
My eyes have gazed
on that which is eternal,
on wisdom concealed from men,
on knowledge and wise design
(hidden) from the sons of men;
on a fountain of righteousness
and on a storehouse of power;
on a spring of glory
(hidden) from the assembly of flesh.

God has given them to His chosen ones
    as an everlasting possession,
and has caused them to inherit
    the lot of the Holy Ones.

                         (1QS 11.5–8)

The sentiments expressed in the Hymns, of love and gratitude and awareness of God's presence, represent a true religiousness, and must have helped the sectary not to allow his life – governed as it was by laws and precepts – to slide into one of mere religious formalism.

Thou hast upheld me with certain truth;
    Thou has delighted me with Thy Holy Spirit
    and [hast opened my heart] till this day . . .
The abundance of Thy forgiveness is with my steps
    and infinite mercy accompanies Thy judgment of me.
Until I am old Thou wilt care for me;
    for my father knew me not
    and my mother abandoned me to Thee.
For Thou art a father
    to all [the sons] of Thy truth,
and as a woman who tenderly loves her babe,
    so dost Thou rejoice in them;
and as a nurse bearing a child in her lap,
    so carest Thou for all Thy creatures.

                         (1QH 9[17].32–36)

Whether the average Essene actually succeeded in fulfilling his high ideals, we cannot of course know: experience past and present has shown that paths to sanctity devised by organized religion are beset with snares. As has been noted earlier (p. 106 on 4Q477), in some individual cases, moral shortcomings were actually recorded. But there can be no doubt of their intention. The aim of a holy life lived within the Covenant was to penetrate the secrets of heaven in this world and to stand before God for ever in the next. Like Isaiah, who beheld the Seraphim proclaiming 'Holy, holy, holy', and like Ezekiel, who in a trance watched the winged Cherubim drawing the divine Throne-Chariot, and like the ancient Jewish mystics who consecrated themselves, despite official disapproval by the rabbis, to the contemplation of the same Throne-Chariot and the heavenly Palaces, the Essenes, too, strove for a similar mystical knowledge, as one of their number testifies in a description of his own vision of the ministers of the 'Glorious Face'.

The [cheru]bim prostrate themselves before him and bless. As they rise, a whispered divine voice [is heard], and there is a roar of praise. When they drop their wings, there is a [whispere]d divine voice. The cherubim bless the image of the throne-chariot above the firmament, [and] they praise [the majes]ty of the luminous firmament beneath his seat of glory. When the wheels advance, angels of holiness come and go. From between his glorious wheels there is as it were a fiery vision of most holy spirits. About them, the appearance of rivulets of fire in the likeness of gleaming brass, and a work of. . . radiance in many-coloured glory, marvellous pigments, clearly mingled. The spirits of the living 'gods' move perpetually with the glory of the marvellous chariot(s). The whispered voice of blessing accompanies the roar of their advance, and they praise the Holy One on their way of return. When they ascend, they ascend marvellously, and when they settle, they stand still. The sound of joyful praise is silenced and there is a whispered blessing of the 'gods' in all the camps of God (4Q405.20 ii–22).

Worship in the Community of the Covenant

In addition to the worship of God offered through a life of holiness, the Qumran sectary had more particularly to perform the ritual acts prescribed by Moses in the correct manner and at the right times. The earthly liturgy was intended to be a replica of that sung by the choirs of angels in the celestial Temple.[5]

To judge from the many references to it, the time element, both calendrical and horary, was crucial. The Community Rule lays down that the Community was not to 'depart from any command of God concerning their appointed times; they shall be neither early nor late for any of their appointed times, they shall stray neither to the right nor to the left of any of His true precepts' (1QS 1.13–15). This injunction asks for exact punctuality in regard to the two daily moments of prayer meant to coincide with and replace the perpetual burnt-offering sacrificed in the Temple at sunrise and sunset (Ex. 29.30; Num. 28.4), but it demands in addition a strict observance of the sect's own liturgical calendar.

> He shall bless Him [with the offering] of the lips at the times ordained by Him: at the beginning of the dominion of light,[6] and at its end when it retires to its appointed place; at the beginning of the watches of darkness when He unlocks their storehouse and spreads them out, and also at their end when they retire before the light; when the heavenly lights shine out from the dwelling-place of Holiness, and also when they retire to the place of Glory; at the entry of the (monthly) seasons on the days of the new moon, and also at their end when they succeed to one another. . . (1QS 9.26–10.4).

To understand the peculiarity of Essenism in this respect, a few words need to be said about the calendar followed by non-sectarian Judaism. Essentially, this was regulated by the movements of the moon; months varied in duration from between twenty-nine and thirty days and the year consisted of twelve months of 354 days. Needless to say, such a lunar year does not correspond to the four seasons determined by the movements of the sun, by solstices and equinoxes. The shortfall of about ten days between the lunar and the solar year was therefore compensated for by means of 'intercalation', i.e. by inserting after Adar (February/March), the twelfth month of the year, a supplementary 'Second Adar' at the end of every thirty-six lunar months.

The Qumran sect rejected this seemingly artificial system and adopted instead a chronological reckoning, probably of priestly origin, based on the sun, a practice attested also in the Book of Jubilees and I Enoch, and fully laid out in the remains of a series of calendrical documents (4Q320–330). The outstanding feature of this solar calendar was its absolute regularity in that, instead of 354 days, not divisible by seven, it consisted of 364 days, i.e. fifty-two weeks precisely. Each of its four seasons was thirteen weeks long divided into three months of thirty days each, plus an additional 'remembrance' day (1QS 10.5) linking one season to another (13 x 7 = 91 = 3 x 30 + 1). In tune in this way with the 'laws of the Great Light of heaven' (1QH 12.5) and not with the 'festivals of the nations' (4QpHos = 4Q171, 2.16), Qumran saw its calendar as corresponding to 'the certain law from the mouth of God' (1QH 12[20].9). Its unbroken rhythm meant furthermore that the first day of the year and of each subsequent season always fell on the same day of the week. For the Essenes this was Wednesday, since according to Genesis 1.14–19 it was on the fourth day that the sun and the moon were created. Needless to add, the same monotonous sequence also implied that all the feasts of the year always fell on the same day of the week: Passover, the fifteenth day of the first month, was always celebrated on a Wednesday; the Feast of Weeks, the fifteenth day of the third month, always on a Sunday; the Day of Atonement, the tenth day of the seventh month, on a Friday; the Feast of Tabernacles, the fifteenth day of the seventh month, on a Wednesday, etc. This solar calendar with its eternal regularity cannot of course stand up to the astronomical calculation of 365 days 5 hours 48 minutes and 48 seconds to the year, but the Scrolls so far published give no indication of how the Essenes proposed to cope with this inconvenience, or whether indeed they were even aware of it.

One practical consequence of the sect's adherence to a calendar at variance with that of the rest of Judaism was that its feast-days were working days for other Jews and vice versa. The Wicked Priest was thus able to travel (journeys of any distance being forbidden on holy days of rest) to the place of exile of the Teacher of Righteousness while he and his followers were celebrating the Day of Atonement (cf. above, p. 133). In fact, it is likely that the persecutors of the sect deliberately chose that date to oblige the sectaries to attend to them on what they considered to be their 'Day of Fasting' and 'Sabbath of repose', and thus 'confuse them and cause them to stumble'. The same sort of story is told in the Mishnah of the Patriarch Gamaliel II, who endeavoured to humiliate Rabbi Joshua ben Hananiah by sending him the following instruction:

I charge you that you come to me with your staff and your money on the Day of Atonement according to your reckoning (Rosh ha-Shanah II. 9).

Another peculiarity of the liturgical calendar of the Community, attested in the Temple Scroll, was the division of the year into seven fifty-day periods – hence the name pentecontad calendar – each marked by an agricultural festival, e.g. the Feast of New Wine, the Feast of Oil,

etc. A similar system is mentioned by Philo in connection with the
Therapeutae in his book, *On the Contemplative Life*. One of these
festivals, the Feast of the New Wheat, coincided with the Feast of Weeks
and was for the Essenes/Therapeutae also the principal holy day of the
year, that of the Renewal of the Covenant, the importance of which is
discussed above (p. 112). From the Book of Jubilees, where, as has been
said, the same calendar is followed, it is clear that Pentecost (the Feast
of Weeks), together with the Feast of the Renewal of the Covenant, was
celebrated on the fifteenth day of the third month (Jub. 6.17–19; cf. also
4Q266 fr.11; 270 fr.7). An outline of the ceremony performed on this
holy day, with its confession of sin and its blessings and curses, is preserved in the Community Rule (1QS 1.16–2.25; cf. also 4Q280,
286–287). The sectaries assemble in the service in strict hierarchical
order: the priests first, ranked in order of status, after them the Levites,
and lastly 'all the people one after another in their Thousands,
Hundreds, Fifties and Tens, that every Israelite may know his place in
the Community of God according to the everlasting design' (1QS 2.22–
23). Blessing God, the priests then recite his acts of loving-kindness to
Israel and the Levites, Israel's rebellions against him. This recognition of
guilt is followed by an act of public repentance appropriate to a community of converts.

> We have strayed! We have [disobeyed]! We and our fathers before us
> have sinned and acted wickedly in walking [counter to the precepts]
> of truth and righteousness. [And God has] judged us and our fathers
> also; but He has bestowed His bountiful mercy on us from everlast-
> ing to everlasting (1QS 1.24–2.1).

After the confession, the priests solemnly bless the converts of Israel,
calling down on them in particular the gifts of wisdom and knowledge:

> May he bless you with all good and preserve you from all evil! May
> He lighten your heart with life-giving wisdom and grant you eternal
> knowledge! May He raise his merciful face towards you for everlast-
> ing bliss! (1QS 2.2–4).

This paraphrase of the blessing of Israel which God commanded
Moses to transmit to Aaron and his sons in Numbers 6.24–26, and

which recalls the fourth of the daily Eighteen Benedictions of traditional Judaism, is accompanied by a Levitical curse on the party of Satan and a special malediction directed by both priests and Levites at any sectary whose conversion may be insincere:

> Cursed be the man who enters this Covenant while walking among the idols of his heart, who sets up before himself his stumbling-block of sin so that he may backslide! Hearing the words of this Covenant, he blesses himself in his heart and says, 'Peace be with me, even though I walk in the stubbornness of my heart' (1QS 2.11–12).

The Cave 4 sources of the Damascus Document also depict the ritual of dismissal from the Community. The priest overseeing the Congregation, addressing God, declares:

> Thou hast cursed those who transgress (the boundary) but we maintain it.

Thereupon 'the dismissed man shall leave and whoever eats from what is his or greets the man who has been dismissed, and agrees with him, . . . his judgment shall be complete' (4Q266 fr. 11 ii; 270 fr. 7 ii).

Each benediction and curse is approved by the whole congregation with a repeated 'Amen'.

The ceremony of the Renewal of the Covenant seems to be the only rite described in any detail among the Scrolls, but as the Essenes laid so much emphasis on the full and punctilious observance of the Law of Moses, it may be taken for granted that they did not omit the many other basic acts of Jewish religion and worship.[7] Circumcision, for example, which was certainly practised, is mentioned in connection with female uncleanness after childbirth when Leviticus 12.3 is cited in passing (4Q266 fr.6). It is also referred to only figuratively in the context of severing the 'foreskin of the evil inclination' (1QS 5.5), or possibly and by implication as the 'Covenant of Abraham' mentioned in connection with (Gentile) manservants (CD 12.11; 16.6). The laws of purity were also assuredly essential to the sect, despite the relative scarcity of exhaustive practical guidance on them (cf., however, TS 46–51, 4Q274–84 and MMT). The same applies to the dietary laws, though a glimpse of information on these comes from the Damascus

Document declaring the eating of 'live creatures' prohibited (e.g. larvae of bees, fish and locusts – CD 12.11–15) or from MMT ordering a live animal foetus to be slaughtered before becoming fit for consumption (4Q396 frs.1–21, cf. also 11QTS 47–48). Josephus also remarks that an Essene was forbidden to eat food prepared by people not belonging to the brotherhood (*War* 2.143).

On three other topics, the Qumran sources are less taciturn: ritual ablutions, Temple worship and the sacred meal. It now remains to consider the doctrinal significance of these rites, discussed in Chapter 4 as part of the life of the sect.

Josephus, as will be recalled, observes that the Essenes took a ritual bath twice daily before meals (cf. *War* 2.129, 132).[8] 4Q414 – entitled 'Baptismal liturgy' – deals definitively with such a bathing ritual, but the text is very mutilated. As regards the bath itself, the Damascus Document adds that the minimum quantity of clean water required for a valid act of purification was to be the amount necessary to cover a man (CD 10.12–13). This is not of course an Essene invention, but typically, where the Mishnah prescribes a minimum of forty seahs (about 120 gallons), the sect's teaching concentrates on the practical purpose of the Mishnaic rule, namely that 'in them men may immerse themselves' (Mikwaot 7.1) and eliminates the obligation of having carefully to measure out what that quantity should be. Of greater interest, however, is the theological aspect, with its insistence on a correlation between the inner condition of a man and the outer rite. The wicked, according to the Community Rule, 'shall not enter the water . . . for they shall not be cleansed unless they turn from their wickedness' (1QS 5.13–14). True purification comes from the 'spirit of holiness' and true cleansing from the 'humble submission' of the soul to all God's precepts.

> For it is through the spirit of true counsel concerning the ways of man that all his sins be expiated . . . He shall be cleansed from all his sins by the spirit of holiness . . and his iniquity shall be expiated by the spirit of uprightness and humility. And when his flesh is sprinkled with purifying water and sanctified by cleansing water, it shall be made clean by the humble submission of his soul to all the precepts of God (1QS 3.6–9).

The second issue has to do with the sect's attitude towards the Temple and Temple sacrifice. While some Essenes, notwithstanding their vow of total fidelity to the Law of Moses, rejected the validity of the sanctuary and refused to participate (temporarily) in its rites (cf. Philo, *Omnis probus* 75; Josephus, *Ant.* 18.19), they evaded the theological dilemma in which this stand might have placed them by contending that until the rededication of the Temple, the only true worship of God was to be offered in their establishment. The Council of the Community was to be the 'Most Holy Dwelling for Aaron' where, 'without the flesh of holocausts and the fat of sacrifice', a 'sweet fragrance' was to be sent up to God, and where prayer was to serve 'as an acceptable fragrance of righteousness' (1QS 8.8–9; 9.4–5). The Community itself was to be the sacrifice offered to God in atonement for Israel's sins (1QS 8.4–5).[9]

Besides this evidence in the Community Rule, the same equation of Council of the Community = the Temple appears in the Habakkuk Commentary (12.3–4) in a most interesting interpretation of the word 'Lebanon'. Traditionally, 'Lebanon' is understood by ancient Jewish interpreters to symbolize 'the Temple'. For example, Deuteronomy 3.25, 'Let me go over . . . and see . . . that goodly mountain and Lebanon', is rendered in Targum Onkelos as 'Let me go over . . . and see . . . that goodly mountain and the Temple'. The Qumran commentator, explaining the Habakkuk text, 'For the violence done to Lebanon shall overwhelm you' (Hab. 2.17), proceeds from the belief that the Council of the Community is the one valid Temple. He then sets out to prove it by directly associating Lebanon with the Council in the conviction that the traditional exegesis will be familiar to all his readers: Lebanon = Temple. Temple = Council of the Community, *ergo* Lebanon = Council of the Community (cf. also 4Q285, fr.5).

The symbolical approach of the sect to sacrificial worship may account for Essene celibacy (where it was practised). Sexual abstinence was imposed on those participating in the Temple services, both priests and laymen; no person who had sexual intercourse (or an involuntary emission, or even any contact with a menstruating woman) could lawfully take part. More importantly still, bearing in mind the central place occupied by prophecy in Essene doctrine, clear indications exist in inter-testamental and rabbinic literature that a similar renunciation was associated with the prophetic state. Thus Moses, in order always to be ready to hear the voice of God, is said by Philo to have cleansed himself of 'all calls of mortal nature, food, drink and intercourse with women' (*Life of Moses* 2.68–9). Consequently, despite the attempt made by this writer and by Josephus to attribute the sect's celibacy to misogyny, a more reasonable explanation would be that it was thought that lives intended to be wholly consecrated to worship and wholly preoccupied with meditation on prophecy should be kept wholly, and not inter-mittently, pure.[10]

The common table of the Essenes, the third special cultic subject to be examined, has already been discussed in Chapter 4 (p. 100), but one remaining point needs to be mentioned, namely that since the rules relating to the daily meal and the messianic meal are the same, it is not unreasonable to infer from the New Testament parallel that the former was thought to prefigure the latter.[11] As is well known, the evangelist Matthew portrays the Last Supper as the prototype of the great eschato-logical feast, quoting Jesus as saying:

I tell you, I shall not drink again of this fruit of the vine until that day when I drink it new with you in my Father's Kingdom (Matt. 26.29).

Future expectations in the Community of the Covenant

The Essene sect was born into a world of eschatological ferment, of intense expectation of the end foretold by the prophets.[12] Using biblical models as vehicles for their own convictions, the Teacher of Righteousness and the Community's sages projected an image of the future which is detailed and colourful, but which cannot always be fully comprehended by us, partly because some of the associations escape us, and partly because of gaps in the extant texts and the complete evidence has not yet been fully investigated. They foresaw their Community as fulfilling the prophetic expectations of the salvation of the righteous. It was from their ranks, swollen by the re-conversion of some of the 'Simple of Ephraim' (4QpNah = 4Q169 3.4–5) who had caused such distress by their previous apostasy, and by other Jewish recruits (1QSa 1.1–5; cf. also 4Q471ᵃ), that the sons of Light would go to battle against the sons of Darkness. The Community, the 'exiles of the desert', would move to Jerusalem after a preliminary attack on the 'army of Satan', symbolized by the 'ungodly of the Covenant' and their foreign allies from the environs of Judaea, followed by an assault on the Kittim occupying the Holy Land. These events were expected to cover a period of six years. The seventh, the first sabbatical year of the War, would see the restoration of the Temple worship.

Of the remaining thirty-three years of its duration, four would be sabbatical years, so the War would be waged during twenty-nine: against the 'sons of Shem' for nine years, against the 'sons of Ham' for ten years, and against the 'sons of Japheth' for another ten years (1QM 1–2). The final conflict would end with the total defeat of the 'King of the Kittim' and of Satan's hosts, and the joyful celebrations of the Hero, God, by the victorious sons of Light.

> Rise up, O Hero!
> Lead off Thy captives, O Glorious One!
> Gather up Thy spoils, O Author of mighty deeds!
> Lay Thy hand on the neck of Thine enemies
>   and Thy feet on the pile of the slain!
> Smite the nations, Thine adversaries,
>   and devour flesh with Thy sword!
> Fill Thy land with glory
>   and Thine inheritance with blessing!
> Let there be a multitude of cattle in Thy fields,
>   and in Thy palaces silver and gold and precious stones!
> O Zion, rejoice greatly!
>   Rejoice all you cities of Judah!
> Keep your gates ever open
>   that the host of the nations may be brought in!
> Their kings shall serve you
>   and all your oppressors shall bow down before you;
>   they shall lick the dust of your feet.
> Shout for joy, O daughters of my people!
> Deck yourselves with glorious jewels
>   and rule over the kingdom of the nations!
> Sovereignty shall be to the Lord
>   and everlasting dominion to Israel.

(1QM 19.2–8)

Such was to be the course of the War in its earthly dimensions. But it would possess in addition a cosmic quality. The hosts of the sons of Light, commanded by the 'Prince of the Congregation', were to be supported by the angelic armies led by the 'Prince of Light', also known in the Scrolls as the archangel Michael or Melkizedek. Similarly, the 'ungodly of the Covenant' and their Gentile associates were to be aided by the demonic forces of Satan, or Belial, or Melkiresha. These two opposing camps were to be evenly matched, and God's intervention alone would bring about the destruction of evil (1QM 18.1–3). Elsewhere the grand finale is represented as a judgment scene in which the heavenly prince Melkizedek recompenses 'the holy ones of God' and executes 'the vengeance of the judgments of God' over Satan and his lot (11QMelch 2.9, 13). Yet in another non-messianic composition (4Q246), the symbolical opponent, usurping the titles, 'son of God' and 'son of the Most High', is said to be overcome by 'the people of God' ready to establish an eternal kingdom with the help of the Great God.[13]

The role of the priests and Levites in this imaginary ultimate grappling of good with evil, described in the War Scroll, emerges as that of non-combatants, but it is difficult to determine the function of the commander-in-chief, the so-called 'Prince of the Congregation'. We learn that on his shield will be inscribed his name, the names of Israel, Levi and Aaron, and those of the twelve tribes and their chiefs (1QM 5.1–2); but little room appears to be left in the War Scroll for him to act as the royal Messiah. God himself is the supreme agent of salvation and after him in importance is Michael.

In some other Scrolls, by contrast, the theme of Messianism is apparent.[14] Complex and *sui generis*, it envisages sometimes one messianic figure, royal, Davidic, triumphant (4Q285, 4QpIsa[a] = 4Q161 and the Damascus Document speaking of the Messiah of Aaron and Israel in the singular, 4Q266 fr.1), again and again two, and once possibly even three, Messiahs. The lay King-Messiah, otherwise known as the 'Branch of David', the 'Messiah of Israel', the 'Prince of [all] the Congregation' and the 'Sceptre', was to usher in, according to the sect's book of Blessings, 'the Kingdom of his people' and 'bring death to the ungodly' and defeat '[the kings of the] nations' (1QSb 5.21, 25, 28). The theory recently advanced that 'the Prince of the Congregation, Branch of David' of 4Q285 is a suffering and executed Messiah is contradicted by both the immediate context and the broader exegetical framework of

Isaiah 10.34–11.2 on which 4Q285 depends (cf. 4Q161, figs. 8–10; 1QSb5.20–29).[15] As befits a priestly sect, however, the Priest-Messiah comes first in the order of precedence, the 'Messiah of Aaron', the 'Priest', the 'Interpreter of the Law' (cf. 1QSa 2.20). The King-Messiah was to defer to him and to the priestly authority in general in all legal matters: 'As they teach him, so shall he judge' (4QpIsa 8–11.23). The 'Messiah of Aaron' was to be the final Teacher, 'he who shall teach righteousness at the end of days' (CD 6.11). But he was also to preside over the battle liturgy (1QM 15.4; 16.13; 18.5) and the eschatological banquet (1QSa 2.12–21).

The third figure, 'the Prophet', is mentioned directly though briefly only once:[16] we are told that his arrival was expected together with that of the Messiahs of Aaron and Israel (1QS 9.11). The whole messianic phrase is absent, however, from the 4Q manuscripts of the Comrnunity Rule. Viewed in the context of inter-testamental Jewish ideas, the Prophet was to be either an Elijah returned as a precursor of the Messiah (Mal. 4.5; I Enoch 90.31,37; Matt. 11.13; 17.12), or a divine guide sent to Israel in the final days (I Macc. 4.46; 14.41; John 1.21) no doubt identical with 'the Prophet' promised by God to Moses ('I will raise up for them a prophet like you . . . He shall convey all my commands to them', Deut. 18.15–18; cf. Acts 3.22–23; 7.37). An identification of 'the Prophet' with a 'new Moses' is supported by the inclusion of the Deuteronomy passage in the Messianic Anthology or Testimonia from Cave 4 as the first of three messianic proof texts, the second being Balaam's prophecy concerning the Star to rise out of Jacob (Num. 24.15–17), and the third, the blessing of Levi by Moses (Deut. 33.11), prefiguring respectively the royal Messiah and the Priest-Messiah.

If it is proper to deduce from these not too explicit data that, if ever expected by the Qumran sect, the messianic Prophet (or prophetic Messiah) was to teach the truth revealed on the eve of the establishment of the Kingdom, it would follow that his part was to all intents and purposes to be the same as that attributed by the Essenes to the Teacher of Righteousness. If this is correct, it would not be unreasonable to suggest that at some point of the sect's history the coming of the Prophet was no longer expected; he was believed to have already appeared in the person of the Teacher of Righteousness.[17]

The evidence available does not permit categorical statements on the sectaries' views of what was to follow the days of the Messiahs. Some kind of metamorphosis was awaited by them, as is clear from the Community Rule – 'until the determined end, and until the Renewal' (1QS 4.25). But one cannot be sure that it was understood as synonymous with the new creation of the Apocalypses of Ezra (7.75) and Baruch (32.6). Similarly, the 'new Jerusalem' described in various manuscripts (1Q32; 2Q24; 4Q554–555; 5Q15; 11Q18) does not match by definition the Holy City descending from above of I Enoch (90.28–29) or Revelation 21, but could be an earthly city rebuilt according to the plans of angelic architects.

As for the after-life proper, and the place it occupied in Essene thought, for many centuries in the biblical age Jews paid little attention to this question.[18] They believed with most peoples in antiquity that after death the just and wicked alike would share a miserable, shadowy existence in Sheol, the underworld, where even God is forgotten: 'Turn, O Lord, save my life,' cries the psalmist, 'for in death there is no remembrance of thee; in Sheol who can give thee praise?' (Ps. 6.5; cf. Isa. 38.18; Ps. 88.10–12, etc.). The general hope was for a long and prosperous life, many children, a peaceful death in the midst of one's family, and burial in the tomb of one's fathers. Needless to say, with this simple outlook went a most sensitive appreciation of the present time as being the only moment in which man can be with God.

Eventually, the innate fear of death, and the dissatisfaction of later biblical thinkers with a divine justice that allowed the wicked to flourish on earth and the just to suffer, led to attempts in the post-exilic era to solve this fundamental dilemma. The idea of resurrection, or rather of the reunification of body and soul after death, first appears as a metaphor in Ezekiel's vision of the rebirth of the Jewish nation after the Babylonian captivity as the reanimation of dry bones (Ezek. 37). Later, after the historical experience of martyrdom under the persecution of Antiochus Epiphanes, resurrection was expected to be the true reward of individuals who freely gave their lives for God – i.e., for their religion (Dan. 12.2; II Macc. 7.9; 12.44; 14.46, etc.). At the same time, the notion of immortality also emerged, the idea that the righteous are to be vindicated and live for ever in God's presence. This view is developed fully in the Greek apocryphal Book of Wisdom (3.1–5.16).

Josephus tells us that the Essenes subscribed to this second school of thought. According to him, they adopted a distinctly Hellenistic concept of immortality, holding the flesh to be a prison out of which the indestructible soul of the just escapes into limitless bliss 'in an abode beyond the ocean' after its final deliverance (*War*, 2.154–8). Resurrection, implying a return of the spirit to a material body, can thus play no part in this scheme.[19]

Until recently, the Scrolls themselves have not been particularly helpful. The Hymns include equivocal statements such as, 'Hoist a banner, O you who lie in the dust! O bodies gnawed by worms, raise up an ensign. . .!' (1QH 6 [14], 34–35; cf. 11 [19], 10–14), which may connote bodily resurrection. On the other hand, the poet's language may just be allegorical. Immortality, as distinct from resurrection, is better attested. The substance of Josephus's account is confirmed, though not surprisingly without any typically Hellenistic colouring (no doubt introduced by him to please his Greek readers). The Community Rule, discussing the reward of the righteous and the wicked, assures the just of 'eternal joy in life without end, a crown of glory and a garment of majesty in unending light' (1QS 4.7–8), and sinners of 'eternal torment and endless disgrace together with shameful extinction in the fire of the dark regions' (1QS 4.12–13).

It is interesting to observe that immortality was not conceived of as an entirely new state, but rather as a direct continuation of the position attained on entry into the Community. From that moment, the sectary was raised to an 'everlasting height' and joined to the 'everlasting Council', the 'Congregation of the Sons of Heaven' (1QH 3 [11].2–22).

The 'liberation' of the Scrolls in 1991 has revealed, however, one poetic text, usually designated as the 'Resurrection fragment' (4Q521), which, echoing Isaiah 61.1, describes God in the age of the Messiah as healing the wounded and *reviving the dead*. If this poem is an Essene composition and not a psalm dating to the late biblical period, it can be said that one out of about 800 Qumran manuscripts definitely testifies to the belief of the sect in bodily resurrection.[20]

In sum, the portrait of the sectary as it is reflected in his religious ideas and ideals bears the marks of a fastidious observance of the Mosaic Law, an overwhelming assurance of the correctness of his beliefs, and certainty of his own eventual salvation. But whereas these characteristics may make little appeal to modern men and women, we would do well not to overlook other traits conspicuous in particular, in his prayers and hymns, which testify to his absolute dependence on God and his total devotion to what he believed to be God's cause.

For without Thee no way is perfect,
　and without Thy will nothing is done.
It is Thou who hast taught all knowledge
　and all things come to pass by Thy will.
There is none beside Thee to dispute Thy counsel
　or to understand all Thy holy design
or to contemplate the depth of Thy mysteries
　and the power of Thy might.
Who can endure Thy glory,
　and what is the son of man
　in the midst of Thy wonderful deeds?
What shall one born of woman
　be accounted before Thee?
Kneaded from the dust,
　his abode is the nourishment of worms.
He is but a shape, but moulded clay,
　and inclines towards the dust.

(1QS 11.17–22)

Qumran and Biblical Studies

In the opening phases of Scrolls research, the adjective 'revolutionary' was on everyone's lips. Today, such an emotive word is out of place and our initial enthusiasm has given way to a more mature assessment.

The opinion at present is that our greatest gain has been, first and foremost, an acquaintance with the life customs, history and beliefs of the Dead Sea Community itself. It should never be forgotten that before 1947 the very word Qumran was known only to geographers.

The second great benefit derived from the Judaean documents, supplemented by the Masada and Bar Kokhba finds, is that they have brought into being two new fields of scholarship: the study of Hebrew manuscripts and of Hebrew script[1] and orthography from the third century BCE to the second century CE. To appreciate what this means it should be recalled that, prior to the discovery, these years were represented by one single scrap of the Nash papyrus (cf. above, pp. 2, 28).

Besides these contributions, three other domains have been profoundly affected by the Judaean discoveries: the text of the Hebrew Bible and the Apocrypha; non-biblical Jewish religious literature of the inter-testamental period, i.e. the Pseudepigrapha; and finally the New Testament.

The Text of the Old Testament[2]

Before 1947, the non-scholarly editions of the Hebrew Bible reproduced the text first printed in Venice in 1524–5, from late mediaeval manuscripts, by Jacob ben Hayyim. We also had a critical edition in the *Biblia Hebraica* issued in 1937 by Paul Kahle. Kahle worked from a biblical codex dated to 1008 CE which was copied 'from correct and clear manuscripts prepared by the master Aaron ben Moses ben Asher'. This

Aaron, and his father Moses, the leading Palestinian Bible scholars of the ninth and tenth centuries, were responsible for putting the final touches to the established text of the Hebrew Scriptures known as *Masoretic,* i.e. the version prepared by *Masoretes* or guardians of tradition. Before that time, all Hebrew manuscripts, biblical scrolls included, were unvocalized; they consequently left the way open to mispronunciation and misinterpretation. The Masoretes met the need for an undisputed pronunciation, and the popular success of their reform led to a rejection of all the older manuscripts and their replacement by codices furnished with vowel signs. Only some sixth to eighth-century fragments from the Cairo Geniza, and the already cited Nash papyrus with its few lines from Deuteronomy, survived by chance. For instance, before the discovery in Cave 1 of the complete text of Isaiah, the oldest extant Hebrew specimen of this book was the Cairo Codex of the Prophets copied by Moses ben Asher in 895 CE.

The unvocalized version on which the Ben Ashers worked, the so-called proto-Masoretic text, had been stabilized for hundreds of years. It is reflected in the various translations and transcriptions of the Old Testament made in the early centuries of the Christian era: Jerome's Latin Vulgate *(c.* 400 CE), the somewhat earlier Syriac rendering, the partial transliteration of the Hebrew text with Greek letters published by the great Christian biblical expert, Origen, in the first half of the third century, and extracts from the second-century revisions or retranslations of the Greek Bible by Aquila, Symmachus and Theodotion, also preserved by Origen and other church Fathers. Their convergent testimony, reinforced by biblical quotations in the writings of the rabbis in the second to the fifth centuries, suggests that the consonantal skeleton of this Bible existed already in around 100 CE.

Further corroboration comes from the Mishnah and the Talmud, which attest that it was at about the same time that the teachers assembled at Jamnia agreed on the exact contents of Holy Scripture; that is, on a list of books to be reckoned henceforth as authoritative sources of Judaism.

Before 1947, the student needing to reach back to the pre-Masoretic and pre-Christian stage of textual development was obliged to rely on the indirect evidence of the Samaritan Pentateuch and the ancient Greek or Septuagint version of the Old Testament.[3] The Samaritan Pentateuch, written in Hebrew and preserved in mediaeval manuscripts, includes variant readings, and also shows deliberate alterations, some of them thought to have been introduced into the text in antiquity. The Septuagint, produced by Greek-speaking Egyptian Jews for their own use until it was appropriated by the Christian church, was translated from the Hebrew between the third and the first century BCE. It differs in both canon and text from the Hebrew counterparts. All the apocryphal books are acknowledged as scripture; Esther and Daniel contain supplements; and discrepant readings occur throughout, with occasionally even more noticeable changes, such as another order of chapters and an abridged text in Jeremiah. The nature of the differences pointed strongly to a Hebrew source other than that of the proto-Masoretic text, but in the absence of manuscript proof, there could be no certainty that they did not result from a wilful interference with the original (interpolation, excision, paraphrase) or even from plain mistranslation.

Today, thanks to the marvellous literary windfall of the Qumran finds, our knowledge of the Hebrew Bible has been extended by another one thousand years or more (a Samuel manuscript from Cave 4 is said to date to about 225 BCE). The eleven caves have yielded something from every book of the scriptures, varying from one small scrap to a complete Scroll. The only exception is *possibly* Esther, for although no identifiable fragment of this book has emerged so far, tiny scraps, containing a letter or two, may belong to it. Many biblical writings are represented by more than one copy, as may be seen from the following list.

Pentateuch

Genesis	15
Exodus	17
Leviticus	13
Numbers	8
Deuteronomy	29

Former Prophets

Joshua	2
Isaiah	21
Judges	3
Samuel	4
Kings	3

Latter Prophets

Jeremiah	6
Ezekiel	6
12 Minor	8

Writings

Psalms	36
Job	4
Proverbs	2
Ruth	4
Song of Songs	4
Ecclesiastes	3
Lamentations	4
Esther	0
Daniel	8
Ezra-Nehemiah	1
Chronicles	1

It should not surprise us that of a total of 202 manuscripts, 72 represent the Pentateuch. This must always be the holiest section of the Bible for all Jews. But the preponderance of Deuteronomy, with its recapitulation of the whole Mosaic legislation, is particularly indicative of Essene interests, as is the popularity of the Latter Prophets, especially Isaiah, and of the Psalms and Daniel in the Writings. A further proof of the sect's absorption in Bible study may be seen in the presence of a large number of commentaries (cf. above, pp. 63–90), and of Greek (Exodus, Leviticus, Numbers) and Aramaic (Leviticus, Job) translations of parts of scripture.

The biblical remains (Hebrew, Aramaic and Greek) amount to around 212 manuscripts, 4 of them more or less complete Scrolls (two Isaiah manuscripts from Cave 1, a Psalms Scroll and an Aramaic Job from Cave 11). And to them must be added exegetical works reproducing biblical texts, and phylacteries and *mezuzoth* (small scrolls to be affixed to door-posts), both containing extracts from the Law.

In the early years of Qumran studies, critical scholars often sought answers to questions that the manuscripts were unable to give.[4] Did the Isaiah Scrolls from Cave 1 shed any light on the problem of the book's composition? Did they confirm that, as modern students argue, it was written by a First, Second and Third Isaiah? They did not. But neither of the Scrolls is old enough to do so, for already at the beginning of the second century BCE Jesus ben Sira, the author of Ecclesiasticus (48.24), appears to assign the whole work to a single prophet. The Septuagint, too, in a translation roughly contemporaneous with the Scrolls, deals with all 66 chapters as though they form one book from one writer. Likewise, although the Qumran fragments of Daniel date to only a few decades after the text was composed (probably in the 160s BCE), they reflect the traditional linguistic division which has baffled scholars for so long. Already in around 100 BCE, an Aramaic section (2.4b–7.28) was sandwiched between two Hebrew sections (1.1–2.4a and 8.1–12.13).

The Scrolls are equally powerless to dispel all our uncertainties about the canon of scripture. It is true that the whole of the Hebrew Old Testament (except perhaps Esther) is attested at Qumran; but this does not mean that the Essene canon was identical with that of traditional Judaism. Apart from passages expressly cited as scripture in the Rules, or used as the basis of biblical commentaries, how are we to know for sure that a composition present in the caves – say Chronicles or Ruth – was held to be canonical? On the other hand we cannot assert that some of the Apocrypha were not treated by the Essenes as an integral part of scripture. After all, the book of Ecclesiasticus or Ben Sira was found in Caves 2 and 11 (and at Masada), five copies of Tobit have surfaced from Cave 4 (four in Aramaic and one in Hebrew) and a small Greek fragment of another of the Apocrypha, the Letter of Jeremiah, has been identified among the contents of Cave 7. The status of several major Pseudepigrapha also remains unsettled; for instance, the Book of Jubilees and the Testament of Levi are both quoted in the Damascus Document as though they were scripture (CD 16.3–4 and 4.16). And the Psalms Scroll from Cave 11 includes a number of apocryphal poems not appended to, but interspersed among, the canonical compositions (cf. above, pp. 13–14).

Have then the cave manuscripts affected in any significant way our understanding of the Bible message? The answer is once more no. Recent Old Testament translators, from 1952 (the American Revised Standard Version) onwards, have all consulted the Qumran evidence, but without introducing changes likely to impinge on religious belief. As an illustration, insiead of 'lawful captives', the equivalent of the traditional Hebrew wording of Isaiah 49.24, the Revised Standard Version follows the big Isaiah Scroll and reads 'the captives of a tyrant'. Similarly, the peculiar phrase 'to lay bare his net', in Habakkuk 1.17, is replaced in the *New English Bible* (1970) by 'to unsheath his sword', after the Habakkuk Commentary. It is not surprising in the circumstances that for biblical specialists, concerned mainly to relieve worried Christians, the Scrolls' most striking contribution to Old Testament studies has been their support of the Masoretic text. In 1955, Millar Burrows, the editor of the first Qumran Scrolls, wrote:

> We did not need the Dead Sea Scrolls to show us that the text has not come down to us unchanged . . The essential truth and the will of God revealed in the Bible . . . have been preserved . . . through all the vicissitudes in the transmission of the text.[5]

On a superficial level Burrows was right. All the same, the differences, which he did not deny, are highly significant, disclosing as they do hitherto unsuspected facets of Jewish intellectual and religious history.

When, in 1953, F. M. Cross published fragments from the Books of Samuel found in Cave 4, the student was confronted for the first time with a Hebrew text representing not the Masoretic version but the original from which the ancient Greek translation of Samuel had been made.[6] The late third-century BCE Qumran manuscript (4QSam[b]) contains ten passages where the Septuagint departs from the traditional Hebrew reading. In eight of these, the Cave 4 fragments reproduce the text underlying the Greek translation; the remaining two agree with the Masoretic version. For example, where in I Samuel 23.14 the traditional Hebrew text gives the divine name as *elohim* (God), and the Septuagint has *kurios* (the Lord, i.e. YHWH), the Qumran fragment supports the Greek version with the Tetragram. Likewise in II Samuel 8.7, the Cave 4 fragment attests the longer text of the Greek Bible.

In the case of Jeremiah, two of the three Jeremiah manuscripts from Cave 4 follow the longer recension of the Masoretes, whilst the third (4QJer[b], dated by Cross to 200 BCE) attests the shorter Septuagint type of the text. In other words, two differing textual traditions co-existed in the religious library of the Essenes.

Besides texts that diverge from one another, some of the writings from Cave 4 testify to mixed versions. An unpublished fragment from Numbers (4QNum[b]) displays characteristics of the Samaritan Pentateuch against the Masoretic and Septuagint evidence: e.g. Joshua's appointment by Moses as his successor (Num. 27.13) is supplemented by appropriate words borrowed from Deuteronomy 3.21. By contrast, in several cases it sides with the Septuagint against the Samaritan and

Masoretic traditions. Another witness to an anti-Masoretic tendency is a Deuteronomy fragment from Cave 5. Here, the original manuscript, assigned by the editor to the first half of the second century BCE, represents the Masoretic text, but a second scribe has furnished it, probably in the first century BCE, with four supralinear corrections to bring it in line with the Hebrew basis of the Septuagint. In Deuteronomy 32.43, the 4Q44 fragment occupies a position between the long Septuagint and the short Masoretic text.

A further illustration of this sort of combination, Deuteronomy 32.8, reveals the cause of the textual variants.

LXX	4Q	MT
Rejoice O heavens	Rejoice O heavens	
with him and *let* all	with him and all	
the *angels of God*	you *'gods'*,	
worship him.	worship him.	
Rejoice O nations		Rejoice O nations
with his people		with his people.
and let all the sons		
of God declare		
him mighty.		
For he shall avenge	For he shall avenge	For he shall avenge
the blood of his	the blood of his	the blood of his
sons	*sons*	*servants*
and shall take	and shall take	and shall take
revenge	revenge	revenge
and pay justice		
to his enemies	*on* his enemies	*on* his enemies
and shall reward	*and shall reward*	
them	*them*	
that hate him	*that hate him*	

In the Song of Moses we read that God established the world's countries according to the number either of the 'sons of Israel' (Masoretic text) or of the 'angels of God' (Septuagint), or of the 'sons of God' (Qumran). Since 'angels of God' and 'sons of God' are synonyms, it is reasonable to conclude that the Septuagint represents the Qumran type of Hebrew. Yet why do the two differ from the Masoretic reading? The number itself, arrived at by counting the names appearing in Genesis 10, is seventy, and both traditions accept this implicitly. But whereas the Masoretic explanation of this figure is Israel-centred, that of Qumran is not. The thought underlying the former text is that the total number of Gentile countries reflects the 'seventy souls' journeying with Jacob from Canaan to Egypt, i.e. the 'seventy sons of Israel' according to Exodus 1.5. The Septuagint, and its Hebrew basis attested by a fragment from Cave 4 (4QEx^a), cannot reproduce this simile in Deuteronomy 32.8 because in their version of Exodus 1.5 the retinue of Jacob amounts to seventy-five, not seventy. Their reasoning therefore runs: the guardian angels of the various peoples were created before man, so when God divided the human race into nations, he ensured that each of the seventy pre-existent angels should have his own special client.

Thus the Masoretic 'sons of Israel' and the Septuagint-Qumran 'angels/sons of God' cannot be explained as stylistic variations: they derive from autonomous traditions. The point to be made here is that the Habakkuk Commentary from Cave 1 has revealed that a tendency to reconcile such deviant records goes back at least as far as the inter-testamental era itself. The commentator, quoting Habakkuk 2.16, follows a Septuagint-type text, 'Drink and stagger (*hera'el*)'; but he shows in his exegesis that he is well aware of the Masoretic reading, 'Drink and show your foreskin' (*he'arel*), since he writes:

For he (the Wicked Priest) did not circumcise the *foreskin* of his heart and walked in the ways of *drunkenness* (1QpHab 11-9-14).

This most ancient library of biblical manuscripts thus testifies to a variety of textual traditions, some proto-Masoretic, some non-Masoretic, the latter being further identifiable as Samaritan or Septuagintal by type. It also provides examples of conflated readings and of the reciprocal impact made by one type on another. At Qumran, in short, but no doubt also elsewhere, a plurality of textual traditions coexisted in the inter-testamental period, a situation which stimulates us to ask how we are to account for, first the plurality, and secondly the unity.

Contemporary scholarship endeavours to explain the plurality, either by the theory of geographically distinct local texts (F. M. Cross), or by the hypothesis that popular recensions were succeeded by an official version (S. Talmon), or by a large diversity of text-forms (E. Tov).[7] It is noteworthy that neither hypothesis advocates an Urtext, an authentic original source from which the variants depart either intentionally or inadvertently. No doubt the reason is that it is thought that a literature, perhaps committed to writing in various places after a period during which it was transmitted orally, cannot be judged according to norms regulating the handing down of records with a written past alone.

F. M. Cross's theory acknowledges three types of text. The first is an ancient Palestinian type, containing frequent explanatory additions and glosses and represented by the 'Samaritan'-type Qumran fragments and the later Samaritan Pentateuch. The second is an Egyptian-type text, imported from Jerusalem and related to the old Palestinian form in so far as it, too, displays the same expansionist tendency. It is this type that underlies the Septuagint. The third type is defined as 'conservative'; it is non-periphrastic and keeps in line with the text which at Jamnia was to become the proto-Masoretic version. As it cannot be either Palestinian or Egyptian, it is assigned to Babylonia.

Emanuel Tov, by contrast, emphasizes that, besides agreements, there are also many disagreements between the Hebrew underlying the Septuagint and 4Q Samuel. Taking together the data of I Samuel 1.22–2.28 and II Samuel 3.23–5.14, the following statistics are obtained:

$$4Q = LXX \neq MT: 35$$
$$4Q = MT \neq LXX: 11$$
$$4Q \neq LXX = MT: 15$$
$$4Q \neq LXX \neq MT: 9$$

In brief, 35 agreements stand against 35 disagreements, including 9 *triple* disagreements.

The alternative thesis of Shemaryahu Talmon postulates that a larger number of textual traditions were current at a stage preceding that of Qumran. Some are believed to have vanished, but it is suggested that those which have survived owe their existence not to geographically distinct centres, but to separate socio-religious groups, each of which came to adopt its own 'official' text: the Samaritans the Samaritan-type, the Hellenistic Jews (and Christians) the Septuagint-type, and the Pharisees and the rabbis the proto-Masoretic type. The fluidity manifest in the Qumran library testifies to the state of affairs obtaining prior to the standardization of the biblical text.

It is unnecessary to stress once more that no definite conclusion can be reached regarding this or any other Qumran problem until all the evidence has been published. Some of the data to be discussed presently will be seen as profoundly meaningful, but we cannot know to what extent they represent the whole truth. Bearing this reservation in mind, it is instructive to ponder on the significance of the relationship between the Qumran Samuel fragments and the parallel Masoretic text of Chronicles.

According to the traditional Hebrew, II Samuel 24.20 reads: 'When Araunah looked down, he saw the king and his servants coming towards him', a reading faithfully echoed by the Septuagint. The Qumran fragment (4QSam^a), reporting the same encounter between David and the Jebusite owner of the threshing-floor on which the Temple was to be built, introduces a concrete fresh detail, '. . . and Ornan (a variant of Araunah) was threshing wheat'. Turning next to I Chronicles 21.20–21 in the Masoretic text, we find the identical incident told in the words of the Qumran fragment of Samuel, and with the name similarly given as Ornan: 'Now Ornan was threshing wheat . . . As David came to Ornan, Ornan looked and saw David . . .'.

This kind of correlation between the Qumran Samuel text and the Masoretic Chronicles, going hand in hand with a divergence from the Masoretic wording of Samuel itself, is not a freak occurrence: it confronts Bible scholars again and again. They therefore have to ask themselves whether the Qumran Samuel text is influenced by a Masoretic-type I Chronicles, or whether the Masoretic I Chronicles, using II Samuel as a source, depends on a Qumran-type text and not on a Masoretic II Samuel!

If the first alternative is correct, and the Qumran Samuel represents a revision of II Samuel (redacted in the sixth century BCE) in the light of I Chronicles (written in about the fourth century BCE), we have in the Qumran fragment an 'updating' of the older narrative according to the more 'modern' edition. This case would then illustrate, on the level of the biblical text itself, a law which I believe to have been discovered in connection with Bible exegesis in ancient Judaism: namely, that the understanding of a composite scriptural narrative by its final redactor 'was inherited by later interpreters of the written Bible, who in turn explicitly introduced the sense of the latest tradition . . . into the former versions'.[8] In other words, the process of harmonization detected in early post-biblical scripture commentary was apparently preceded by a similar effort within the Bible text itself.

The second alternative, that the Masoretic Chronicles is dependent on a non-Masoretic Samuel, would be still more sensational, for it would imply that the redactor of I Chronicles in the fourth century BCE was either unacquainted with the Masoretic version of II Samuel or discarded it deliberately in favour of the Qumran type of text.

To bring this fairly dry statement home more forcefully, let us rephrase it in theological jargon. If we subscribe to the belief that the traditional (i.e. Masoretic) Hebrew Bible is authentic scripture, the word of God, then we have to explain the discrepancy of the word of God preserved in I Chronicles from the word of God surviving in the inspired (i.e. Masoretic) text of II Samuel, and its conformity with a recension (attested at Qumran) which neither synagogue nor church recognizes as sacred. In the pre-Qumran days, Bible translators could still try, like Jerome, to reproduce the 'Hebrew truth' (*hebraica veritas*). Today, convinced that plurality antedated unity, we are compelled to ask: Which Hebrew truth?

In considering next the problem of how the text was unified, it should first be borne in mind that the Bible canonized by the rabbis in around 100 CE was not a new creation. As has been mentioned, the proto-Masoretic type is well attested at Qumran, especially for parts of the Pentateuch and the Latter Prophets. The Hebrew Bible as we have it is not constructed from readings selected from various types of manuscripts. Nor is it a conflation of several streams of tradition. It is a one-type text that includes a few, mostly minor, variant readings preserved as marginal notes in the form of instructions that the written word (*ketib*) should be read aloud (*qere*) in a certain way.

Rabbinic tradition hints obliquely that the authentic biblical text was determined by consultation of three rolls especially esteemed and kept in the Temple. When doubts arose concerning small inconsistencies, they were settled by choosing as official and binding the reading attested by at least two of the model scrolls (Sifre on Deut. 356; yTaanit 68a).[9] It would appear therefore that unification was the work of religious authority. Thereafter, every text which departed from the canonized scripture was held to be an unauthorized version.

Historically, all these issues were decided by the rabbis at Jamnia in the final decades of the first century CE. In regard to the text, they confirmed one of the prevailing types; in regard to the canon, they sanctioned established custom, rejecting hesitations over the scriptural status of the Song of Songs because of its erotic overtones, and over Ecclesiastes because of its apparent agnosticism (mYadayim 3.5). And the prompt implementation of their decrees is evident from the nature of the Murabbaʻat and Bar Kokhba caches dating to the early second century, which consisted, in the domain of religious literature, almost exclusively of biblical fragments exhibiting the proto-Masoretic Hebrew text of Jamnia.

The Pseudepigrapha

It is not only knowledge of the Bible and the Apocrypha[10] that has benefited so greatly from the discoveries at the Dead Sea. The same may be said of the Pseudepigrapha,[11] Jewish religious compositions written between 200 BCE and 100 CE which, although popular and influential, failed to be accepted into either the Palestinian or Hellenistic canon of scripture. More than this, where the Apocrypha had survived in Greek as part of the Bible of the Hellenistic church, many of the Hebrew or Aramaic Pseudepigrapha, shunned by the rabbis, had been preserved sometimes in Greek, but more often on the peripheries of Christian religious literature as secondary translations into Ethiopic, Syriac, Armenian, Slavonic, etc. Thus the main source of Jubilees, a doctrinal paraphrase of Genesis, and of I Enoch, is in Ethiopic, though there are also Greek and other fragments extant. The ethical Testaments of the Twelve Patriarchs can be read in full in Greek and in Armenian, but sections of the Testament of Levi from the same work, identified among the fragments of the Cairo Geniza, appear also in Aramaic.

The general absence of texts in the original languages, and the revisions of complete re-editions of these Jewish writings made by Christian copyists, had rendered their use for the study of intertestamental Judaism fairly complicated. Now, however, we are assured that Jubilees, for instance, was first written in Hebrew: fragments representing no less than twelve manuscripts were found in Caves 1–4 and 11. Again, the original of the Testament of Levi has proved to be Aramaic: three manuscripts from Cave 4 confirm the antiquity of the recension preserved in the mediaeval Geniza fragments. The Testament of

Naphtali in Hebrew has emerged from Cave 4. As for the Book of Enoch, it has survived in Cave 4 in a dozen Aramaic manuscripts.

Beyond providing definite proof of the Jewish and Semitic origin of these documents, the Qumran finds have gone some way to help solve various literary enigmas connected with them, and in particular with Enoch. This latter composition, important enough to have been quoted as an authority in the New Testament (Jude 14), is divided in its Ethiopic version into five books – like the Law and the Psalms in the Bible. The Aramaic fragments from Cave 4 testify to the same five-fold division, but the Book of Parables, the second section of the Ethiopic Enoch (chapters 37–71), does not figure among them. Instead we find a Book of Giants. Now if we accept the conclusion advanced by J. T. Milik, the editor of the Qumran Enoch, that the absence of the Parables from the Aramaic version points to a post-Qumran date for that section in the Ethiopic, the repercussions on the interpretation of the Gospels are considerable, for it is in these same Parables of Enoch that the 'Son of Man' appears, the figure formerly thought to be the prototype of the Gospels' 'Son of Man' about whom New Testament scholars have speculated so exhaustively.[12]

In general, we can say of the Pseudepigrapha remains of Qumran that they have re-awakened scholarly interest in a potentially very rich area of studies, from which our understanding of Jewish history, religion and culture in the age immediately preceding the emergence of rabbinic Judaism and the formation of the New Testament is bound to reap enormous profit.

The New Testament

From the beginning, the relationship between the Dead Sea Scrolls and the New Testament has been the subject of voluminous, occasionally fanciful, and frequently heated argument. As a final contribution, this review will seek to re-appraise the major aspects of the debate and summarize our conclusions.[13]

Qumran Essenism and Palestinian Christianity can be related in three different ways. They are either identical, the Community being the church and Jesus the Teacher of Righteousness. Or Christianity is an offshoot of Essenism. Or Essenism and Christianity both spring from the same common stock, the Judaism of that period.

As has been anticipated in Chapter 5 and confirmed by the survey of the history and teachings of Essenism, the theory of their identity is so implausible as to need no further rebuttal: the time-factor is unsuitable, the two ideologies differ fundamentally, and no New Testament fragment has been discovered in any of the Qumran Caves. In the latter respect, the claim made by the Spanish Jesuit, José O'Callaghan, that Greek papyrus scraps from Cave 7, almost entirely illegible, derive from manuscripts representing Mark, Acts, Romans, I Timothy, James and II Peter, has been justly rejected as totally unacceptable by the leading authorities in the field.[14]

Can Qumran then be the parent of Christianity? This view has been advanced most forcibly by André Dupont-Sommer, who reminds us of Ernest Renan's famous dictum, 'Christianity is an Essenism that has largely succeeded.'[15] For him, the bond linking the Teacher of Righteousness to Jesus is 'quite unique', though he will not have it that Jesus was merely 'a mythical double of the Essene prophet'.[16] Having clarified this point, Dupont-Sommer continues:

> The documents from Qumran make it plain that the primitive Christian Church was rooted in the Jewish sect of the New Covenant, the Essene sect, to a degree none would have suspected, and that it borrowed from it a large part of its organization, rites, doctrines, 'patterns of thought' and its mystical and ethical ideas.[17]

Essenism as the mother of Christianity is not, of course, an impossible notion. On the other hand, the same arguments used to contest the theory of their identity operate here also: namely that the heavy emphasis on the punctilious observance of the Mosaic Law at Qumran is so greatly in contrast to the place given to it in the Gospels that a linear descent from one to the other seems extremely improbable.[18]

The third possibility presupposes that the Qumran sectarian writings and the New Testament represent two independent movements in pursuit of similar ideals. But even here, the question of a direct Essene influence on the early church is possible, but arises only when their common features cannot be otherwise explained. A re-examination of some fundamental problems occurring in both literatures will help to illustrate this point.

The first concerns the part played by the Bible in Essene and Christian theological thought.[19] As at Qumran, scripture is of central importance in the teaching of Jesus and especially of his disciples, but while the New Testament message is less directly concerned with actual observances than with their moral and religious significance, Jesus' essential approach to the Law, the permanent validity of which is asserted by him (Matt. 5.18), shows similarities with as well as dissimilarities from the Scrolls.

Thus in connection with marriage laws, both the New Testament and the Scrolls accentuate the inner import, though their angles of approach differ. One example of this appears in the Damascus Document, where 'male and female created he them' (Gen. 1.27) is interpreted as forbidding polygamy (CD 4.20–21), whilst the New Testament cites the same text in support of an absolute, or conditional, ban on divorce (Mark 10.2–12; Matt. 19.3–9). Likewise, the logic of the sectarian teachers that the biblical ban on marriage between aunt and nephew must also apply between uncle and niece, and that if one union is fornication, so must the other be, is taken even further by Jesus in his statement that one who has looked at a woman with lust has already committed adultery with her in his heart (Matt. 5.27–28).

Jesus, expounding his understanding of the Torah, lays stress on inward religion; he aims at combating the hypocrisy caricatured in Matthew 23, which may produce a beautiful outward appearance but conceals iniquity within (Matt. 23.27–28). The Qumran masters, addressing men accustomed to hold external observances in high esteem, also seek to do the same, but by way of preaching the necessity for those outer observances to be accompanied by corresponding spiritual attitudes.

The parallelism in the use of prophecy at Qumran and in the New Testament has often been noted. The Community and the church were convinced that, consciously or unconsciously, the prophets were referring to the history and doctrine of their own groups when they proclaimed the final realities. The fulfilment interpretation or *pesher* is as familiar in the Gospels and Acts as at Qumran. The prophecy, 'A voice crying in the wilderness: "Prepare the way of the Lord"' (Isa. 40.3), was heard at Qumran as meaning the retirement into the desert of the Teacher of Righteousness and his followers to prepare for the coming of the messianic age. For the New Testament, the voice is that of John the

Baptist carrying out a similar mission (Mark 1.3–8; Matt. 3.1–12; Luke 3.2–17). In both literatures, apologetic considerations often obtrude: the authors set out to prove the predestined nature of the Community or church by demonstrating that its history conforms to prophetic prediction. The presentation of the argument varies in style. The Scrolls, addressed to initiates, can develop it summarily and even elliptically; the Gospels, with an eye on the unconverted, are inclined to make sure that they are understood: 'All this took place to fulfil what the Lord had spoken by the prophet' (Matt. 1.22), or 'For these things took place that the scripture might be fulfilled' (John 19.36).

Another feature common to the Essenes and Christianity is that they both claimed to be the exclusive community of the elect, the sole beneficiaries of a new Covenant in the final age. As the sectaries saw themselves divided into twelve tribes led by twelve chiefs, so the Epistle of James is sent to 'the twelve tribes in the dispersion' (James 1.1), and Jesus promises his twelve apostles that they will 'sit on twelve thrones, judging the twelve tribes of Israel' (Matt. 19.28; Luke 22.30).

On the plane of eschatology, the outlook of the two movements was also similar, in so far as each expected its founder to be ushering in the last days. The followers of Jesus were convinced that the Kingdom of God had already dawned and that their departed Master would return in glory during their own lifetime to judge the world. As the coming of the end was delayed, we find both groups being exhorted to perseverance. The Qumran Habakkuk Commentary urges:

> If it (the end) tarries, wait for it, for it shall surely come and shall not be late (Hab. 2.3) – Interpreted, this concerns the men of truth who keep the Law, whose hands shall not slacken in the service of truth when the final age is prolonged. For all the ages of God reach their appointed end as He determines for them in the mysteries of His wisdom (1QpHab 7.9–14).

The writer of II Peter, echoing the same concern, encourages his readers likewise:

> You must understand . . . that scoffers will come in the last days with scoffing . . . and saying, 'Where is the promise of his coming?' . . . But do not ignore this fact, beloved, that with the Lord one day is like a

thousand years and a thousand years as one day . . . The Lord is not slow about his promise . . . but is forbearing toward you . . . that all should reach repentance (II Peter 3.3–9).

The attitude of the Scrolls to the Jerusalem Temple and official worship also overlaps to a large extent with that displayed in the New Testament. The Essenes, as we know, were not of one mind in this respect: some continued to participate in sacrifices while for others the Council of the Community was the sanctuary where atonement was to be offered by means of a holy life.

The New Testament is also equivocal. Jesus himself behaved in a conventionally Jewish way, visiting the Temple and teaching there, and his disciples continued to pray in the sanctuary even after his death. Paul went further: he is said to have 'purified himself' and made arrangements with the priests for a sacrificial offering in fulfilment of a vow (Acts 18.18; 21.26). Yet at the same time he was promoting a doctrine recalling that taught at Qumran, in which Jesus and the 'apostles and prophets', like the inner Council of the Community Rule, are represented as the foundations, and the Christians as the building stones, of a new sanctuary, a 'holy Temple', a 'dwelling-place of the Lord in the spirit' (Eph. 2.20–22), where their bodies were to be presented 'as a living sacrifice, holy and acceptable' (Rom. 12.1).

Beyond this point the Scrolls and the New Testament part company in their approach to the Temple. Qumran predicts the restoration of Temple worship. The Book of Revelation dreams of a new Jerusalem where no sanctuary is needed, 'for its Temple is the Lord God the Almighty and the Lamb' (Rev. 21.22).

The organization of community life is yet another field where the customs of one movement find an echo in those of the other. The Essene superior, the *mebaqqer,* responsible for admissions, teaching, administration, distribution of charitable funds, is adjured to be the father and shepherd of his congregation. The last title is applied once to Jesus, 'shepherd and guardian of . . . souls' (I Peter 2–2.5), but the normal Pauline usage for a leader is *episkopos*, bishop. Appointed to take charge of the 'flock' and to 'feed the church' (Acts 20.28), he too was to be an 'apt teacher' and a good 'manager' (I Tim. 3.2), 'able to give instruction in sound doctrine', a blameless 'steward of God' (Titus 1.7, 9).

Again, the Essene rule provided for both the private ownership of property and voluntary communism. The New Testament's testimony is similar. Jesus himself exhorted his hearers to sell their belongings and to distribute the proceeds among the poor and follow him, thus proving their total reliance on God (Matt. 19.21; Mark 10.21; Luke 18.22), while the Fourth Gospel implies that his closest circle drew from a common purse entrusted to Judas (John 12.6; 13.19). At the other extreme, however, we find the Christians of the Pauline Epistles living in community but otherwise conforming to normal secular behaviour: earning a living, caring for their families and contributing to help the poor. Thus between the two poles of an absolute renunciation of possessions and a retention of personal wealth, the early days of Christianity saw a system of religious communism or quasi-communism identical with that of Qumran in the Jerusalem church. Jesus' command that a disciple should divest himself of all he had and pass the money to the poor was re-interpreted to advocate, as did the rule of the monastic Essenes, a common ownership of property within the brotherhood:

All who believed were together and had all things in common; and they sold their possessions and goods and distributed them to all, as any had need (Acts 2.44–45).

In this connection, an interesting parallel may be drawn between the Qumran 'lying in matters of property', punished by the relatively severe sentence of a year's exclusion from 'purity' and the reduction of food by one quarter, and the same offence and its punishment in Christian circles. When the Jerusalem couple, Ananias and Sapphira, pretended to hand over all their riches to the church leaders but kept back part of it, God caused them both to drop dead (Acts 5.1–11)!

In regard to celibacy as it is treated in the Essene literature and the New Testament, we know that many sectaries were married, but learn from the classical sources that celibacy was compulsory in one of the branches. Similarly in the New Testament marriage is nowhere openly condemned; even Paul, who professes that 'it is well for a man not to touch a woman', is forced to concede that married life is not ungodly (I Cor. 7.1–7). But he, and apparently Jesus too, saw celibacy as preferable in the eschatological age. Indeed, the chief difference between Paul and Jesus on this subject appears to be that Paul does not favour the severing of marital ties (I Cor. 7.1–11), notwithstanding his advice to married men to live as though they had no wives (I Cor. 7.29), whereas Jesus does, positively praising those enthusiasts for the Kingdom of Heaven who have made themselves 'eunuchs' and forsaken wives and family (Matt. 19.12; Luke 14.26; 18.29). Whether this advocacy of the separation of the sexes is to be understood literally or is a rhetorical exaggeration, is not clear. It could simply mean that if earthly bonds hinder a man in his search for God, they should be sacrificed. But it could also be intended, as was the exclusion of women from the camp of the sons of Light during the final war, as a necessary part of the preparation for the coming of the Kingdom.

It is to be doubted that celibacy was widespread among Christians of the apostolic generation. Paul declares himself to be single (I Cor. 7.8), but he allows even his bishops to marry once (though not twice) (I Tim. 3.2; Titus 1.6). As for Jesus, the Gospels remain silent and imply that he had no wife.

If Essene and Christian motives for sexual abstinence are compared, the only element common to both groups seems to be the eschatological factor. In the Scrolls, the sectaries' association with the heavenly hosts demanded a degree of ritual purity attainable only in a life of angelic celibacy. Likewise, if Jesus was genuinely advising his disciples to renounce marriage, it was in order to stress the overriding importance of a wholehearted quest for the Kingdom. Also, before it became an established custom in the church, celibacy was recommended simply as a sensible measure in view of the 'impending distress' (I Cor. 7.26) – 'Alas for those who are with child . . . in those days' (Mark 13.17; Matt. 24.19; Luke 21.23) – though practical Christianity of Pauline inspiration continued to see it as an advantage to those desirous to devote themselves entirely to the 'affairs of the Lord' (I Cor. 7.32–34).

Some of the parallels noticed in this survey between the Scrolls and the New Testament may be accounted for by general sectarian principles. To both the Essenes and the first Christians scripture was central, and they both taught that their institutions fulfilled prophecy; they were both the chosen people and had inherited its privileges. Moreover, coming into being as they did in a climate of eschatological upheaval in Palestine, it is normal that they should both have awaited an imminent end of time. In their attitudes towards the Temple too, sectarian logic no doubt played a part; though not unexpectedly, the issue affected the priestly brotherhood of the Essenes more deeply than the group of Galileans, whose lack of sophistication in matters of worship and sacrifice, no doubt attributable to the distance separating their province from Jerusalem, was notorious. Nevertheless, the parallelism between Paul's theology and that of Qumran is too pronounced to be no more than a coincidence. It is probable that he was acquainted with Qumran Temple symbolism and adapted it in shaping his own teaching on spiritual worship.

The most likely domain of Qumran influence on Christianity is that of organization and religious practice. After all, the Qumran sect was already a well-tried institution when the Judaeo-Christian church was struggling to establish itself, and it would have been only sensible for the inexperienced men of the fellowship of Jesus to observe and imitate existing patterns. Thus the monarchical government of the Pauline churches – Jewish communities were administered not by single leaders but by a group of elders – may easily have been modelled on the Essene pattern of a Guardian as pastor of each individual camp, with Paul himself playing the part of the 'Guardian of all the camps' within the Gentile church. It is also difficult to accept that the common life and religious communism described in Acts in regard to the Jerusalem church owed nothing to the by then world-famous Essene life 'without money'. Finally, since lasting celibacy was completely alien to Jewish thinking, its occurrence in Christianity is likely to be an adaptation of the eschatological asceticism for which the sectaries from the Dead Sea were renowned even outside the frontiers of Palestine. 'A unique people' – to quote Pliny – 'more admirable than any other in the whole world, without women and renouncing sex altogether (*sine ulla femina, omni venere abdicata*) . . . an eternal people in which no one is born' (*Natural History* 5. 73).

In conclusion, although no Qumran impact on the primitive church can be proved, and although the bulk of Jewish traditions incorporated into Christianity was not sectarian, a presumed Essene influence on the New Testament writers on some at least of the points mentioned explains them more satisfactorily than any other theory. The information available to us suggests that the main contact occurred, not between the sect and Jesus, a Galilean charismatic for whom a great deal of Essene doctrine would have been repugnant,[19] but between Essenism and Judaean Christianity. Some have thought that the original channel was John the Baptist, but for this he would have to have abandoned the Essene life and its seclusion to preach to all Israel. This of course is pure speculation; John's apparently Essene characteristics can just as well be explained as the habits of a Judaean hermit devoted to ritual ablution in the river Jordan.

It has often been remarked that the New Testament makes no mention of the Essenes. This is another mystery which we cannot yet solve. Unless we conclude from the unsubstantiated statement that the 'great many priests . . . obedient to the faith' referred to in the Acts of the Apostles (6.7) were wholly or in part Essenes, we are left with the following theories. First, there is no reason whatever to suppose that Jesus, in Galilee, ever encountered any Essenes, since no such establishment is attested there. Secondly, as New Testament allusions to other religious parties (the Pharisees, Sadducees, Herodians, etc.) are made largely in the context of polemics and apologetics, silence apropos of the Essenes may be due to their known unwillingness to engage in controversy with outsiders. And if the later church organizers followed Essene models, they probably preferred to keep this dark. This is clearly not the full answer, but those who look to find something particularly mysterious in this lacuna should bear in mind that the great mass of rabbinic literature may not mention the Essenes either, for none of its vague phrases and titles – 'the Silent', 'the Builders', 'the Holy Congregation' – can be proved, in the absence of any specific statement, to apply to them and them alone.

This brings to a close our summary examination of Qumran's contribution to New Testament studies. An improved comprehension of the Essene sect has opened up a new approach to the origins of Christianity. The parallelisms, established or adumbrated, will enable us more reliably to insert Jesus and the movement that arose in his wake into the historical world of Judaism. The fresh insights obtained, combined with a familiarity with the larger fields of Jewish and Gentile civilizations in the first century CE, will help not only to disclose interacting links and influences but also to single out all that is peculiar to the inspiration of two very different spiritual masters. Contrasted with the austere figure of the Teacher of Righteousness, a priest who sought to instil in his people a thorough knowledge of the Torah and urged them to combine a strict observance of the externals of the Law with inner spiritual authenticity, Jesus the Galilean holy man, who addressed not the learned or the seekers of perfection, but the simple country people, including publicans, sinners and whores, appears as someone whose concern was with other humans and their need to be taught how to live as the children of God. At the heart of Essenism rested elements of intolerance, rigidity and exclusiveness. This, perhaps, is why it vanished, whereas the flexible and dynamic Judaism of the rabbis and cosmopolitan Christianity were able to live on.

Scrolls Catalogue

Perhaps the greatest disservice rendered to scholarship by Roland de Vaux and his successors was their obstinate refusal to release the list of the unpublished texts from Caves 4 and 11. 'Outsiders' not only were denied access to them but were not even allowed to know what exactly they were not permitted to see! We had to wait until the spring of 1992 for Emanuel Tov, editor-in-chief of the Qumran Publication Project since 1990, to correct this injustice by disclosing the long-awaited 'secrets' and publishing them, at my invitation, in the *Journal of Jewish Studies*.[1] Here follows a complete inventory of the manuscripts and fragments discovered in the eleven Qumran caves together with source references to all the published texts.[2]

Cave 1

Scrolls

1QIsa^a Complete Isaiah	Millar Burrows et al., *The Dead Sea Scrolls of St Mark's Monastery* I, American Schools of Oriental Research 1950.
1QIsa^b Incomplete Isaiah	E. L. Sukenik, *The Dead Sea Scrolls of the Hebrew University*, Magnes Press 1955; Hebrew edition 1954.
1QapGen	Genesis Apocryphon in N. Avigad and Y. Yadin, *A Genesis Apocryphon*, Magnes Press 1956.
1QpHab	Commentary of Habakkuk in Millar Burrows et al., *The Dead Sea Scrolls of St Mark's Monastery* I, American Schools of Oriental Research 1950.
1QS	Community Rule in Millar Burrows, *The Dead Sea Scroll of St Mark's Monastery* II, fasc. 2, 1951.
1QH	Thanksgiving Hymns in E. L. Sukenik, *The Dead Sea*

Scrolls of the Hebrew University, Magnes Press 1955; Hebrew edition 1954.

1QM — War Scroll in E. L. Sukenik, *The Dead Sea Scrolls of the Hebrew University,* Magnes Press 1955; Hebrew edition 1954.

Fragments

DJD I

No. and siglum	Title
1Q	
1 = 1QGen	Genesis
2 = 1QEx	Exodus
3 = 1QpaleoLev	Leviticus in palaeo-Hebrew script
4–5 = 1QDeut^{a–b}	Deuteronomy
6 = 1QJudg	Judges
7 = 1QSam	I and II Samuel
8 = 1QIsa^b	Fragments belonging to the incomplete Isaiah Scroll
9 = 1QEzek	Ezekiel
10–12 = 1QPs^{a–c}	Psalms
13 = 1QPhyl	Phylactery
14 = 1QpMic	Commentary on Micah
15 = 1QpZeph	Commentary on Zephaniah
16 = 1QpPs	Commentary on Psalms
17–18 = 1QJub^{a–b}	Jubilees
19 and 19bis = 1QNoah	Book of Noah
20 = 1QapGen	Genesis Apocryphon
21 = 1QTLevi ar	Aramaic Testament of Levi
22 = 1QDM	*Divre Mosheh* (Sayings of Moses)
23–24 = 1QEnGiants	Book of Giants (Enoch)
25	Apocryphal prophecy
26	Wisdom text
27 = 1QMyst	Book of mysteries
28a = 1QSa	Rule of the Congregation (Annex to Community Rule)

28b = 1QSb	Benedictions (Annex to Community Rule)
29	Liturgical text
30–31	Liturgical texts
32 = 1QJNar	Aramaic New Jerusalem
33 = 1QMfrgs	War Scroll
33–34 bis = 1QLitPr a–b	Liturgical prayers
35 = 1QHfrgs	Thanksgiving Hymns (1QH)
36–40	Hymns
41–62	Unidentified Hebrew fragments
63–68	Unidentified Aramaic fragments
69	Unidentified Hebrew fragments
70–70bis	Unidentified papyrus fragments
71–72 = 1QDana–b	Daniel

Cave 2

DJD III

1 = 2QGen	Genesis
2–4 = 2QExa–c	Exodus
5 = 2QpaleoLev	Leviticus in palaeo-Hebrew script
6–9 = 2QNuma–d	Numbers
10–12 = 2QDeuta–c	Deuteronomy
13 = 2QJer	Jeremiah
14 = 2QPs	Psalms
15 = 2QJob	Job
16–17 = 2QRuth a–b	Ruth
18 = 2QSir	Ben Sira
19–20 = 2QJuba–b	Jubilees
21 = 2QapMoses	Moses apocryphon
22 = 2QapDavid	David apocryphon
23 = 2QapProph	Apocryphal prophecy
24 = 2QJNar	Aramaic text on the New Jerusalem
25	Legal document
26 = 2QEnGiants	Book of Giants (Enoch)

27–33   Unidentified small fragments

Cave 3
DJD III

Cave 4
DJD XII

23 = Lev-Num^a	Leviticus-Numbers
24–26 = Lev ^b–d	Leviticus
27 = Num^b	Numbers

DJD XIV

No. and siglum	Title
4Q	
28 = Deut^a	Deuteronomy
29 = Deut^b	Deuteronomy
30–31 = Deut^c–d	Deuteronomy
32 = Deut^e	Deuteronomy
33–34 = Deut^f–g	Deuteronomy
35 = Deut^h	Deuteronomy
36 = Deut^i	Deuteronomy
37–40 = Deut^i–m	Deuteronomy
41 = Deut^n	Deuteronomy
42–43 = Deut^o–p	Deuteronomy
44 = Deut^q	Deuteronomy
45 = Josh^a	Joshua
48 = Josh^b	Joshua
49–50 = Judg^a–b	Judges
51–52 = Sam^a–b	Samuel
53 = Sam^c	Samuel

DJD XV

No. and siglum	Title
4Q	
54 = Kgs	Kings
55 = Isa^a	Isaiah
56–69b = Isa^b–r	Isaiah
70 = Jer^a	Jeremiah
71–71a–b = Jer^b,d–e	Jeremiah
72 = Jer^b	Jeremiah
73–74 = Ezek^a–b	Ezekiel

75 = Ezek^c	Ezekiel	
76–81 = XII^{a–f}	Minor Prophets	

No. and siglum	Title	Preliminary publication
82 = XII^g	Minor Prophets	
83 = Ps^a	Psalms	
84 = Ps^b	Psalms	Skehan[3]
85–87 = Ps^{c–e}	Psalms	
88 = Ps^f	Psalms	Starcky[4]
89–97 = Ps^{g–p}	Psalms	
98 = Ps^q	Psalms	Milik[5]
98a = Ps^r	Psalms	
98b = Ps^s	Psalms	Skehan[6]
98c–d = Ps frg 1–2	Psalms	
99–100 = Job^{a–b}	Job	
102–103 = Prov^{a–b}	Proverbs	
104 105 = Ruth^{a–b}	Ruth	
106–108 = Cant ^{a–c}	Song of Songs	
109 = Qoh^a	Ecclesiastes	Muilenburg[7]
110 = Qoh^b	Ecclesiastes	
111 = Lam	Lamentations	Cross[8]
112 = Dan^a	Daniel	Ulrich[9]
113–114 = Dan^{b–c}	Daniel	Ulrich[10]
115–116 = Dan^{d–e}	Daniel	
117 = Ezra	Ezra	
118 = Chr	Chronicles	Trebolle[11]

DJD IX

No. and siglum	Title
4Q	
11 = paleoGen-Ex^l	Genesis-Exodus
22 = paleoEx^m	Exodus
45–46 = paleoDeut^{r–s}	Deuteronomy

101 = paleoJob^c	Job
119 = LXXLev^a	Greek Leviticus
120 = papLXXLev^b	Greek Leviticus
121 = LXXNum	Greek Numbers
122 = LXXDeut	Greek Deuteronomy
123 paleoParaJosh	Parabiblical Joshua fragments
124–125 = paleoUnid 1–2	Unidentified fragments
126 = Unid gr	Unidentified Greek fragments
127 = papPara Exgr	Greek parabiblical Exodus fragments

DJD VI

No. and siglum	Title
4Q	
128–148 phyl^a–u	Phylacteries
149–155 = mez^a–g	Mezuzot
156 = tgLev	Targum of Leviticus
157 = tgJob	Targum of Job

DJD V

No. and siglurn	Title
4Q	
158 = BibPar	Biblical paraphrases
159 = Ord^a	Ordinances
160 = VisSam	Vision of Samuel
161–165 = plsa^a–e	Commentaries on Isaiah
166–167 = pHos^a–b	Commentaries on Hosea
168 = pMic	Commentary on Micah
169 = pNah	Commentary on Nahum
170 = pZeph	Commentary on Zephaniah
171 = pPs^a	Commentary on Psalms
172 = pUnid	Commentary on unidentified texts
173 = pPs^b	Commentary on Psalms
174 = Flor	Florilegium
175 = Testim	Testimonia

176 = Tanh	Tanhumim[12]
177 = Cat[a]	Catena A
178	Unnamed
179 = apLam[a]	Apocryphal lamentations
180 = AgesCreat	Ages of the creation
181	Unnamed (here The Wicked and the Holy)
182 = Cat[b]	Catena B
183	Unnamed
184 = Wiles	Wiles of the wicked woman
185	Unnamed
186 = Cryptic	Cryptic texts[13]

DJD XIX

No. and siglum	Title	
4Q		
196 = Tob ar[a]	Tobit in Aramaic	
197–199 = Tob[b–d]	Tobit in Aramaic	
200 = Tob heb	Tobit in Hebrew	

No. and siglum	Title	Prelim. publication
4Q		
201–202 = En[a–b]	Enoch	Milik[14]
203 En Giants[a]	Enoch (Giants)	Ibid.
204–207 = En[c–f]	Enoch	Ibid.
208–211 = Enastr[a–d]	Astrological Enoch	Ibid.
212 = En[g] + Letter	Enoch and his Letter	Ibid.

DJD XXII

No. and siglum	Title
4Q	
213 = TLevi ar[a]	Aramaic Testament of Levi
214 = TLevi ar[b]	Aramaic Testament of Levi
215 = TNaph	Testament of Naphtali

DJD XIII

No. and siglum	Title
4Q	
216 = Jub^a	Jubilees
217–218 = Jub^b–c	Jubilees
219 = Jub^d	Jubilees
220 = Jub^e	Jubilees
221 = Jub^f	Jubilees
222 = Jub^g	Jubilees
223 = Papjub^h	Jubilees
224 = papJub^h?	Jubilees
225–226 = psJub^a–b?	Pseudo-Jubilees^a–b
227 = psJub^c?	Pseudo-Jubilees^c
228 = cit of Jub	Work citing Jubilees

No. and siglum	Title
4Q	
229 = pseudep	Pseudepigraphic work in Mishnaic Hebrew
230–231 = CatSpir^a–b	Catalogue of Spirits
232 = JN Hebr.	New Jerusalem in Hebrew
233 = Toponyms	Fragments with place names
234 = Gen27.20f.	Scribal exercise
235 = frgs of Kings	Book of Kings
236 = Psalm 89	Psalm 89
237 = Psalter	Psalter
238 = Hab 3 and songs	Habakkuk 3 and songs
239 = Pesh	Pesharim on the true Israel
240 = Comm. Cant.?	Commentary on the Song of Songs?
241 Lamcit	Fragments citing Lamentations

DJD XXII

No. and siglum	Title
4Q	
242 = PrNab	Prayer of Nabonidus
243–245 = psDan ar^{a-c}	Daniel in Aramaic
246 = ArApocal	Aramaic apocalypse

No. and siglum	Title	Prelim. publication
4Q		
247 = Apoc Weeks	Apocalypse of Weeks	Milik[15]
248 = ActsGrKing	Acts of a Greek King	Broshi and Eshel[16]
249 = apMSMcryp A	Midrash Sefer Mosheh A	
250 = versoMSM	Text written on verso of 249	
251 = legComm	Legal commentary on Torah	Baumgarten[17]

DJD XXII

No. and siglum	Title
4Q	
252 = pGen^a	Commentary on Genesis
253–254 = pGen^{b-c}	Commentary on Genesis

DJD XXVI

4Q

No. and siglum	Title
255 = papS^a	Serekh^a
256 = S^b	Serekh^b
257 = S^c	Serekh^c
258 = S^d	Serekh ^{d}
259 = S^e	Serekh^e
260–264 = S^{f-i}	Serekh^{f-i}

No. and siglum	Title	Prelim. publication
4Q		
265 = SD	Serekh-Damascus	Baumgarten[18]

DJD XVIII

No. and siglum	Title
4Q	
266 = Dᵃ	Damascusᵃ
267–268 = Dᵇ⁻ᶜ	Damascus ᵇ⁻ᶜ
269 = Dᵈ	Damascusᵈ
270 = Dᵉ	Damascusᵉ
271 = Dᶠ	Damascusᶠ
272–273 = Dᵍ–papʰ	Damascusᵍ

No. and siglum	Title	Prelim. publication
4Q		
274 = Toh A	Tohorot A	Baumgarten[19]
275 = Toh Bᵃ	Tohorot Bᵃ	Milik[20]
276–279 = Toh B ᵇ⁻ᶜ-C–Dᵃ	Tohorot B ᵇ⁻ᶜ-C–Dᵃ	Eisenman[21]
280 = Toh Dᵇ?	Tohorot Dᵇ?	Eisenman[22]
281–283 = Toh E ᵃ⁻ᵇ?–F	TohohotE ᵃ⁻ᵇ?–F	
284 = Nidd	Serekh he-Niddot	
284a = Leq	Leqet	
285 = SMilh	Sepher ha-Milhamah	Vermes[23]

DJD XI

No. and siglum	Title	Prelim. publication
4Q		
286–287 = Berᵃ⁻ᵇ	Berakhot	Nitzan[24]
288–290 = Berᶜ⁻ᵉ	Berakhot	Ibid.

No. and siglum	Title	Prelim. publication
4Q		
291–293 = Prayers	Work containing prayers	
294–297 = Rules	Rules and Euchologies?	
298 = Words of Sage	Words of a Sage to sons of Dawn	Pfann[25]
299–300 = Myst[a–b]	Mysteries A–B	Schiffmann[26]
301	Mysteries C	
302 = papPraise	Praise of God	Nitzan[27]
302a = Parable	Parable of the Tree	Ibid.
303–305 = CreatA[a–b]B	Meditation on Creation A–B	
306 = Wisd	Fragments concerning people who err	
307–308 = Sap	Sapiential fragments	
309 = Ar work	Aramaic work in cursive script	
310 = Ar pap	Aramaic work on papyrus	
311 – Hebr pap	Hebrew text on papyrus	
312 = Hebr	Hebrew text in Phoenician cursive	
313 = Cryp fr	Cryptic Text A	
314–315 = parcels	Four parcels of uninscribed leather	
316 = Hebr fr	Fragments in Hebrew	
317 = Moon crypt	Fragments on the phases of the Moon (cryptic)	Milik[28]
318 = Zod and Bront	Zodiology and Brontology	Greenfield and Sokolov[29]
319 = Otot	Otot	Glessner[30]
320–330 = Cal	Calendar	Wacholder and Abegg, Talmon[31]
331 = pap list[a]	Historical work on papyrus A	
332–333 = Hist [b–c]	Historical work on papyrus B–C	
334 = Ordo	Ordo	

335–336 = Astr?	Astronomical works
337 = frCal	Calendar
338 = Geneal	Genealogical list

DJD XIX

No. and siglum	Title
4Q	
339 = False Prophs	List of False Prophets
340 = Netin	List of Netinim

No. and siglum	Title	Prelim. publication
4Q		
341 = Names	List of proper names	Naveh[32]

DJD XXVII

No. and siglum	Title
4Q	
342 = Letter ar	Letter in Judaeo-Aramaic
343 = Letter nab	Letter in Nabataean
344 = Debt	Acknowledgment of debt
345 = Sale ar/heb	Sale of land in Aramaic or Hebrew
346 Sale ar	Deed of sale in Aramaic
346a	Unidentified fragment
347 = papDoc ar	Aramaic deed on papyrus
348 = Deed Hebr	Ownership document in Hebrew
351–352 = Cereal	Accounts of cereal
352a	Account in Aramaic or Hebrew
353	Account of cereal in Aramaic or Hebrew
354	Account of cereal in Aramaic or Hebrew
356–358	Account in Aramaic or Hebrew
359	Deed in Aramaic or Hebrew
360a	Unidentified fragment in Aramaic

No. and siglum	*Title*	
4Q		
361 = papDoodles	Doodles on papyrus	
362–363 = Crypt B	Undeciphered Cryptic B	

DJD XIII

364–365 = PentPara[a–b]	Pentateuchal paraphrase[a–b]	
366–367 = PentPara[c–d]	Pentateuchal paraphrase[c–d]	
368 = PentAp	Pentateuch Apocryphon	

DJD XIII

369 = Apoc	Apocryphon[a]	

DJD XIX

370 = Flood Ap	Flood Apocryphon	
371 = JosAp[a]	Joseph Apocryphon[a]	
372 = JosAp[b]	Joseph Apocryphon[b]	Schuller[33]
373 = JosAp[c]	Joseph Apocryphon[c]	Schuller[34]

DJD XIX

374 = MosAp A	Moses Apocryphon A	
375–376 = MosApB	Moses Apocryphon B	
377 = MosApC	Moses Apocryphon C	

DJD XXII

378–379 = PsJos[a–b]	Psalms of Joshua[a–b]	

No. and siglum	*Title*	*Prelim. publication*
4Q		
380–381 = apPs	Apocryphal Psalms	Schuller[35]
382 = paraKings	Papyrus paraKings	
383 = pap apJer A	Apocryphal Jeremiah A?	

DJD XIX

No. and siglum	Title
4Q	
384 = pap apJer B	Apocryphal Jeremiah B? on papyrus

No. and siglum	Title	Prelim. publication
4Q		
385 = psEzek[a]	Pseudo-Ezekiel[a]	Strugnell[36]
385a = psMos[a]	Pseudo-Moses[a]	
385b = apJer[c]	Apocryphal Jeremiah[c]	
386–387 = psEzek[b–c]	Pseudo-Ezekiel[b–c]	
387a = psMos[b]	Pseudo-Moses[b]	
387b = apJer[d]	Apocryphal Jeremiah[d]	
388 = psEzek[d]	Pseudo-Ezekiel[d]	
388a–389 = psMos[c–d]	Pseudo-Moses[c–d]	
389a = apJer[e]	Apocryphal Jeremiah[e]	
390 = psMos[e]	Pseudo-Moses[e]	Eisenman[37]

DJD XIX

No. and siglum	Title
4Q	
391 = pap psEzek[g]	Pseudo-Ezekiel?[g] on papyrus
392–393 = Lit	Liturgical works

DJD X

No. and siglum	Title
4Q	
394 = MMT[a]	MMT[a]
395–397 = MMT[b–d]	MMT[b–d]
398 = papMMT[e]	MMT[e] on papyrus
399 = MMT[f]	MMT[f]

DJD XI

No. and siglum	Title	Prelim. publication
4Q		
400–407 = ShirShab^{a–h}	Songs of Sabbath Sacrifice^{a–h}	Newsom[38]
408 = Wisd	Sapiential work	Steudel[39]
409 = Lit	Liturgy	Qimron[40]
410–413 = Wisd	Sapiential work	
414 = Bapt	Baptismal liturgy	Eisenman[41]
415 = WisdB^{a–b}	Sapiential work B^{a–b}	
416–418 = Wisd^{a–c}	Sapiential work A^{a–c}	Eisenman[42]
419 = Wisd A^d	Sapiential work A^d	
420–421 = Right^{a–b}	Ways of Righteousness^{a–b}	Elgvin[43]

DJD XIII

No. and siglum	Title
4Q	
422 = GenExodComm	Paraphrase of Genesis and Exodus

No. and siglum	Title	Prelim. publication
4Q		
422a = ExComm	Exodus Commentary	
423 = Farmer	Rule for the Farmer	
423a = Wisd E	Sapiential work E	
424 = Wisd	Sapiential work	Eisenman[44]
425 = Wisd C	Sapiential work C	
426 = Wisd	Sapiential work	
427–432 = Hod^{a–f}	Thanksgiving hymns^{a–f}	
433 = Hod-like	Hodayot-like fragment	
434–438 = Barki^{a–e}	Barki nafshi^{a–e}	Eisenman[45]
439 = Barki-like	Work similar to Barki nafshi	
440 = Hod-like	Work similar to Hodayot	
441–444 = Pr	Prayers	

445–447 = Poet frs	Poetic fragments

DJD XI

No. and siglum	Title	
4Q		
448 = apPs and Jon	Apocryphal Psalm – King Jonathan	
449–456 = Prs	Prayers	
457 = Narrs	Narratives	
458 = Narr	Narrative	Eisenman[46]
459–460 = Pseudep	Pseudepigraphic work	
461 = Narr	Narrative	Eisenman[47]

DJD XIX

No. and siglum	Title
4Q	
462–463	Narrative
464 = Apoc^b	Apocryphon^b

No. and siglum	Title	Prelim. publication
4Q		
465 = unid	Unidentified text	
466–467 = Apoc?	Apocryphon	
468 = Hist	4Q Historical text B	Broshi[48]

DJD XIX

No. and siglum	Title
4Q	
470 = Zedk fr	Fragment mentioning Zedekiah

No. *and siglum*	*Title*	*Prelim. publication*
4Q		
471 = M^g	War^g	Eshel[49]
471a = Polem. fr	Polemical fragment	Eshel and Kister[50]
471b = PrMich	Prayer of Michael	Eshel[51]
472 = Wisd	Sapiential work	

DJD XXII

No. *and siglum*	*Title*
4Q	
473 = 2 ways	Sapiential work: Two Ways

No. *and siglum*	*Title*	*Prelim. publication*
4Q		
474 = Wisd	Joseph apocryphon?	Elgvin[52]
475–476 = Wisd	Sapiential work	
477 = Sect decr	Decrees of the sect	Eshel[53]

DJD XXII

No. *and siglum*	*Title*
4Q	
478 = papFestivlas	Papyrus mentioning festivals
479 = Fr.David of David	Text mentioning descendants
480 = Narrative	Narrative
481 = Mixed kinds	Text on mixed kinds
481a = Elisha frg	Fragment mentioning Elisha
481b = Narr	Narrative
481c = Prayer	Prayer for mercy
481d = Red	Fragments with red ink
4813 = Narrative	Narrative
481f = Misc	Miscellaneous fragments

DJD VII

No. and siglum	Title
4Q	
482–483 = papJub?	Jubilees? on papyrus
484 = TJudah?	Testament of Judah?
485 = Proph	Prophetic or sapiential text
486–487 = Sap a–b	Sapiential work[a–b]
488 = Ap ar	Aramaic apocryphon
489 = papApoc ar	Aramaic apocalypse
490	Related fragment?
491–497 = Ma–g	War[a–g]
498 = HymSap	Hymns or sapiential work
499 = papHymPr	Fragments of Hymns and Prayers
500 = papBen	Benediction
501 = Lamb	Lamentation[b]
502 = papRitMar	Marriage Ritual
503 = papPrQuot	Daily Prayers
504–506 = DivHama–c	Words of the Heavenly Lights[a–c]
507–509 = PrFesta–c	Prayers for Festivals[a–c]
510–511 = Shira–b	Canticle of the Sage[a–b]
512 = papRitPur	Ritual of Purification
513–514 = Ordb–c	Ordinances[b–c]
515–520 = pap	Undeciphered papyrus fragments

DJD XXV

521 = MessApoc	Messianic Apocalypse
522 = Proph of Joshua	Prophecy of Joshua
523 = Jonathan	Jonathan
524 = Temple	Temple scroll
525 = Beat	Beatitudes
526 = Test	Testament?
527 = Litur	Liturgical text
528 = Hymn	Hymn or Wisdom work

No. and siglum	Title	Prelim. publication
4Q		
529 = Mich	Words of Michael	Eisenman[54]
530–531 = Giants^b–c	Book of Giants (Enoch)^b–c	Milik[55]
532 = Giants^e	Book of Giants (Enoch)^e	Eisenman[56]
533 = psEn	Book of Giants or Pseudo-Enoch	
534 = Elect	Elect of God	Starcky[57]
535–536 = Ar NC	Aramaic texts N and C	Eisenman[58]
537 = AJa	Aramaic Jacob	Puech[59]
538 = AJu	Aramaic Judah	Milik[60]
539 = AJo	Aramaic Joseph	Milik[61]
540–541 = TLevi^c–d?	Testament of Levi?^c–d	Puech[62]
542 = TQahat	Testament of Qahat	Puech[63]
543–548 = Amram^a–f	Visions of Amram^a–f	Milik[64]
549 = HurMir	Work mentioning Hur and Miriam	
550 = PrEsth	Proto-Esther^a–e+f	Milik[65]
551 = DanSus?	Susannah episode in Daniel?	Milik[66]
552–553 = 4Kgd^a b	Four Kingdoms^a–b	
554 = JNa	New Jerusalem^a	Starcky[67]
555 = JNb	New Jerusalem^b	
556–557 = Vis ^a–c	Visions	
559 = papChronol	Biblical Chronology	Eisenman[68]
560 = Provs	Proverbs?	Elsenman[69]
561 = Physiogn	Physiognomic horoscope	Eisenman[70]
562–575 = Ar D–Z	Aramaic fragments D–Z	

DJD XXV

No. and siglum	Title
4Q	
576 = Gen	Genesis[n]
577 = Flood	Text mentioning the Flood
578 = Hist	Historical work
579 = Hym	Poetic work

Cave 5

DJD III

No. and siglum	Title
5Q	
1 = Deut	Deuteronomy
2 = Kgs	Kings
3 = Isa	Isaiah
4 = Am	Amos
5 = Ps	Psalms
6–7 = Lam[a–b]	Lamentations a–b
8 = Phyl	Phylactery
9 = Toponyms	Place names
10 = apMal	Apocryphal Malachi
11 = S	Serekh
12 = D	Damascus
13 = S-like	Fragment similar to S
14 = Curses	Liturgical curses
15 = JN ar	Aramaic New Jerusalem
16–25 = Unid	Small unidentified and unclassified fragments

Cave 6

DJD III

No. and siglum	*Title*
6Q	
1 = paleoGen	Genesis in palaeo-Hebrew
2 = paleoLev	Leviticus in palaeo-Hebrew
3 = Deut	Deuteronomy
4 = Kgs	Kings
5 = Ps	Psalms
6 = Cant	Song of Songs
7 = papDan	Daniel on papyrus
3 = pap EnGiants	Book of Giants (Enoch)
9 = papSam/Kgs	Samuel-Kings Apocryphon on papyrus
10 = apProph	Apocryphal prophecy
11 = Vine	Allegory of the Vine
12 = apProph	Apocryphal Prophecy
13 = PriestProph	Priestly Prophecy
14 = Apoc at	Aramaic Apocalypse
15 = D	Damascus
16 = papBen	Benedictions on papyrus
17 = Cal	Calendar
18 = papHym	Hymns on papyrus
19 = Gen? ar	Aramaic text related to Genesis?
20 = Deut?	Deuteronomy?
21 = frgProph	Prophetic fragment
22 = Unid Hebr	Unidentified Hebrew text
23 = Unid ar	Unidentified Aramaic texts
24–31 = misc	Diverse fragments

Cave 7

DJD III

No. and siglum	Title
7Q	
1 = papLXXEx	Greek Exodus
2 = papLXXEpJer	Greek Epistle of Jeremiah
3–5 = papGr Bib frgs?	Unidentified Greek biblical fragments?[71]
6–18 = papUnid	Unidentified tiny fragments[72]
19 = Gr impr	Imprints of Greek papyrus on plaster

Cave 8

DJD III

No. and siglum	Title
8Q	
1 = Gen	Genesis
2 = Ps	Psalms
3 = phyl	Phylactery
4 = mez	Mezuzah
5 = Hym	Liturgical poem

Cave 9

DJD III

9Q1	Papyrus fragment

Cave 10

DJD III

10Q1	Ostrakon

Cave 11

No. and siglum	Title	Prelim. publication
11Q		
1 = paleoLev	Leviticus a in palaeo-Hebrew	Freedman[73]

DJD XXIII

No. and siglum	Title
11Q	
2 = Lev	Leviticus
3 = Deut	Deuteronomy
4 = Ezek	Ezekiel

DJD IV

5 = Ps[a]	Psalms[a]

DJD XXIII

5a = Ps[a] Frs E,F	Psalms[a]
6 = Ps[b]	Psalms[b]
7 = Ps[c]	Psalms[c]
8–9 = Ps[d–e]	Psalms[d–e]
10 = tgJob	Targum of Job
11 = apPs[a]	Apocryphal Psalms
12 = Jub	Jubilees
13 = Melch	Melkizedek
14 = SephMilh	Sepher ha-Milhamah
15–16 = Hym[a–b]	Hymns[a–b]
17 = ShirShab	Songs of the Sabbath Sacrifice
18 = JN	New Jerusalem

No. and siglum	Title	Prelim. publication
19 = Temple[a]	Temple Scroll	Yadin[74]

DJD XXIII

No. and siglum	Title
20 = Temple[b]	Temple Scroll fragments
21 = Temple[c]	Temple Scroll[c]?
22–28 = Unid	Unidentified fragments
29 = Serekh	Fragment related to Serekh ha-Yaḥad
30 = Unid	Unidentified fragments
31 = Unid	Unidentified words

Notes

1. The Dead Sea Scrolls: 1947–1999

1. E. L. Sukenik, *Megillot genuzot* I, Jerusalem 1948; W. F. Albright, *BASOR* 110, April 1948, 1–3; G. E. Wright, 'A Sensational Discovery', *BA*, 1948, 21–3.

2. Cf. the interview with the discoverer reported by John C. Trever, *The Dead Sea Scrolls: A Personal Account*, Eerdmans, Grand Rapids 1979, 191–4.

3. Cf. *Observations sur le Manuel de discipline découvert près de La Mer Morte*, Paris 1951. His major synthesis in English is *The Essene Writings from Qumran*. For the latest survey, see G. Vermes and Martin Goodman, *The Essenes according to the Classical Sources*, Sheffield 1989.

4. *Archaeology and the Dead Sea Scrolls*, OUP, Oxford 1973.

5. *Les manuscrits du désert de Juda*, Desclée, Tournai-Paris 1953; *Discovery in the Judean Desert*, Desclée, New York 1956.

6. *Dix ans de découvertes dans le désert de Juda*, Paris 1957, ET *Ten Years of Discovery in the Wilderness of Judaea*; F. M. Cross, *The Ancient Library of Qumran and Modern Biblical Studies*; R. de Vaux, *Archaeology and the Dead Sea Scrolls* (n. 4).

7. *The Dead Sea Scrolls of St Mark's Monastery* I, II/2.

8. *The Dead Sea Scrolls of the Hebrew University*.

9. N. Avigad and Y. Yadin, *A Genesis Apocryphon*. See now J. C. Greenfield and E. Qimron, 'The Genesis Apocryphon Col. XII', in *Studies in Qumran Aramaic*, ed. T. Muraoka, 70–7; M. Morgenstern et al., 'The Hitherto Unpublished Columns of the Genesis Apocryphon', *Abr-Nahrain* 33, 1995, 30–52.

10. *DJD I*.

11. M. Baillet, J. T. Milik, R. de Vaux, *DJD III*.

12. J. A. Sanders, *DJD IV*.

13. J. M. Allegro and A. A. Anderson, *DJD V*.

14. *Megillat ha~Miqdash I–III*, Jerusalem. ET *The Temple Scroll I–III*.

15. J. P. M. van der Ploeg, A. S. van der Woude and B. Jongeling, *Le Targum de Job de la grotte XI de Qumrân*; D. N. Freedman and K. A. Matthews, *The Paleo-Hebrew Leviticus Scroll (11QpaleoLev)*.

16. In the 1970s, only J. T. Milik remained productive: cf. *The Books of Enoch: Aramaic Fragments of Qumran Cave 4*; *DJD VI*, before he, too, entered a state of hibernation. By 1991, he was persuaded to relinquish all his unpublished documents, which were re-assigned to new editors.

17. *The Dead Sea Scrolls: Qumran in Perspective*, London 1977, 24 (originally the 1977 Margaret Harris Lectures delivered at the University of Dundee).
18. *A Preliminary Edition of the Unpublished Dead Sea Scrolls I: The Hebrew and Aramaic Texts from Cave 4.*
19. *A Preliminary Concordance to the Hebrew and Aramaic Fragments from Qumran Caves II to X* distributed by H. Stegemann, Göttingen 1988.
20. Robert H. Eisenman and James M. Robinson, *A Facsimile Edition of the Dead Sea Scrolls I–II.*
21. Patrick W. Skehan, Eugene Ulrich and Judith E. Sanderson, *DJD IX.*
22. This document has been published by F. M. Cross and Esther Eshel, *IEJ* 47, 1997, 17–28.
23. See Ada Yardeni, ibid., 233–7.
24. Cf. Emanuel Tov, 'The Unpublished Qumran Texts from Caves 4 and 11', *JJS* 43, 1992, 101–36. It seems that 4Q342–361 did not originate from Qumran, but from other caves in the Judaean desert.
25. The exception is the Damascus Document, well attested in Caves 4, 5 and 6, which has been known from two incomplete mediaeval manuscripts found in the Cairo Genizah, and first published by S. Schechter as *Documents of Jewish Sectaries Vol.1: Fragments of a Zadokite Work*, Cambridge 1910, reprinted with a Prolegomenon by J. A. Fitzmyer, New York 1970. For a better edition see Magen Broshi, *The Damascus Document Reconsidered*, 1992.
26. 'The Development of the Jewish Scripts', in *The Bible and the Ancient Near East: Essays in Honor of W. F. Albright*, Doubleday, Garden City 1961, 133–202.
27. Cf. O. R. Sellers, 'Radiocarbon Dating of Cloth from the 'Ain Feshka Cave', *BASOR* 123, 1951, 22–4.
28. G. Boriani et al., 'Radiocarbon Dating of the Dead Sea Scrolls', *Atiqot* XX, 1991, 25–32.
29. The tests performed at the University of Arizona in 1994 dated the Habakkuk Commentary, one of the main sources of Qumran history, between 120 BCE and 5 CE. See A. J. T. Jull et al., 'Radiocarbon Dating of the Scrolls . . .', *Radiocarbon* 37, 1995, 11–17.
30. Cf. most recently in *The Essenes according to the Classical Sources* (n. 3),12–23.
31. During recent years several further establishments, tentatively identified as Essene, were discovered in the Judaean desert and in Jerusalem, but none of them is comparable to Qumran in size or importance and none has yielded manuscripts.
32. G. Vermes, *The Dead Sea Scrolls. Qumran in Perspective* (n. 17), 130; see p. 126 below.
33. For a major restatement of the whole subject, see Emanuel Tov, *Textual Criticism of the Hebrew Bible*, Minneapolis and Assen/Maastricht 1992.
34. Cf. 'Biblical Proof-texts in Qumran Literature', *JSS* 34, 1989, 493–508. It should, however, he observed that the Damascus Document also quotes the Book of Jubilees and a work attributed to the Patriarch Levi. It is unclear what their status was.
35. See J. A. Fitzmyer, *DJD XIX*, 1–76 (4Q196–200).

36. See J. A. Sanders, *DJD* IV, 79–85. Cf. also a Masada manuscript edited by Y. Yadin, *The Ben Sira Scroll from Masada*, Jerusalem 1965.
37. Cf J. T. Milik, *The Books of Enoch: Aramaic Fragments of Qumran Cave 4*.
38. Cf. *HJP* III, 250–68.
39. Cf. 'Qumran Forum Miscellanea II: The so-called King Jonathan Fragment (4Q448)', *JJS* 44, 1993, 294–300.
40. Cf. *War* 2.567; 3.11,19.
41. Cf. *War* 2.1152–3.
42. Though rejecting the sect's Essene identity, the so-called 'Groningen hypothesis' is basically a variation on the common opinion. Cf. F. García Martínez, 'Qumran Origins and Early History: A Groningen Hypothesis', *Folia Orientalia* 25, 1988, 113–36; id. and A. S. van der Woude, 'A Groningen Hypothesis of Qumran Origins and Early History', *RQ* 14, 1990, 521–42.
43. G. R. Driver, *The Judaean Scrolls: The Problem and a Solution*; C. Roth, *The Historical Background of the Dead Sea Scrolls*, Oxford 1958.
44. See his numerous articles in *JJS* between 1951 and 1955.
45. *The Sacred Mushroom and the Cross*, London 1970.
46. *Jesus the Man: A New Interpretation from the Dead Sea Scrolls*, London and New York 1992 = *Jesus and the Riddle of the Dead Sea Scrolls*, New York 1992.
47. *DSSU.*
48. See my review of Eiseman and Wise in the *TLS* of 4 December 1992.
49. 'The Problem of Origin and Identification of the Dead Sea Scrolls', *Proceedings of the American Philosophical Society*, 124/1, 1980, 1–24; 'Who hid the Dead Sea Scrolls?', *BA* 48, 1982, 68–82; 'Khirbet Qumran and the Manuscripts of the Judaean Wilderness: Observations on the Logic of their Investigation', *JNES* 49, 1990, 103–14; *Who Wrote the Dead Sea Scrolls?*. One of Golb's objections to the Essene occupation of Qumran, viz., the absence of letters and economic documents, will require some readjustment since we now know that 4Q341–349 consist of letters, lists of names, deeds of sale and various accounts. For a criticism of the hypothesis, see Timothy H. Lim, 'The Qumran Scrolls: Two Hypotheses', *Studies in Religion* 21/4, 1992, 455–66.
50. At the Scrolls Symposium held at the Library of Congress in Washington on 21–22 April 1993, Magen Broshi, Director of the Shrine of the Book at the Israel Museum in Jerusalem, delivered a powerful and wholly convincing rebuttal of the Golb conjecture and the speculation advanced at another conference, held in New York in December 1992, by Dr Pauline Donceel-Voûte concerning the identification of Qumran as a winter villa built for wealthy inhabitants of Jerusalem and the room which de Vaux identified as a scriptorium, a dining hall, cf. 'Archaeology of Qumran', in M. O. Wise (ed.), 'Methods of Investigation of the Khirbet Qumran Site', *Annals of the New York Academy of Sciences*, 1994, 1–38; 'Coenaculum – La salle à l'étage du locus 30 à Khirbet Qumrân', *Banquets d'Orient, Res Orientales* 4, 1992, 61–84. Against the latter theory see R. Reich in *JJS* 46, 1995, 157–60. For a discussion by four archeologists about the nature of the Qumran site see 'The Enigma of Qumran', *Biblical Archaeology Review* 24, 1998, 24–37, 78–84.

51. Cf. e.g. John Strugnell, 'Moses Pseudepigrapha at Qumran', in *Archaeology and History in the Dead Sea Scrolls*, ed. Lawrence H. Schiffman, 221.
52. 'Hebrew Biblical Manuscripts from the Judaean Desert: Their Contribution to Textual Criticism', *JJS* 39, 1988, 1–19.
53. It may also be wondered why the librarians of Jerusalem should have chosen such a distant place to hide their manuscripts when equally inaccessible caves could have been found closer to home.
54. Cf. J. T. Milik, 'La prière de Nabonide', *RB* 63, 1956, 407–11.
55. Cf. G. Vermes, *Jesus the Jew*, London and Philadelphia 1983, 67–9; *The Religion of Jesus the Jew*, London and Minneapolis 1993, 192–3.
56. *DSSU*, 19–23; C. Vermes, 'Qumran Forum Miscellanea I', *JJS* 43, 1992, 303–4; Michael O. Wise and James D. Tabor, 'The Messiah at Qumran', *BAR* 18 (Nov/Dec. 1992), 60–5; Emile Puech, 'Une apocalypse messianique', *RQ* 15, 1992, 475–522.
57. Targum Neofiti, Fragmentary Targum and Pseudo-Jonathan on Gen. 3.15.
58. S. Talmon in F. M. Cross and S. Talmon, *Qumran and the Origin of the Biblical Text*, Cambridge, Mass. 1975, 380.
59. *The Dead Sea Scrolls Forty Years On*, Oxford 1987, 15–16.
60. On this, see G. Vermes, *The Religion of Jesus the Jew* (n. 55).

2. Authenticity and Dating of the Scrolls

1. A brief account of the vicissitudes of the Shapira Deuteronomy may be found in *EncJud* 14, 1971, 1301–2 (F. F. Bruce, 'Shapira Fragments'). For a contemporary presentation read C. Clermont-Ganneau's fascinating book, *Les fraudes archéologiques en Palestine*, Paris 1885. After the discovery of Qumran fragments written in archaic Hebrew characters, M. Mansoor endeavoured to reopen the old Shapira story with a view to setting the record straight. See his article, 'The Case of Shapira's Dead Sea (Deuteronomy) Scroll of 1883', in *Transactions of the Wisconsin Academy of Sciences, Arts and Letters* 47, 1959, 183–229. The spuriousness of the Shapira scroll is re-confirmed by M. H. Goshen-Gottstein in 'The Shapira Forgery and the Qumran Scrolls', *JJS* 7, 1956, 187–93. Cf. also A. D. Crown, 'The Fate of the Shapira Scroll', *RQ* 7, 1970, 421–3.
2. The preliminary issues relating to the authenticity of the Scrolls and their relationship with the Qumran caves are treated authoritatively by R. de Vaux, *Archaeology and the Dead Sea Scrolls*, 95–102.
3. The result of the carbon-14 test was originally described by O. R. Sellers in 'Radiocarbon Dating of the Cloth from the "Ain Feshkha Cave"', *BASOR* 23, 1951, 24–6. For a subsequent analysis of charred wood from the Qumran building, see F. E. Zeuner, 'Notes on Qumran', *PEQ* 92, 1960, 27–8 (16 CE plus or minus eighty years).
4. G. Boriani *et al.*, 'Radiocarbon Dating of the Dead Sea Scrolls', *'Atiqot* 20, 1991, 27–32. For a second test, in general agreement with the first and with palaeographical dating, see J. A. T. Jull et al., 'Radiocarbon Dating of the Scrolls . . .', *Radiocarbon* 37, 1995, 11–17. Cf. above, 219 n. 28.

5. *IEJ* 12, 1962, 249.
6. *RB* XX, 1949, 236.
7. Ibid., 429.
8. R. de Vaux's initial views are contained in 'La cachette des manuscrits hébreux', *RB* 56,1949, 234–6; 'La grotte des manuscrits hébreux', ibid., 586–609. A more satisfactory archaeological dating was proposed by W. F. Albright in his Postscript to *BASOR Supplementary Studies* 10–12, 1951–1958. On the basis of literary data, A. Dupont-Sommer argued that the Scrolls must have been concealed during the first Jewish war: *Aperçus préliminaires sur les manuscrits de la Mer Morte*, Paris 1950, 105: *The Dead Sea Scrolls*, Oxford 1952, 85.

   The most influential interpretation of the Qumran excavations is given in the revised English translation of R. de Vaux's 1959 Schweich Lectures, *Archaeology and the Dead Sea Scrolls*. See also E.-M. Laperrousaz, *Qumrân: L'Établissement essénien des bords de la Mer Morte. Histoire et archéologie du site*, Paris 1976. Cf. also M. Broshi, 'The Archaeology of Qumran – A Reconsideration', in D. Dimant and U. Rappaport (eds), *The Dead Sea Scrolls: Forty Years of Research*, Leiden 1992, 103–15.

9. *Archaeology and the Dead Sea Scrolls*, 10.
10. The view of de Vaux that the mud brick table came from a *scriptorium* is rejected by G. R. Driver in 'Myths of Qumran', *Dead Sea Scroll Studies 1969*, *ALUOS* 6, 1969, 23–7. Driver's arguments in favour of an upper-storey dining-room table are answered by de Vaux, *Archaeology and the Dead Sea Scrolls*, 29 n. 1. A similar objection was voiced by Pauline Donceel-Voûte in a BBC television documentary in early 1993. For further divergent opinions, see N. Golb, 'The Problem of Origin and Identification of the Dead Sea Scrolls', *Proceedings of the American Philosophical Society* 124/1, 1980, 1–24; P. R. Davies, 'How not to do Archaeology: The Story of Qumran', *BA* 51, 1988, 203–7.
11. The Qumran numismatic finds are as follows (cf. de Vaux, *Archaeology and the Dead Sea Scrolls*, 18–44; Laperrousaz, *Qumrân: L'Établissement essénien des bords de la Mer Morte* [n. 5], 149–54): The earliest group consists of twelve Seleucid coins, six bronze and six silver. Three of the latter are dated to the reign of Antiochus VII Sidetes, viz. to 132–131, 131–130 and 130–129 BCE. The oldest Jewish pieces, according to de Vaux, are a coin of John Hyrcanus I (134–104 BCE) and one of Judah Aristobulus (104–103 BCE). This identification is founded on the theory, held generally, that Hasmonaean coinage began under John Hyrcanus (cf. B. Kanael, 'The Beginning of Maccabean Coinage', *IEJ* 1, 1951, 170–5). It would clash, however, with the rival thesis advanced by Y. Meshorer, *The Jewish Coins of the Second Temple Period*, Jerusalem 1967, 41–55, according to which Alexander Jannaeus (103–76 BCE) was the first ruler to strike his own coins, with the consequence that the pieces marked John and Judah are to be attributed to John Hyrcanus II (63–40 BCE) and Judah Aristobulus II (67–63 BCE).

   One hundred and forty-three coins derive from the rule of Alexander Jannaeus. For the rest of the Hasmonaeans, we have one coin minted by

Alexandra-Salome with her son Hyrcanus II (76–67 BCE); five by Hyrcanus II and four by Antigonus Mattathias (40–37 BCE).

The reign of Herod the Great (37–4 BCE) is represented by ten coins; the ethnarchy of Archelaus (4 BCE–6 CE) by sixteen; the reign of Agrippa I (41–44 CE) by seventy-eight; the period of Roman prefects (6–41 CE) and procurators (44–66 CE) by ninety-one; and the first Jewish war against Rome by ninety-four bronze coins, most of them struck in 67 and 68 CE.

The Roman occupation of Qumran is attested by nine coins from Caesarea and four from Dora dated to 67–68 CE; two undated coins from Nero's reign; one silver coin of Vespasian and Titus (69–70 CE); another, undated, of Vespasian; two coins from Ashkelon (72–73 CE); and four undated, but clearly post-70, coins celebrating the Roman conquest of the Jewish state with the legend *Judaea capta*. To the same era belongs a single coin of the last Herodian ruler, Agrippa II (50–92/93 CE), dated to 87 CE, but since it was found outside the building area, it may not be relevant to the chronology of Qumran.

In addition to these coins, the archaeologists also discovered three pots containing a hoard of 561 silver pieces. They are almost exclusively Tyrian and the most recent of them dates to 9–8 BCE.

A short survey of Hebrew coins is given in *HJP* I, 602–6.

12. During the last few years a number of fresh ideas concerning the identity of the Qumran establishment have been floated (rich man's villa, customs post and hostellery, etc.), without making much impact on mainstream opinion.

13. The most comprehensive tractate on Hebrew palaeography is that by S. A. Birnbaum, *The Hebrew Script. Part One. The Text*, Leiden 1971; *Part Two: The Plates*, London 1954–7.

    For the study of Qumran palaeography consult S. A. Birnbaum, 'The Qumran (Dead Sea) Scrolls and Palaeography', *BASOR Supplementary Studies* 13–14, 1952; F. M. Cross, 'The Oldest Manuscript from Qumran', *JBL* 74, 1955, 147–72 = F. M. Cross and S. Talmon (eds), *Qumran and the History of the Biblical Text*, Cambridge, Mass. and London 1975, 147–76; N. Avigad, 'The Palaeography of the Dead Sea Scrolls and Related Documents', in *Aspects of the Dead Sea Scrolls, Scripta Hierosolymitana* IV, 1958, 56–87.

    A pioneering study of palaeography in the light of the new discoveries is F. M. Cross, 'The Development of Jewish Script', *The Bible and the Ancient Near East: Essays in Honor of William Foxwell Albright*, ed. G. E. Wright, Doubleday, New York 1961, 133–202.

14. The Nash papyrus was originally published by S. A. Cook, 'A Pre-Massoretic Biblical Papyrus', *Proceedings of the Society of Biblical Archaeology* 25, 1903, 34–56. The photograph is reproduced in E. Würthwein, *The Text of the Old Testament*, London and Grand Rapids 1980, plate 6. For the most thorough study, see W. F. Albright, 'A Biblical Fragment from the Maccabaean Age: The Nash Papyrus', *JBL* 56, 1937, 145–76, and 'On the Date of the Scrolls from Ain Feshkha and the Nash Papyrus', *BASOR* 115, 1949, 10–19.

15. For the third-century CE epigraphical material from Dura Europos, see E. G. Kraeling, *The Excavations at Dura Europos* VIII, 1, *The Synagogue*, New Haven 1956.

16. The sources of the Masada and Bar Kokhba texts are: Y. Yadin, 'The Excavation of Masada – 1963/64: Preliminary Report', *IEJ* 15, 1965, 1–120; Y. Yadin, J. Naveh and Y. Meshorer, *Masada I*, Jerusalem 1989; H. M. Cotton and J. Geiger, *Masada II*, Jerusalem 1989. – P. Benoit et al., *DJD* II; N. Avigad, Y. Yadin et al., 'The Expedition to the Judaean Desert', *IEJ* 11,1961, 1–81; 12, 1962, 167–262; N. Lewis, *The Documents from the Bar Kokhba Period in the Cave of Letters: Greek Papyri*, Jerusalem 1989.

17. The oldest Qumran manuscripts are discussed by F. M. Cross, 'The Oldest Manuscript from Qumran' (n. 13), 147–72, and J. Muilenburg, 'A Qoheleth Scroll from Qumran', *BASOR* 135, 1954, 2–8. The revival of the archaic Hebrew script is discussed by F. M. Cross, 'The Development of Jewish Script' (n. 13), 189 n. 4.

18. The divine Name is written with square Hebrew characters in the Greek Papyrus Fouad 266 published by W. G. Waddell, 'The Tetragrammaton in the LXX', *JTS* 45, 1944, 157–61. In fragments discovered in the Cairo Geniza, the name YHWH is reproduced with archaic Hebrew letters in the Greek translation of the Bible by Aquila. See F. C. Burkitt, *Fragments of the Books of Kings according to the Translation of Aquila*, Cambridge 1897, and C. Taylor, *Hebrew-Greek Cairo Genizah Palimpsests*, Cambridge 1900. The custom of spelling the name of God in Hebrew in Greek biblical manuscripts is mentioned by Origen in his commentary on Psalm 2.2 *(Patrologia Graeca* XII, 1104). See also, E. Tov, 'Hebrew Biblical Manuscripts from the Judaean Desert', *JJS* 39, 1988, 13–14. Palaeo-Hebrew letters are also used occasionally at Qumran for *el* (God).

4. The Community

1. A full account of the priestly government of the Jews during the Persian and Hellenistic eras may be found in *HJP* II, 227–313. The question of the Zadokite priesthood is discussed ibid. 251–2 and n. 56. For the Zadokite genealogy of Ezra, see Ezra 7.1–5. The Qumran use of the phrase 'sons of Zadok' is examined by J. Liver, 'The "Sons of Zadok the Priests" in the Dead Sea Sect', *RQ* 6, 1967, 3–30. The following general works may also be consulted: J. Jeremias, *Jerusalem in the Time of Jesus*, London and Philadelphia 1969, 147–221; A. Cody, *A History of the Old Testament* Priesthood, Rome 1969.

2. For the various offices, see J. F. Priest, '*Mebaqqer*, Paquid, and the Messiah', *JBL* 81, 1962, 55–61; A. S. Kapelrud, 'Die aktuellen und die eschatologischen Behörden der Qumrangemeinde', *Qumran-Probleme*, ed. H. Bardtke, Berlin 1963, 259–67; P. Osten-Sacken, 'Bemerkungen zur Stellung des *Mebaqqer* in der Sektenschrift', *ZNW* 55, 1964, 18–26; M. Weinfeld, *The Organizational Pattern and the Penal Code of the Qumran Sect*, Göttingen 1986, 19–21. There are two schools of thought concerning the function of the Law interpreter (1QS 6.6; 8.12). According to one, no special person *was* entrusted with this task; all the sectaries had their study periods in rotation. The other view is that a particular individual, no doubt a priest, was chosen to meditate on Scripture 'day and night', thus foreshadowing the work of the priestly Messiah known

also as the 'Interpreter of the Law' (CD 7.18; 4QFlor 1–11). For a comparison with Essene and Christian leadership, see Chapters 5 and 8.

3. On the terminology 'Community', 'Congregation', etc., consult A. Dupont-Sommer, *The Essene Writings from Qumran*, 44; P. Wernberg-Møller, 'The Nature of YAHAD . . .', *ALUOS* 6, 1969, 6–81.

4. For the problem of excommunication see G. Forkman, *The Limits of the Religious Community. Expulsion from the Religious Community within the Qumran Sect, within Rabbinic Judaism and within Primitive Christianity*, Lund 1972; L. H. Schiffman, *Sectarian Law in The Dead Sea Scrolls*, Chico 1983, 168–73; M. Weinfeld, *The Organizational Pattern and the Penal Code of the Qumran Sect* (n. 2), 41–3. For a general survey see *EncJud 8*, 344–55, and *HJP* II, 1979, 431–3.

5. In regard to the *tirosh* drunk at the common table, the rabbis explain that in the 'language of men', i.e. in ordinary spoken Hebrew, *tirosh* is a sweet, unfermented drink distinct from wine. If a person vowed to abstain from *tirosh*, he might not touch any kind of fruit juice, but was free to drink as much wine as he liked. If, on the other hand, he formulated his vow in the 'language of the Torah', i.e. biblical Hebrew, where *tirosh* is synonymous with wine, he was not to take any alcohol (tNedarim 4.3; yNedarim 40b; Sifre to Deut. 42 on Deut.11.14). It should also be noted in support of our hypothesis that the Qumran sectaries drank grape juice and that priests participating in Temple worship were to abstain from wine according to Lev. 10.8–11, the 'sons of Zadok' in particular, in Ezek. 44.21.

6. For 'purity' and 'the drink of the Congregation', see S. Lieberman, 'The Discipline in the so-called Dead Sea Manual of Discipline', *JBL* 71, 1951, 199–206 = *Texts and Studies*, New York 1974, 200–7. Cf. also J. Licht, '*Ḥumrat mashqeh harabbim miṭohorat harabbim beSerekh hayyaḥad*', *Sefer Segal*, ed. J. M. Grintz, Jerusalem 1964, 300–9.

7. The terminology relating to the training and admission of candidates is analysed by M. Delcor, 'Le vocabulaire juridique, cultuel et mystique de l'initiation dans la secte de Qumrân', in *Qumran-Probleme*, ed. H. Bardtke (n. 2), 109–34; cf. M. Weinfeld, *The Organizational Pattern and the Penal Code of the Qumran Sect* (n. 2), 21–3.

Apropos of initiation, the view has been advanced that the Feast of the Renewal of the Covenant was the occasion for new members to make their sworn pledge (cf. Milik, *Ten Years of Discovery in the Wilderness of Judaea*, 114). This is not, however, borne out by the evidence. The Covenant ritual mentions no oath and the Damascus Document expressly states that the oath was to be taken on the very day the candidate was accepted by the Guardian (CD 15.7–8). It would be reasonable to suppose that the noviciate began on that particular feast-day and ended exactly two years later, but this too is purely speculative.

Essene 'communism' will be examined in Chapter 5 and the use of the common purse in the Jerusalem church in Chapter 8. For the Qumran evidence see L. M. Pákozdy, 'Der wirtschaftliche Hintergrund der Gemeinschaft von Qumran', in *Qumran-Probleme*, 26–91; W. Tyloch, 'Quelques remarques sur le caractère social du mouvement de Qumrân'; ibid., 341–51; J. G. Greehy, 'Community of Goods – Qumran and Acts', *Irish Theological Quarterly* 32, 1965, 230–40; J. A. Fitzmyer, 'Jewish Christianity in Acts in the Light of the Qumran Scrolls', *Essays on the Semitic Background of the New Testament,* London 1971, 271–303.

8. For a discussion of Essene celibacy, see Chapter 5, p. 123 and Chapter 7, pp. 162–3.

9. R de Vaux, *Archaeology and the Dead Sea Scrolls,* 47–8; J.-P. Humbert, *Fouilles de Khirbet Qumrân,* 346–52.

10. On the similarities and differences between the Qumran Community and the rabbinic *ḥaburoth* or guilds devoted to the strict observance of purity and tithe-laws, cf. S. Lieberman, 'The Discipline in the so-called Dead Sea Manual of Discipline', (n. 6); G. Vermes, *Discovery in the Judean Desert,* 48–52; C. Rabin, 'Yahad, Haburah and Essenes', *Studies in the Dead Sea Scrolls . . . in Memory of E. L. Sukenik,* Jerusalem 1957, 104–22 (in Hebrew). On the *haburoth* in general, see *HJP* II, 1979, 398–9.

11. On Qumran halakhah, see L. H. Schiffman, *The Halakhah at Qumran,* Leiden 1975; *Sectarian Law and the Dead Sea Scrolls,* Atlanta 1983; J. M. Baumgarten, *Studies in Qumran Law,* Leiden 1977; M. Bernstein, F. García Martínez and J. Kampen, *Legal Texts and Legal Issues,* Leiden 1997.

12. The ban on sexual intercourse 'in the city of the Sanctuary' has been interpreted as referring to fornication (R. H. Charles, *Apocrypha and Psendepigrapha* II, Oxford 1913, 828), but as has been suggested, it more probably alludes to intercourse between married pilgrims in the holy city (C. Rabin, *Zadokite Documents,* 59).

13. On the age of twenty as marking a youth's majority, see S. B. Hoenig, 'On the Age of Mature Responsibility in 1QSa', *JQR* 48, 1957, 371–5; 'The Age of Twenty in Rabbinic Tradition and 1QSa', *JQR* 49, 1958, 209–14. The recommended age for marriage for a man is eighteen years in rabbinic tradition (mAbot 5.21).

    The problem of divorce is nowhere treated explicitly in the Scrolls. A number of scholars see in the prohibition on taking two wives 'in their lifetime' (CD 4.20–5.2) an outlawing of both polygamy and divorce, but a careful analysis of the passage makes it plain that the author is arguing against polygamy alone, and was not concerned with the question of a divorce followed by re-marriage. For specialized literature on the subject, see Y. Yadin, 'L'attitude essénienne envers la polygamie et le divorce', *RB* 79, 1972, 98–9; G. Vermes, 'Sectarian Matrimonial Halakhah in the Damascus Rule', JJS 25, 1974, 197–202 [= *PBJS,* 50–56]; J. A. Fitzmyer, 'The Matthean Divorce Texts and some new Palestininan Evidence', *Theological Studies* 37, 1976, 197–226.

14. The nature and identity of the 'Book of Meditation *(Hagu)*' are still debated. It has been suggested that this is an alternative title for the Community Rule (A. Dupont-Sommer, *The Essene Writings from Qumran,* 70) or a 'written corpus of Torah exegesis' (P. Wernberg-Møller, *ALUOS* 6, 1969, 79–80 n. 32). However, the fact that it is represented as the basic text-book studied at the one extreme by the Guardian and the Judges, and at the other by young children,

points to the Bible, and more particularly the Pentateuch. Note also that Moses instructed Joshua, and the Psalmist the just man in general, to *meditate* on the Law day and night (Josh. 1.8; Ps. 1.2). In fact, a rabbinic dictum goes so far as to restrict all meditation' *(hege)* to 'the words of the Law' (Gen. R. 49.17). Cf. L. H. Schiffman, *The Halakhah at Qumran* (n. 11), 44 n. 144.

15. Rabbinic legislation for the composition of Jewish tribunals is contained in the tractate Sanhedrin (Mishnah, Tosefta and Talmud). The special court of ten judges is mentioned in mMegillah 4.3; mSanhedrin 1.3. The Ordinances of Cave 4 know also of a tribunal of twelve, two priests and ten laymen, apparently endowed with capital jurisdiction (4Q159).

   For a comparison of Qumran with the primitive church, see M. Delcor, 'Les tribunaux de l'église de Corinthe et les tribunaux de Qumrân', in *Studiorum Paulinorum Congressus Catholicus 1961*, Rome 1963, 535–48 (= *Paul and Qumran*, ed. J. Murphy-O'Connor, London 1968, 69–84); J. M. Baumgarten, The Duodecimal Courts of Qumran, Revelation and the Sanhedrin', *JBL* 95, 1976, 57–78. See further, J. Pouilly, 'L'évolution de la législation pénale dans la Communauté de Qumrân', *RB* 82, 1975, 522–51.

16. Apropos of the death penalty, the interpretation of CD 9.1 is controversial. C. Rabin *(Zadokite Fragments,* in loc.*)* understands it to mean that criminals condemned to death by the sect were to be handed over to the Gentiles for execution. But the exegesis advanced by P. Winter makes better sense: the mere laying of a capital charge against a sectary (or perhaps simply against another Jew) before a Gentile court constituted a crime punishable by death: cf. 'Ṣadoqite Fragment IX. 1', *RQ* 6, 1967, 131–6. See also Z. W. Falk, *'Beḥuqei hagoyim* in Damascus Document IX. 1' ibid., 1969, 569.

   In connection with Qumran allusions to crucifixion, the following points are to be borne in mind. Josephus twice records that Alexander Jannaeus crucified eight hundred of his political opponents (Pharisees) in *c.* 88 BCE. *(Ant.* 13.380; *War* I. 97). 4QpNah 1.7–8 appears to echo this event, if the phrase 'to hang man alive (on the tree)' is interpreted in the light of Sifre to Deut. 221, where this form of death penalty is represented as characteristic of the Roman authorities. If, as is likely, the legislation recorded in the Temple Scroll (64.6–13) concerns the future age, its choice of 'hanging/crucifixion' for the execution of persons guilty of crimes against the Jewish state may be seen as inspired by Roman law. Cf. D. J. Halperin, 'Crucifixion, the Nahum Pesher, and the Penalty of Strangulation', *JJS* 31, 1981, 32–46. On crucifixion in general, see P. Winter, *On the Trial of Jesus,* Berlin 1974, 90–6; M. Hengel, *Crucifixion,* London and Philadelphia 1977. For the Qumran texts, cf. N. Wieder, 'Notes on the New Documents from the Fourth Cave of Qumran', *JJS* 7, 1956, 71–2; Y. Yadin, 'Pesher Nahum Reconsidered', *IEJ* 21, 1971, 1–12; *HJP* I, 224–5. J. M. Baumgarten takes the Hebrew verb 'to hang' in the sense of an execution by hanging because he finds crucifixion repugnant to Jewish law: cf. 'Does *tlh* in the Temple Scroll refer to Crucifixion?', *JBL* 91, 1972, 472–81.

17. The problem of single witnesses has been considered by several scholars: B. Levine, 'Damascus Document IX, 17–22: A New Translation and Comments',

RQ 8, 1973, 195–6; J. Neusner, 'By the Testimony of Two Witnesses in the Damascus Document IX, 17–22 and in Pharisaic-Rabbinic Law', ibid., 197–217; L. H. Schiffman, 'The Qumran Law of Testimony', ibid., 603–12; N. L. Rabinovitch, 'Damascus Document IX, 17–22 and Rabbinic Parallels', *RQ* 9, 1977, 113–16; B. S. Jackson, '*Testes singulares* in Early Jewish Law and the New Testament', in *Essays in Jewish and Comparative Legal History,* Leiden 1975,172–201. Both Neusner and Jackson explain the text as demanding that three separate single witnesses report the commission on three separate occasions of the same capital crime by the same sectary. If the witnesses were trustworthy, the Guardian could start proceedings against the accused.

18. For the liturgical calendar of the sect and its connection with the Book of Jubilees, see Chapter 7, pp. 157–8, 237 n. 5.
19. The stipulation that the Guardian of all the camps should be versed in all the languages of humankind may be compared to the statement in the Babylonian Talmud (bSanhedrin 17a) that only men acquainted with the seventy languages of the creation were eligible to sit on the Jerusalem Sanhedrin.
20. J. T. Milik, *Ten Years of Discovery in the Wilderness of Judaea,* 117–89.
21. For the female skeletons in the Qumran cemetery, see in addition to de Vaux *(Archaeology,* 47–8), S. H. Steckoll, 'Preliminary Excavation Report in the Qumran Cemetery', *RQ* 6, 1968, 323–44; N. Haas and H. Nathan, 'Anthropological Survey of the Human Skeletal Remains from Qumran', ibid., 345–52. Steckoll claims to have excavated in 1966 and 1967 nine further tombs at Qumran which yielded the bones of six men, two women, one of them buried with a baby, and a little girl. R. de Vaux expressed serious doubts about the researches of 'this Sherlock Holmes of archaeology' *(Archaeology and the Dead Sea Scrolls,* 48). In view of the confused evidence, further archaeological investigation of the cemetery is essential.
22. It is worth noting that lay heads of the sect appear only in the Messianic Rule and the War Rule – the chiefs of tribes, Thousands, Hundreds, Fifties and Tens. Interestingly, the eschatological lay leader, the Messiah of Israel, is never called 'king'. His title is 'prince' *(nasi,* 1QSb 5.20; 1QM 5.1; CD 7.20), following the model of Ezek. 34.24. The same style was used by the commander of the second Jewish revolution, Simeon ben Kosiba, as witnessed by his coins and the Murabba'at and Nahal Hever papyri. Cf. *HJP* I, 544, 606.

5. Identification of the Community

1. Among the many general works devoted to inter-testamental Judaism, the following are particularly recommended: *HJP* I (political history from 175 BCE to 135 CE); II (institutions and movements). On a less technical level see *The Jewish People in the First Century,* ed. S. Safrai and M. Stern, Assen and Philadelphia, I, 1974; II, 1977. See also M. Simon, *Les sectes juives au temps de Jésus Christ,* Paris 1960 and J. Jeremias, *Jerusalem in the Time of Jesus,* London and Philadelphia 1969. For the reconstruction of Judaism at Jamnia, cf. J. Neusner, *A Life of Yohanan ben Zakkai,* Leiden 1970.
2. For the organization of the synagogue and its worship, including the Eighteen

Benedictions, see *HJP* II, 447–63.

3. The identification of the Qumran sect as a Christian community was first advanced in a series of articles by J. L. Teicher in *JJS* 2–5, 1950–4. The same view has been expressed by Y. Baer, 'Serekh ha-Yaḥad – The Manual of Discipline. A Jewish-Christian Document from the Beginning of the Second Century CE', *Zion* 29, 1960, 1–60 (in Hebrew). For extravagant variations, see Barbara Thiering, *Jesus the Man*, Sydney 1992, and Robert H. Eisenman, *Maccabees, Zadokites, Christians and Qumran*, Leiden 1983; *James the Just and the Habakkuk Pesher*, Leiden 1986; *DSSU*.

4. For a general discussion, see *HJP* II, 404–14, with full bibliography. J. Le Moyne, *Les Sadducéens*, Paris 1972 (a comprehensive survey). See also R. Meyer, 'Sadducee', *TDNT* VII, 1971, 35–54; A. J. Saldarini, *Pharisees, Scribes and Sadducees in Palestinian Society*, Edinburgh 1989.

5. Among the endeavours to identify the Qumran sectaries and Sadducees, see R. North, 'The Qumran Sadducees', *CBQ* 17, 1955, 164–88; L. H. Schiffman, 'The Sadducean Origins of the Dead Sea Scroll Sect', in Hershel Shanks (ed.), *Understanding the Dead Sea Scrolls*, New York 1992, 35–49.

6. Again see *HJP* II, 388–403 for a general examination of the subject and bibliography. The following are a few of a large number of monographs: R. T. Herford, *The Pharisees*, London 1924; L. Finkelstein, *The Pharisees* I–II, Philadelphia 1962; A. Michel – J. Le Moyne, 'Pharisiens', Dictionnaire de la Bible, Supplément VII, 1966, 1022–115; J. Neusner, *The Rabbinic Traditions about the Pharisees before 70 I–III*, Leiden 1970; *From Politics to Piety: The Emergence of Pharisaic Judaism*, Englewood Cliffs, NJ 1973; R. Meyer and H. F. Weiss, 'Pharisee', *TDNT* IX, 1974, 11–48; E. Rivkin, 'Pharisees', *IDBS*, 1976, 657–63; A. J. Saldarini, *Pharisees, Scribes and Sadducees in Palestinian Society* (n. 4).

7. The constitution of the *ḥaburoth* is outlined in *HJP* II, 398–400. The relationship of the Qumran sect to the *ḥaburah* has been discussed by S. Lieberman, 'The Discipline of the so-called Manual of Discipline', *JBL* 71, 1952, 199–206 (= *Texts and Studies*, Ktav, New York 1974, 200–7); C. Rabin, Qumran Studies, Oxford University Press, Oxford 1957.

8. For the rabbinic attitude towards celibacy, see G. F. Moore, *Judaism* II, Cambridge, Mass. 1927, 119–20, 270; G. Vermes, *Jesus the Jew*, London and Philadelphia 1981, 101–2; E. Rivkin, *The Hidden Revolution*, Nashville 1978.

9. *HJP* II, 598–606 contains an Appendix on the Zealots compiled by C. T. R. Hayward.

The most important and extensive monograph is by M. Hengel, *Die Zeloten*, Leiden 1961, ²1976, ET *The Zealots*, Edinburgh 1989; cf. also 'Zeloten und Sikarier', *Josephus-Studien (O. Michel Festschrift)*, ed.O. Betz et al., Göttingen 1974, 175–96. The following general studies are available in English: W. R. Farmer, *Maccabees, Zealots, Josephus*, New York 1956; S. G. F. Brandon, *Jesus and the Zealots*, Manchester 1967; M. Stern, 'Zealots', *Encyclopaedia Judaica Yearbook*, Jerusalem 1973, 135–52; E. M. Smallwood, *The Jews under Roman Rule*, Leiden 1976, 153–5, 312–69; E. M. Rhoads, *Israel in Revolution 6–74 CE*, Philadelphia 1976.

Among the learned articles published in recent years the most important are: M. Smith, 'Zealots and Sicarii: their Origins and Relations', *HTR* 64, 1971, 1–19; M. Borg, 'The Currency of the Term Zealot', *JTS* 22, 1971, 504–12; S. Applebaum, 'The Zealots: the Case for Revaluation', *JRS* 61, 1971, 195–70; V. Nikiprowetzky, 'Sicaires et Zélotes – une reconsidération', *Semitica* 23, 1973, 51–64.

10. The results of the archaeological excavations at Masada are summarized and illustrated in Y. Yadin, *Masada: Herod's Fortress and the Zealots' Last Stand*, London 1966; id., *Masada I–II. The Yigael Yadin Excavations 1963–1965, Final Report*, 1989.

11. The theory identifying the Qumran sect with the Zealots was the creation in the mid-1950s of my greatly missed colleague G. R. (later Sir Godfrey) Driver and my predecessor at Oxford, the late Cecil Roth. Their plan for a joint publication misfired when Roth released his thesis unilaterally in *The Historical Background of the Dead Sea Scrolls*, Oxford 1958, claiming that the theory was his own and that he was the first to voice it in seminars in early 1957. 'At the same time,' Roth explains in the Introduction, 'I communicated my views to my colleague Professor G. R. Driver, who accepted them generously . .' (p. vii). Driver's much more substantial book (614 pages against Roth's 87) had to wait another seven years before completion: *The Judaean Scrolls: The Problem and a Solution*, Oxford 1965. In the Preface, Driver's version of the same incident reads: '. . . in 1953 I showed that the same document (the Commentary on Habakkuk) alluded to an event which took place in A D 70 . . . When . . . early in 1957 Dr C. Roth, who knew my views, drew my attention to the same solution, I saw at once that a fresh investigation would be required, and I invited him to join me in carrying it out' (p. ix). Cf. also R. H. Eisenman, in n. 3 above.

12. As a preamble to an Essene bibliography a few notes are called for on the ancient writers who serve as primary sources.

Flavius Josephus, originally called Joseph son of Mattathias before adopting a Roman name, was a Jewish priest. He was born in 37–38 C E and died c. 100. During the war against the Romans he was the rebel commander-in-chief of Galilee, but surrendered, and afterwards settled in Rome. He wrote four works in Greek. 1. *The Jewish War*, mostly devoted to the history of the revolution, was completed in the late 70s. Book 2.119–61 discusses the Essenes. 2. *Jewish Antiquities*, concluded in 93–94 C E, relates the history of the Jewish people from its beginning to A D 66, the outbreak of the first revolution. The two main but brief notices on the Essenes appear in 12.171–2 and 18.18–22. 3. The *Life* deals mainly with Josephus's activities in 66–70 C E as commander of Galilee. It was written in the second half of the 90s. Sections 11–12 allude to Josephus's association with the Essenes. 4. *Against Apion*, a vindication of Judaism, was composed after *Antiquities*, which it cites. A bilingual Greek-English edition of the whole of Josephus is available in the Loeb Classical Library in ten volumes. For an introduction see *HJP* I, 43–63.

Philo of Alexandria, the Jewish philosopher and interpreter of the Bible, was probably born in the 20s B C E. The date of his death is unknown, but he was still alive in 40 C E, for in that year he led an Alexandrian Jewish embassy to the emperor Gaius Caligula. His principal treatise on the Essenes is entitled *Every Good Man is Free*, or, *Quod omnis probus liber sit*, 75–91. Extracts from a shorter account contained in his *Hypothetica* or *Apology for the Jews* have been saved for posterity by the church historian Eusebius in his *Praeparatio evangelica* 8.11.1–18. Philo is also the author of *On the Contemplative Life*, in which he describes the Therapeutae, a Jewish group of ascetics living in Egypt. Like Josephus, Philo wrote in Greek. His writings, with an English translation, fill twelve volumes of the Loeb Classical Library.

Pliny the Elder (23/4–79 CE) is the author of a famous *Natural History* in Latin. Consisting of thirty-seven books, it was completed two years before his death in the eruption of Vesuvius which also buried Pompeii and Herculaneum. His paragraph on the Essenes appears in a geographical description of Judaea (5. 73). The same Loeb Library includes *Naturalis Historia* in a Latin-English edition.

All the Greek and Latin texts are assembled in a handy booklet by A. Adam and C. Burchard, *Antike Berichte über die Essener*, Berlin 1972. For the primary texts with English translation, see Geza Vermes and Martin Goodman, *The Essenes according to the Classical Sources*, Sheffield Academic Press 1989. An English translation of all the main texts is also included in A. Dupont-Sommer, *The Essene Writings from Qumran*, 21–38. For a historical survey of the research into Essenism from the end of the eighteenth to the beginning of the twentieth century, cf. S. Wagner, *Die Essener in der wissenschaftlichen Diskussion*, Berlin 1960.

A comprehensive bibliography is appended to the work of Adam and Burchard quoted above (pp. 66–88). For a general introduction with a selected book list, see *HJP* II, 555–97 and G. Vermes and M. Goodman, *The Essenes according to the Classical Sources* (above).

13. For a full discussion of the meaning of the term Essene, see Vermes, *PBJS*, 8–36.

14. The identification of the Qumran Community as an Essene sect was first suggested by E. L. Sukenik, *Megillot genuzot* [Hidden Scrolls] I, Jerusalem 1948, 16, and more systematically advanced by A. Dupont-Sommer, *Aperçus preliminaires sur les manuscrits de la Mer Morte*, Paris 1950, 105–17. His thesis is fully developed in *The Essene Writings from Qumran*.

15. Pliny's evidence is examined and applied to Qumran by R. de Vaux, *Archaeology and the Dead Sea Scrolls*, 133–7. For the two baths identified at Qumran, cf. ibid. 9–10, 131–2.

16. On the question of celibacy see Chapter 7, pp. 162–3; Vermes, *Jesus the Jew*, 99–102, 245–6.

17. For attempts to prove that the Qumran sectaries were not Essenes, see M. H. Goshen-Gottstein, 'Anti-Essene Traits in the Dead Sea Scrolls', *VT* 4, 1954, 141–7; C. Roth, 'Why the Qumran Sect cannot have been Essenes', *RQ* 1, 1959, 417–22; 'Were the Qumran Sectaries Essenes?', *JTS* 10, 1959, 87–93; G. R. Driver, *The Judaean Scrolls*, 100–21; N. Golb, 'The Problem of Origin and Identification of the Dead Sea Scrolls', *Proceedings of the American Philosophical Society* 124/1, 1980, 1–24; *Who wrote the Dead Sea Scrolls?*; P. H. E. Donceel-Voûte, 'Coenaculum – La salle à l'étage du *locus* 30 à Khirbet

Qumrân', *Banquets d'Orient, Res Orientales*, 1992, 61–84. Contra R. Reich, 'A Note on the Function of Room 30', *JJS* 46, 1995, 157–60.

18. This bibliographical survey would remain incomplete without some reference to that other ascetic group described by Philo, the Therapeutae, i.e. Worshippers/Healers, whom he associates with the Essenes in regard to aims and inspirations. The essential difference between them as he presents it is that the Essenes were active, i.e. combined prayer and study with manual work, whereas the contemplative Therapeutae spent all their life in meditation and worship. For a bilingual Greek-English edition of *On the Contemplative Life*, see Vol. IX of Philo in the Loeb Library. See also P. Geoltrain, 'Le Traité de la Vie contemplative de Philon d'Alexandrie', *Semitica* 10, 1960, 5–67; F. Daumas and P. Miquel, *Les Oeuvres de Philon d'Alexandrie*, Vol.29, Paris 1963; G. Vermes and M. Goodman, *The Essenes according to the Classical Sources* (n. 12 above), 75–99. According to Philo (*Contemp.Life* 13,68) the Therapeutae formed separate male and female communities: mature men and aged virgins. 4Q502, alluding to old men and women ('daughters of truth'), may refer to the Therapeutae (cf. J. M. Baumgarten, '4Q 502, Marriage or Golden Age Ritual?', *JJS* 34, 1983, 125–35).

For a link between Therapeutae, Essenes and Qumran, see Vermes, 'Essenes-Therapeutae-Qumran', *Durham University Journal* 21, 1960, 97–115; *PBJS*, 30–6; *HJP* II, 591–7, G. Vermes and M. Goodman, *The Essenes according to the Classical Sources* (n. 12), 15–17.

The church historian Eusebius erroneously identified the Therapeutae as Egyptian Jewish ascetics converted to Christianity (*Ecclesiastical History* 2.16 17). Whilst his thesis is untenable, an influence of the Therapeutae on Christian monasticism still remains a serious possibility. See F. Daumas, 'La solitude des Thérapeutes et les antécédents égyptiens du monachisme chrétien', *Philon d'Alexandrie – Lyon 11–15 September 1966, Colloques Nationaux du CNRS*, Paris 1967, 347–58; A. Guillaumont, 'Philon et les origines du monachisme', ibid. 361–73.

6. The History of the Community

1. The most comprehensive scholarly exposition of Jewish history from 175 BCE to 135 CE is the first volume of *HJP*. For a less technical treatment of the epoch in question see S. Safrai and M. Stern (eds), *The Jewish People in the First Century*, Assen and Philadelphia, I, 1974; II, 1977; H. H. Ben Sasson, *A History of the Jewish People*, London 1976, Part III.

The reader may also consult the following monographs devoted to particular aspects of inter-testamental history. V. Tcherikover, *Hellenistic Civilization and the Jews*, Philadelphia 1959; A. H. M. Jones, *The Herods of Judaea*, Oxford 1967; A. Schalit, *König Herodes*, Berlin 1969; J. Jeremias, *Jerusalem in the Time of Jesus*, London and Philadelphia 1969; M. Hengel, *Judaism and Hellenism* I–II, London and Philadelphia 1974; E. M. Smallwood, *The Jews under Roman Rule*, Leiden 1976. The classic commentary on the Books of the Maccabees is F.-M. Abel, *Les Livres des Maccabées*, Paris 1949; cf. also J. A.

Goldstein, *II Maccabees,* New York 1983. For the temple of Onias in
Leontopolis see M. Delcor, 'Le temple d'Onias en Égypte', *RB* 75, 1968,
188–205; Vermes, *PBJS,* 83–4; R. Hayward, 'The Jewish Temple of
Leontopolis', *JJS* 33, 1982, 429–43.

2. All the general studies on the Scrolls contain a section on historical issues, as
do dictionary articles on Qumran. Cf. also *HJP* II, 585–88. Further important
special studies of Qumran history include H. H. Rowley, 'The History of the
Qumran Sect', *BJRL* 49, 1966, 203–32; F. M. Cross, 'The Early History of the
Qumran Community', in *New Directions in Biblical Archaeology,* ed. D. N.
Freedman and J. C. Greenfield, Garden City 1971, 70–89; H. Stegemann, *Die
Entstehung der Qumrangemeinde,* Bonn Dissertation, privately published 1971;
J. Murphy-O'Connor, 'The Essenes and their History', *RB* 81, 1974, 215–44; H.
Burgmann, 'Gerichtsherr und Generalankläger: Jonathan und Simon', *RQ* 9,
1977, 3–72; G. Vermes, 'The Essenes and History', *JJS* 32, 1981, 18–31; P. R.
Callaway, *The History of the Qumran Community: An Investigation,* Sheffield
1988; Stegemann, *The Library of Qumran,* Leiden 1998, 142–62.

3. The phrase '390 years' in CD 1.5 requires a brief discussion. We may safely dis-
card the idea that 390 is a symbolic figure borrowed from Ezekiel 4.4, where it
corresponds to the number of days during which the prophet, lying on his left
side, atoned for the 390 years of iniquity of the House of Israel. Indeed there is
no indication whatever that the fate of the Northern kingdom played any part
in the sect's speculation concerning its own origins. Similarly, the view that the
390 years are to be counted not from, but to, the time of Nebuchadnezzar
seems to run counter to the whole logic of the account in the Damascus
Document. For the thesis in question see I. Rabinowitz, 'A Reconsideration of
"Damascus" and "390 Years" in the "Damascus" (Zadokite) Fragments', *JBL*
73, 1954, 11–35; E. Wiesenberg, 'Chronological Data in the Zadokite
Fragments', *VT* 5, 1955, 284–308.

The unreliability of the post-exilic chronology of ancient Jewish writers may
be illustrated by two examples. The third century BCE Jewish Hellenist
Demetrius calculates the total number of years between the fall of Samaria
(722/1 BCE) and the accession of Ptolemy IV of Egypt (221 BCE) to have been
573 instead of the actual 500; cf. Clement of Alexandria, *Stromateis* I, 141, 2;
see N. Walter, 'Fragmente jüdisch-hellenistischer Exegeten', *Jüdische Schriften
aus hellenistisch-römischer Zeit,* ed. W. G. Kümmel, III. 2, Gütersloh 1975,
292. Even the careful Josephus in the first century CE was unable to produce
precise figures. He reckoned 481 *(Ant.* 13.301) or 471 *(War* 1.70) years, instead
of 435, between the return from the Babylonian exile (538 BCE) and the death
of Aristobulus I(103 BCE), and 343 years, i.e. roughly a hundred years too
many, for the duration (approximately 160 BCE–73 CE) of the Leontopolis
Temple *(War* 7.436). As for the chronology contained in the Seder Olam
Rabbah 30 of Rabbi Yose the Galilean (second century CE), the lapse of time
from Nebuchadnezzar to the destruction of the Temple amounts there to the
mystical 70 times 7, i.e. 490 years, echoing Daniel 9.24. R. Yose's data are:
Babylonian rule, 70 years; Persian rule, 34 years; Greek rule, 180 years;
Hasmonaean rule, 103 years; Herodian rule, 103 years. Cf. G. R. Driver, *The*

Judaean Scrolls: The Problem and a Solution, Oxford 1965, 311–16, though his use of the evidence is to be taken with a pinch of salt, since he did not seem to realize that we are dealing with a theological time-schedule.

4. Cf. E. and H. Eshel, 'A Qumran Composition containing . . . a Prayer for King Jonathan and his Kingdom', *IEJ* 42, 1992, 199–229; G. Vermes, 'The So-called King Jonathan Fragment', *JJS* 44, 1993, 294–300.

5. In the early years of Qumran research, some scholars argued that the Kittim were Greek Seleucids. See e.g. E. Stauffer, 'Zur Frühdatierung des Haba-kukmidrasch', *TLZ* 76, 1951, 667–74; H. H. Rowley, *The Zadokite Fragments and the Dead Sea Scrolls*, Oxford 1952. The Roman theory, strongly favoured since the beginning, has now become the dominant one. Cf. A. Dupont-Sommer, *The Essene Writings from Qumran*, 341–51; R. Goossens, 'Les Kittim du Commentaire d'Habacuc', *Nouvelle Clio* 2, 1952, 137–70; G. Vermes, *Discovery*, 79–84; *PBJS*, 215–16.

6. For a discussion of the 'last Priests of Jerusalem', see G. Vermes, *Discovery in the Judaean Desert*, 78–9, and for possible allusions to the Teacher of Righteousness in the Qumran Hymns, ibid., 216–20; Dupont-Sommer, *The Essene Writings from Qumran*, 358–67. For a more recent survey, see E. P. Sanders, *Paul and Palestinian Judaism*, London and Philadelphia 1977, 321–3.

7. The Zadokite affiliation of the Teacher of Righteousness may be supported by circumstantial evidence. According to the older version of the Community Rule, represented by 4Q258 and 256, the democratic 'Congregation' consti-tuted the supreme authority of the Community, with priests, sons of Aaron, forming the top layer in the administration. This position is attributed to the 'sons of Zadok', members of the high-priestly family, in the revised 1QS5. In other words, at some early stage in the sect's history there was a Zadokite takeover. Combining this information with the account of CD 1 (supported by 4QD), we may reasonably surmise that the change occurred with the arrival of the Teacher of Righteousness. The crisis in the Zadokite ranks in the 160s BCE, following the secession of Onias IV to Egypt, provides the likeliest background for these events (cf. G. Vermes, 'Sons of Zadok – Priests – Congregation: The Leadership of the Qumran Community', in *Geschichte-Tradition-Reflexion (Martin Hengel Festschrift)*, I, Tübingen 1996, 375–84). In this connection it may not be irrelevant to note that according to 4Q266 fr. 5 ii priests who had emigrated among the Gentiles were disqualified.

8. Various views concerning the meaning of the phrase 'Land of Damascus' have been advanced. Cf. I. Rabinowitz, 'A Reconsideration of Damascus', *JBL* 73, 1954, 11–35 (locality of the exile of the Judaeans after 586 BCE); A. Jaubert, 'Le pays de Damas', *RB* 65, 1958, 214–48; J. Murphy-O'Connor, 'The Essenes and their History', *RB* 81, 1974, 21–23 (Damascus = Babylonia); R. North, 'The Damascus of Qumran Geography', *PEQ* 87, 1955, 33–48 (Damascus = Qumran); R. de Vaux, *Archaeology and the Dead Sea Scrolls*, 113–14; C. Milikowsky, 'Again *Damascus* in the Damascus Document and in Rabbinic Literature', *RQ* 11, 1982–4. For the exegetical symbolism Damascus = Jerusalem (Qumran), cf. G. Vermes, *Scripture and Tradition in Judaism*, Leiden 1961, 43–9, 97–106.

9. Although in my opinion the Teacher of Righteousness is likely to remain anonymous, the following (unconvincing) identifications have been proposed: Onias III, high priest, murdered in 171 BCE (H. H. Rowley, *The Zadokite Fragments and the Dead Sea Scrolls* [n. 5], 67–8); Yose ben Yoezer, priest, one of the first Pharisaic masters (E. Stauffer, 'Der gekreuzigte Thoralehrer', *ZRGG* 8, 1956, 250–3; an anonymous high priest who succeeded Alcimus in c. 160 BCE (J. Murphy-O'Connor, 'The Essenes and their History' [n. 8], 229–30; 'Demetrius I and the Teacher of Righteousness', *RB* 83, 1976, 400–20; cf. J. G. Bunge, 'Zur Geschichte und Chronologie der Oniaden und des Aufstiegs der Hasmonäer', *JSJ* 6, 1975, 27–43; the Pharisee Eleazar, a critic of John Hyrcanus I, or the Essene prophet Judas at the end of the second century BCE (W. H. Brownlee, 'The Historical Allusions of the Dead Sea Habakkuk Midrash', *BASOR* 126, 1952, 18; Onias the Just, a miracle-worker executed in 65 BCE (R. Goossens, 'Onias le Juste, le Messie de la Nouvelle Alliance, lapidé à Jérusalem en 65 avant J.-C.', *Nouvelle Clio* 1–2, 1949–50, 336–53; Menahem son of Judas the Galilean murdered in 66 CE (C. Roth, *The Historical Background of the Dead Sea Scrolls*, Oxford 1958, 60–3; G. R. Driver, *The Judaean Scrolls: The Problem and a Solution*, 267–81, see p. 229 above). Writers identifying the sect with Christianity advance firm, but diverse, views regarding the Teacher: John the Baptist (Barbara Thiering, *Jesus the Man*, 1992); Jesus (J. L. Teicher, 'Jesus in the Habakkuk Scroll', *JJS* 3, 1952, 53–5); James the brother of Jesus (R. H. Eisenman, *James the Just in the Habakkuk Pesher*, Leiden 1986).

10. Regarding the historicity of Josephus's notice on Jesus, see *HJP* I, 428–41, with a full bibliography, to which should be added E. Bammel, 'Zurn Testimonium Flavianum', *Josephus-Studien. Festschrift für O. Michel*, Göttingen 1974, 9–22, and G. Vermes, 'The Jesus Notice of Josephus Re-examined', *JJS* 38, 1987, 1–10.

11. For the history of the Essenes consult *HJP* 11, 1979, 585–8; G. Vermes, 'The Essenes and History', *JJS* 32, 1981, 18–31.

12. To these four eminent Essenes we may now add the three guilty sectaries (Yohanan and the two Hananaiahs, 4Q477) and (possibly) Eleazar ben Nahmani (cf. Ostrakon) and Honi (ibid.).

13. A succinct bibliography of the various historical theories advanced during the last four decades may appropriately conclude this section.

1. Pre-Maccabaean theory
H. H. Rowley, *The Zadokite Fragments and the Dead Sea Scrolls* (n. 5); 'The History of the Qumran Sect', *BJRL* 49, 1966, 203–32; I. Rabinowitz, 'The Meaning of the Key ("Demetrius") Passage of the Qumran Nahuni Pesher', *Journal of the American Oriental Society* 98, 1978, 394–9.

2. Maccabaean theory (Wicked Priest = Jonathan or Simon)
G. Vermes, *Les Manuscrits du désert de Juda*, 1953; *Discovery in the Judaean Desert*, 89–97; J. T. Milik, *Dix ans de découvertes dans le desert de Juda*, 1957; *Ten Years of Discovery in the Wilderness of Judaea*, 84–7; F. M. Cross, *The*

Ancient Library of Qumran, 135–53; *Canaanite Myth and Hebrew Epic*, Cambridge, Mass. 1973, 626–42; R. de Vaux, *L'Archéologie et les manuscrits de la Mer Morte*, 1961; *Archaeology and the Dead Sea Scrolls*, 116–17; G. Jeremias, *Der Lehrer der Gerechtigkeit*, Göttingen 1963; H. Stegemann, *Die Entstehung der Qumrangemeinde*, Heidelberg 1971; M. Hengel, *Judaism and Hellenism* I, London and Philadelphia 1974, 224–7; J. Murphy-O'Connor, 'The Essenes and their History', *RB* 81, 1974, 215–44; 'Demetrius I and the Teacher of Righteousness', *RB* 83, 1976, 400–20; 'The Essenes in Palestine', *BA* 40, 1977, 100–24; H. Burgmann, 'The Wicked Woman: Der Makkahier Simon?', *RQ* 8, 1974, 323–59; 'Gerichtsherr und Generalankläger: Jonathan und Simon', *RQ* 9, 1977, 3–72; G. W. F. Nickelsburg, 'Simon – A Priest with a Reputation for Faithfulness', *BASOR* 223, 1976, 67–8; J. Starcky, 'Le Maître de justice et la chronologie de Qumran', *Qumran* (ed. M. Delcor), 1978, 249–56; J. Campbell, *Deciphering the Dead Sea Scrolls*, London 1996, 88–94.

3. Hasmonaean theory (a. Wicked Priest = Alexander Jannaeus)
M. Delcor, *Le Midrash d'Habacuc*, 1951; J. Carmignac, *Les Textes de Qumran* I, 1963, 48–55.
(b. Wicked Priest = Hyrcanus II)
A. Dupont-Sommer, *The Essene Writings from Qumran*, 351–7; M. Wise, M. Abegg and E. Cook, *The Dead Sea Scrolls*, London 1996, 26–34.

4. The Groningen Hypothesis
F. García Martínez, 'Qumran Origins and Early History: A Groningen Hypothesis', *Folia Orientalia* 25, 1988, 113–36; F. García Martínez and A. S. van der Woude, 'A Groningen Hypothesis of Qumran Origins and Early History', *RQ* 14, 1990, 521–42.

5. Zealot theory
C. Roth, *The Historical Background of the Dead Sea Scrolls*, Oxford 1958; G. R. Driver, *The Judaean Scrolls: The Problem and a Solution*, Oxford 1965.

6 Judaeo-Christian theory
See above p. 115.

7. The Religious Ideas of the Community

1. For the religious ideas of inter-testamental Judaism the reader may consult R. Travers Herford, *Talmud and Apocrypha*, London 1933; W. Bousset and H. Gressmann, *Die Religion des Judentums im späthellenistischen Zeitalter*, Tübingen ⁴1966; *HJP* II, 464–554; G. W. F. Nickelsburg and M. F. Stone, *Faith and Piety in Early Judaism*, Philadelphia 1983; G. Boccaccini, *Middle Judaism: Jewish Thought 300 BCE to 200 CE*, Minneapolis 1992; E. P. Sanders, *Judaism: Practice and Belief 63 BCE–66 CE*, London and Philadelphia 1992.

   The standard works on rabbinic theology are: G. F. Moore, *Judaism in the First Centuries of the Christian Era* I–III, Cambridge, Mass. 1927–30; E. F.

Urbach, *The Sages: Their Concepts and Beliefs* I–II, Jerusalem 1975; J. Neusner, *Judaism: The Evidence of the Mishnah*, Chicago 1981; *Judaism in Society*, Chicago 1983; *Judaism and Scripture*, Chicago 1986. For a modern attempt, see L. Jacobs, *A Jewish Theology*, London 1973. Cf. also H. Küng, *Judaism*, London and New York 1991.

For the New Testament see R. Bultmann, *Theology of the New Testament* I–II, London 1952–5; H. Conzelmann, *An Outline of the Theology of the New Testament*, London 1969; J. Jeremias, *New Testament Theology*, Vol.1, London 1971. Readers well versed in Hebrew and Greek are recommended to use *TDNT*. The work also deals also with biblical, inter-Testamental and rabbinic religion. For a parallel survey, see H. Shanks (ed.), *Christianity and Rabbinic Judaism*, Washington and London 1992.

There is no comprehensive study of the theology of the Scrolls. Most general works on Qumran include a chapter on doctrines and beliefs. The following books deserve special mention: F. Nötscher, *Zur theologischen Terminologie der Qumran-Texte*, Bonn 1956; *Gotteswege und Menschenwege in der Bibel und Qumran*, Bonn 1958; H. Ringgren, *The Faith of Qumran: Theology of the Dead Sea Scrolls*, Philadelphia 1963; J. Jeremias, 'Qumrân et la théologie', *NRT* 85, 1963, 474–90; A.-M. Denis, *Les thèmes de connaissance dans le Document de Damas*, Louvain 1967; P. von der Osten-Sacken, *Gott und Belial: Traditionsgeschichtliche Untersuchungen zum Dualismus in den Texten aus Qumran*, Göttingen 1969; G. Klinzing, *Die Umdeutung des Kultus in der Qumrangemeinde und im Neuen Testament*, Göttingen 1971; F. H. Merrill, *Qumran and Predestination*, Leiden 1975; E. P. Sanders, *Paul and Palestinian Judaism*, London and Philadelphia 1977, 239–321; P. Garnet, *Salvation and Atonement in the Qumran Scrolls*, Tübingen 1977; M. Delcor (ed.), *Qumrân: Sa piété, sa théologie et son milieu*, Paris and Gembloux 1978; A. E. Sekki, *The Meaning of* Ruah *at Qumran*, Atlanta 1989; S. Talmon, *The World of Qumran from Within*, Jerusalem and Leiden 1989; M. J. Davidson, *Angels at Qumran*, Sheffield 1992; E. Ulrich and J. VanderKam (eds), *The Community of the Renewed Covenant*, Notre Dame 1994; J. H. Charlesworth et al. (eds), *Qumran-Messianism*, Tübingen 1998.

2. For a recent discussion of the biblical notion, see M. Weinfeld, 'Covenant', *EncJud* 5, 1012–22; cf. also the relevant sections in works on biblical theology and in *TDNT*. The Qumran notion has been discussed by R. F. Collins, 'The Berith-Notion of the Cairo Damascus Covenant and its Comparison with the New Testament', *Ephemerides Theologicae Lovanienses* 39, 1963, 555–94; J. G. Harris, 'The Covenant Concept among the Qumran Sectaries', *Evangelical Quarterly* 39, 1967, 86–92; J. A. Huntjens, 'Contrasting Notions of Covenant and Law in the Texts from Qumran', *RQ* 8, 1974, 361–80; L. H. Schiffman, *Halakhah at Qumran*, Leiden 1975.

3. On the function of Bible interpretation in ancient Judaism and Qumran, see the following studies: F. F. Bruce, *Biblical Exegesis in the Qumran Texts*, London 1959; O. Betz, *Offenbarung und Schriftforschung in der Qumransekte*, Tübingen 1960; G. Vermes, *Scripture and Tradition in Judaism*, Leiden 1961, ²1973; *PBJS*; 'Interpretation (History of) at Qumran and in the Targums',

IDBS, 1976, 438–43; S. Lowy, 'Some Aspects of Normative and Sectarian Interpretation of the Scriptures', *ALUOS* 6, 1969, 84–163; W. H. Brownlee, 'The Background of Biblical Interpretation at Qumran', *Qumran* (ed. M. Delcor), 1978, 183–93; M. P. Horgan, *Pesharim: Qumran Interpretation of Biblical Books*, Washington 1979; H. Gabrion, 'L'interprétation de l'Écriture dans la littérature de Qumran', *Aufstieg und Niedergang der römischen Welt*, ed. H. Temporini and W. Haase, XIX/1, Berlin 1979, 779–848; G. J. Brooke, *Exegesis at Qumran: 4Q Florilegium in its Jewish Context*, Sheffield 1985; G. Vermes, 'Bible Interpretation at Qumran', *Y. Yadin Memorial Volume, Erets-Israel* XX, Jerusalem 1989, 184*–91*; 'Biblical Proof-Texts in Qumran Literature', *JSS* 34, 1989, 493–508; T. H. Lieu, *Holy Scripture in the Qumran Commentaries and Pauline Letters*, Oxford 1997; S. E. Porter and C. A. Evans (eds), *The Scrolls and the Scriptures*, Sheffield 1997.

4. On the doctrine of the two spirits, see J. Licht, 'An Analysis of the Treatise of the Two Spirits in DSD', *Scripta Hierosolymitana* 4, 1958, 88–100; H. W. Huppenbauer, *Der Mensch zwischen zwei Welten*, Zurich 1959; P. Wernberg-Møller, 'A Reconsideration of the Two Spirits in the Rule of the Community', *RQ* 3, 1962, 433–41; J. H. Charlesworth, 'A Critical Comparison of the Dualism in I QS III, 13 – IV, 26 and the "Dualism" contained in the Fourth Gospel', *NTS* 15, 1969, 389–418; A. E. Sekki, *The Meaning of* Ruah *at Qumran*, Atlanta 1989, 193–219.

The Instruction on the Two Spirits appears to supply a doctrinal underpinning for the Guardian in his effort to discern the spiritual qualities of his subjects.

5. A considerable literature is devoted to the problem of the Qumran calendar. For a general survey in the context of the Jewish calendar as such see *HJP* I, 587–601. The most important special studies are by Annie Jaubert, 'Le calendrier des Jubilés et de la secte de Qumrân: ses origines bibliques', *VT* 3, 1955, 250–64; A. R. C. Leaney, *The Rule of Qumran and its Meaning*, London 1966, 80–90; J. M. Baumgarten, '4Q Halakah[a] 5, the Law of Hadash and the Pentecontad Calendar', *JJS* 27, 1976, 3–46; J. C. VanderKam, 'The Origin, Character and Early History of the 364-Day Calendar', *CBQ* 41, 1979, 390–411; S. Talmon, 'The Calendar of the Covenanters of the Judaean Desert', in *The World of Qumran from Within*, 1989, 147–85.

The regularity of the system will appear from the following table.

Months

	I, IV, VII, X	II, V, VIII, XI	III, VI, IX, XII
Wednesday	1 8 15 22 29	6 13 20 27	4 11 18 25
Thursday	2 9 16 23 30	7 14 21 28	5 12 19 26
Friday	3 10 17 24	1 8 15 22 29	6 13 20 27
Sabbath	4 11 18 25	2 9 16 23 30	7 14 21 28
Sunday	5 12 19 26	3 10 17 24	1 8 15 22 29
Monday	6 13 20 27	4 11 18 25	2 9 16 23 30
Tuesday	7 14 21 28	5 12 19 26	3 10 17 24 31

The 31st day in the last column corresponds to the additional day linking one season of three months to the next.

For a detailed bibliography, including a section on the issue of the date of the Last Supper in the Gospels, see J. A. Fitzmyer, *The Dead Sea Scrolls: Major Publications and Tools for Study*, 80–6.

6. Dawn as marking a specific moment of prayer in heaven appears in the ancient Aramaic paraphrases of Gen. 32.25 and 27, the story of Jacob's struggle with an angel, Sariel according to Targum Neofiti I. The biblical text 'Let me go for the day is breaking' is interpreted as 'Let me go for the rising of the column of the dawn has come; for the time has come for the angels on high to praise, and I am the chief of those who praise.' Cf. G. Vermes, 'The Archangel Sariel', in *Christianity, Judaism and other Greco-Roman Cults*, ed. J. Neusner, Leiden 1975, 159–66.

7. The ritual of the Renewal of the Covenant is treated in the commentaries on the Community Rule. Cf. in particular, A. R. C. Leaney, *The Rule of Qumran* (n. 5), 95–107. See further M. Weise, *Kultzeiten und kultischer Bundesschluss in der 'Ordensregel' vom Toten Meer*, Leiden 1961; M. Delcor, 'Das Bundesfest in Qumran und das Pfingstfest', *Bibel und Leben* 4, 1963, 188–204; 'Pentecôte', *DBSuppl* VII, 858–79. One of the Cave 4 manuscripts of the Damascus Document (4Q266) explicitly places this festival in the third month, and according to the Qumran calendar the Feast of Weeks falls on the fifteenth day (Sunday) of the third month.

8. For Jewish notions of purification, see J. Neusner, *The Idea of Purity in Ancient Judaism*, Leiden 1973; O. Betz, 'Die Proselytentaufe der Qumransekte und die Taufe im Neuen Testament', *RQ* 1, 1959, 213–34; E. F. Sutcliffe, 'Baptism and Baptismal Rites at Qumran', *Heythrop Journal* 1, 1960, 69–101; J. Gnilka, 'Die essenischen Tauchbäder und die Johannestaufe', *RQ* 3, 1961, 185–207; A. Dupont-Sommer, 'Culpabilité et rites de purification dans la secte juive de Qoumrân', *Semitica* 15, 1965, 61–70; J. A. Fitzmyer, *Essays on the Semitic Background of the New Testament*, London 1971, 469–73; E. P. Sanders, *Judaism: Practice and Belief*, London and Philadelphia 1992, 352–60. On Jewish and Christian baptizing sects, see J. Thomas, *Le mouvement baptiste en Palestine et Syrie (150 a. J.-C. – 300 apr. J.-C.)*, Gembloux 1935.

9. Regarding the spiritualization of Temple and worship, see in addition to the monograph of Klinzing quoted above (p. 236), B. Gärtner, *The Temple and the Community in Qumran and the New Testament*, Cambridge 1965 and G. Vermes, *PBJS*, 83–5. Cf. also *Scripture and Tradition in Judaism* (n. 3), concerning the symbolism Lebanon = Council of the Community Temple (pp. 26–39). On various Jewish and Christian attitudes to the Temple, see J. Neusner, *Early Rabbinic Judaism*, Leiden 1975, 34–49.

10. On the question of celibacy, see H. R. Moehring, 'Josephus on the Marriage Customs of the Essenes', *Early Christian Origins. Studies in Honor of H. R. Willoughby*, Chicago 1961, 120–7; A. Marx, 'Les racines du célibat essénien', *RQ* 7, 1970, 323–42; A. Guillaumont, 'A propos du célibat des Esséniens', in *Hommages à André Dupont-Sommer*, Paris 1971, 395–404; G. Vermes, *Jesus the Jew*, London 1973, reissued London and Philadelphia 1994, 99–102;

J. Coppens, 'Le célibat essénien', in *Qumrân*, ed. M. Delcor, 1978, 295–303. On rules relating to abstinence from sex among married Essenes, see M. Kister, 'Notes on Some New Texts from Qumran', *JJS* 44, 1993, 280–1.

11. For the Qumran meal and its New Testament associations see J. van der Ploeg, 'The Meals of the Essenes', *JJS* 2, 1957, 163–75; K. G. Kuhn, 'The Lord's Supper and the Communal Meal at Qumran', in *The Scrolls and the New Testament*, ed. K. Stendhal, 65–93; J. Gnilka, 'Das Gemeinschaftsmahl der Essener', *Biblische Zeitschrift* 5, 1961, 39–55; J. F. Priest, 'The Messiah and the Meal in 1QSa', *JBL* 82, 1963, 95–100; M. Delcor, 'Repas cultuels esséniens et thérapeutes', *RQ* 6, 1969, 401–25; L. H. Schiffman, *The Eschatological Community of the Dead Sea Scrolls*, Atlanta 1989, 53–67.

12. On Jewish eschatology and apocalyptic in general see P. Volz, *Die Eschatologie der jüdischen Gemeinde im neutestamentlichen Zeitalter*, Tübingen ²1934; D. S. Russell, *The Method and Message of Jewish Apocalyptic*, London 1964; M. Delcor, 'Le milieu d'origine et le développement de l'apocalyptique juive', *La littérature juive entre Tenach et Mischna*, ed. W. C. van Unnik, Leiden 1974, 101–17. For a useful bibliography, see J. H. Charlesworth, *The Pseudepigrapha and Modern Research*, Missoula 1976, 66–8.

For Essene and Qumran eschatology, the reader may turn to P. Grelot, 'L'eschatologie des Esséniens et le livre d'Enoch', *RQ* 1, 1958, 112–31; I. Hahn, 'Josephus und die Eschatologie von Qumran', *Qumran-Probleme*, ed. H. Bardtke, Berlin 1963, 167–91; J. Licht, 'Time and Eschatology in Apocalyptic Literature and Qumran', *JJS* 16, 1967, 117–82; J. Pryke, 'Eschatology in the Dead Sea Scrolls', in *The Scrolls and Christianity*, ed. M. Black, London 1969, 45–57; J. J. Collins, *The Apocalyptic Imagination*, New York 1984, 115–41; *Apocalypticism in the Dead Sea Scrolls*, London 1997

13. For the eschatological function of angels, see in particular Y. Yadin, *The Scroll of the War of the Sons of Light against the Sons of Darkness*, Oxford 1962, 229–42; J. T. Milik, '*Milkî-ṣedeq et Milkî-resha*' dans les anciens écrits juifs et chrétiens', *JJS* 23, 1972; G. Vermes, 'The Archangel Sariel. A Targumic Parallel to the Dead Sea Scrolls', in *Christianity, Judaism and other Greco-Roman Cults* III, Leiden 1975, 159–66; M. J. Davidson, *Angels at Qumran*, Sheffield 1992. See also the Melkizedek document: cf. Chapter 3, pp. 89–90, and F. L. Horton, *The Melchizedek Tradition*, Cambridge 1976, 64–82.

14. Among the general works dealing with Messianism, see in particular S. Mowinckel, *He that Cometh*, Oxford 1956; J. Klausner, *The Messianic Idea in Israel*, London 1956; M. de Jonge, 'The Use of the Word "Anointed" in the Time of Jesus', *NT* 8, 1966, 132–48; *HJP* II, 1979, 488–554.

For New Testament Messianism, see W. Grundmann, F. Hesse, M. de Jonge, A. S. van der Woude, 'Christos', *TDNT* 9, 1974, 493–580. Cf. G. Vermes, *Jesus the Jew* (n. 10), 129–59, 250–6.

15. For a study of Qumran Messianism, see: A. S. van der Woude, *Die messianischen Vorstellungen der Gemeinde von Qumran*, Assen 1957; 'Le Maître de Justice et les deux messies de la communauté de Qumrân', in *La secte de Qumran et les origines du Christianisme*, ed. J. van der Ploeg, Bruges 1959, 121–34; J. Liver, 'The Doctrine of the Two Messiahs in the Sectarian Literature

in the Time of the Second Commonwealth', *HTR* 52, 1959, 149–85; J. Starcky, 'Les quatre étapes du messianisme à Qumrân', *RB* 70, 1963, 48–305; R. E. Brown, 'The Teacher of Righteousness and the Messiah(s)', in *The Scrolls and Christianity*, ed. M. Black, London 1969, 37–44, 109–12; J. A. Fitzmyer, *Essays on the Semitic Background of the New Testament*, London 1971, 127–60; J. R. Villalón, 'Sources vétérotestamentaires de la doctrine qumranienne des deux Messies', *RQ* 8, 1972, 53–63; A. Caquot, 'Le messianisme qumranien', in *Qumran*, ed. M. Delcor (n. 1), 231–47; G. Vermes, 'The Oxford Forum for Qumran Research: Seminar on the Rule of War (4Q285)', *JJS* 43, 1992, 85–90; J. H. Charlesworth et al. (eds), *Qumran-Messianism*, Tübingen 1998.

16. On the messianic Prophet, see Vermes, *Jesus the Jew* (n. 14), 94–7, 137–9. In earlier publications I have suggested that the role of *Geber* (Man) in the Community Rule, i.e. the teacher of the elect at the end of time (1QS 4.20–22), corresponds to that of the Prophet, and that in the Commentary on Psalm 37 *Geber* is identified as the Teacher of Righteousness. Cf. *Discovery*, 220–2; *Scripture and Tradition*, 56–66. See also W. H. Brownlee, 'The Servant of the Lord in the Qumran Scrolls'. *BASOR* 135, 1954, 36–8; *The Meaning of the Qumran Scrolls for the Bible*, New York 1964, 261–70.

17. Two particular problems, one raised by the Damascus Document, the other by the Messianic Rule, need further comment. Instead of the plural form, 'Messiahs of Aaron and Israel' attested in 1QS 9.11, the Damascus Rule regularly uses the singular, 'Messiah of Aaron and Israel' (CD 12.23–13.1; 19 [B1].10; 20 [B2].1). This is apparently not a doctrinal correction introduced by the mediaeval copyists of the Cairo Geniza manuscripts, since a fragment from Cave 4 confirms the singular reading. Nevertheless, if on the one hand the language of the Damascus Rule appears to exclude belief in several Messiahs, the same document speaks also of the coming of the 'Interpreter of the Law' and the 'Prince of the whole Congregation' (CD 6.7; 7.18–20). Thus it cannot be argued that CD ignores the doctrine of multiple Messianism. Perhaps it should further be pointed out that CD 7.18–20 discovers in the single verse of Num. 24.17 ('A *star* shall come forth out of Jacob and a *sceptre* shall rise out of Israel') the announcement of the coming of both the 'Interpreter of the Law' (= the Star) and the 'Prince of the whole Congregation' (= the Sceptre), while the same passage of Numbers cited in 4QTest is usually understood to refer to the king Messiah only.

There has also been much discussion concerning an obscure and badly preserved passage in the Messianic Rule about God's 'begetting' the Messiah. In 1QSa 1.11–12 the *editio princeps* (*DJD* I, 110, 117–18) contains the reading 'when (God) shall beget (*ywlyd*) the Messiah', but a computer-enhanced image of the word appears to confirm *ywlyd*.

18. The question of an after-life in inter-testamental Judaism has been the subject of a full monograph by G. W. E. Nickelsburg, *Resurrection, Immortality and Eternal Life in Inter-testamental Judaism*, Cambridge, Mass. 1972. For the Qumran doctrine see M. Delcor, 'L'immortalité de l'âme dans le Livre de la Sagesse et les documents de Qumrân', *NRT* 77, 1955, 614–30; R. B. Laurin,

'The Question of Immortality in the Qumran *Hodayot*', *JSS* 3, 1958, 344–66; K. Schubert, 'Das Problem der Auferstehungshoffnung in der Qumrantexten und in der frührabbinischen Literatur', *Wiener Zeitschrift für die Kunde des Morgenlandes* 56, 1960, 154–67; J. van der Ploeg, 'The Belief in Immortality in the Writings of Qumran', *Bibliotheca Orientalis* 18, 1961, 18–24; E. Puech, *La croyance des esséniens en la vie future: immortalité, résurrection, vie éternelle*, Paris 1993.

19. Recalling Josephus's description of the Essene concept of immortality, the late first-century B C E epitaph of a young Egyptian Jewish woman, Arsinoe, written in Greek verse, speaks of her soul as having departed towards the holy ones *(eis hosious)*. Cf. J. B. Frey, *Corpus Inscriptionum Iudaicarum* II, Rome 1952, 421.

20. Cf. G. Vermes, 'Qumran Forum Miscellanea I', *JJS* 43, 1992, 303–4; E. Puech, 'Une apocalypse messianique', *RQ* 15, 1992, 475–522; *DJD* XXV.

8. Qumran and Biblical Studies

1. References to Qumran codicology and palaeography appear on pp. 13, 28–30. For matters of orthography, see M. Martin, *The Scribal Character of the Dead Sea Scrolls* I–II, Louvain 1958; E. Tov, 'Hebrew Biblical Manuscripts from the Judaean Desert: Their Contribution to Textual Criticism', *JJS* 39, 1988, 23–5.

2. For a summary introduction to the Masoretic text, see O. Eissfeldt, *The Old Testament. An Introduction*, Oxford 1966, 678–93; for the ancient versions, see ibid., 696–719; E. Wurthwein, *The Text of the Old Testament*, London and Grand Rapids 1979. For the canon of the Bible, cf. *HJP* II, 1979, 314–21. See also S. Z. Leiman, *The Canonization of Hebrew Scripture*, Transactions of the Connecticut Academy of Arts and Sciences 47, 1976; R. Beckwith, *The Old Testament Canon of the New Testament Church*, London 1985.

3. For general information on the Samaritan Pentateuch, consult Eissfeldt, *The Old Testament* (n. 2), 694–5; F. Tov, *Textual Criticism of the Hebrew Bible*, Minneapolis 1992, 80–100. On the Septuagint, see S. Jellicoe, *The Septuagint and Modern Study*, Oxford 1968, and S. P. Brock, C. T. Fritsch, S. Jellicoe, *A Classified Bibliography of the Septuagint*, Leiden 1973; G. Dorival, M. Harl and A. Munnich, *La Bible grecque des Septante*, Paris 1988.

4. The most important work dealing with the Qumran contribution to the study of the Hebrew Bible and of its Greek translations is E. Tov, *Textual Criticism of the Hebrew Bible* (n. 2). Among earlier studies, see F. M. Cross and S. Talmon, *Qumran and the History of the Biblical Text*, Cambridge, Mass 1975. See also D. Barthélemy, *Les devanciers d'Aquila*, Leiden 1963; W. H. Brownlee, *The Meaning of the Qumran Scrolls for the Bible*, New York 1964; J. G. Janzen, *Studies in the Text of Jeremiah*, Cambridge, Mass. 1973; E. Y. Kutscher, *The Language and Linguistic Background of the Isaiah Scroll*, Leiden 1974; E. N. Freedman, 'Variant Readings in the Leviticus Scroll from Qumran Cave 11', *CBQ* 36, 1974, 525–34; P. W. Skehan, 'Qumran and Old Testament Criticism', in *Qumrân*, ed. M. Delcor, 1978, 163–82; G. Vermes, *The Dead Sea Scrolls Forty Years On*, Oxford 1987, 6–16.

5. Millar Burrows, *The Dead Sea Scrolls*, 320.

6. In connection with F. M. Cross's influential studies two reservations may be expressed. The first is provoked by a certain vagueness in his technical vocabulary, cf. D. W. Gooding, 'An Appeal for Stricter Terminology in the Textual Criticism of the Old Testament', *JSS* 21, 1976, 15–25. The second concerns the lack of clear distinction between the old Palestinian and the Egyptian types of text. Since they are both presented as possessing roughly the same characteristics, is it justified to designate them as two different types rather than subdivisions within the same type?

7. See 'A Modern Textual Outlook based on the Qumran Scrolls', *HUCA* 53, 1982, 11–27, esp. p. 21 n. 45.

8. G. Vermes, *Scripture and Tradition in Judaism*, 176.

9. On rabbinic traditions relating to the master copies of the Torah kept in the Sanctuary, see in particular S. Talmon, 'The Three Scrolls of the Law that were found in the Temple Court', *Textus* 2, 1962, 14–27.

10. See above, 9–10.

11. A brief introduction to the Pseudepigrapha is contained in Eissfeldt, *The Old Testament* (n. 2), 606–37. For more detailed studies see A.-M. Denis, *Introduction aux pseudépigraphes grecs d'Ancien Testament*, Leiden 1970, and J. H. Charlesworth, *The Pseudepigrapha and Modern Research*, Missoula 1976, with full bibliography. For English translations of the collected Pseudepigrapha, see R. H. Charles (ed.), *The Apocrypha and Pseudepigrapha of the Old Testament* II, Oxford 1913; J. H. Charlesworth (ed.), *The Old Testament Pseudepigrapha* I–II, New York 1983 and London 1985; H. F. D. Sparks (ed.), *The Apocryphal Old Testament*, Oxford 1984

12. On the Qumran fragments of the Pseudepigrapha, see Fitzmyer's bibliography and *HJP* III, 1–2. The Aramaic fragments of the Testament of Levi from the Cairo Geniza were first published by A. Cowley and R. H. Charles, 'An Early Source of the Testaments of the Patriarchs', *JQR* 19, 1907, 566–83; cf. P. Grelot, 'Notes sur le Testament araméen de Lévi', *RB* 63, 1956, 391–406. J. C. Greenfield and M. E. Stone, 'Remarks on the Aramaic Testament of Levi from the Geniza', *RB* 86, 1979, 214–30. For the Qumran Testament of Levi, see F. Puech, 'Fragments d'un apocryphe de Lévi et le personnage eschatologique', in J. T. Barrera and L. V. Montaner (eds), *The Madrid Qumran Congress* II, Leiden 1992, 449–501; M. E. Stone and J. C. Greenfield, *DJD* XXII, 1996, 1–72 (4Q213–214). For Jubilees, see J. C. VanderKam, 'The Jubilees Fragments from Qumran Cave 4', in *The Madrid Qumran Congress* II (above), 635–48; J. C. VanderKam and J. T. Milik, 'The First *Jubilees* Manuscript from Qumran Cave 4: A Preliminary Publication', *JBL* 110, 1991, 243–70; J. VanderKam and J. T. Milik, *DJD* XIII, 1994, 1–185 (4Q216–228); for 4Q 225–227 cf. G. Vermes, 'New Light on the Aqedah from 4Q 225', *JJS* 47, 1996, 140–6. The fragments of I Enoch have been edited by J. T. Milik, *The Books of Enoch: Aramaic Fragments of Qumran Cave 4*, Clarendon Press, Oxford 1976. Cf. also M. A. Knibb, *The Ethiopic Book of Enoch: A New Edition in the Light of the Aramaic Dead Sea Fragments I–II*, Oxford University Press, Oxford 1978, Milik's dating of the Parables in the Ethiopic Enoch to 'around AD 270' (p. 96) is based on a flimsy argument, and in my view the most suitable period for these

chapters appears to be the last quarter of the first century CE. For an identical dating, cf. M. A. Knibb, 'The Date of the Parables of Enoch: A Critical Review', *NTS* 25, 1979, 345–59.

The 'son of man' problem has been examined in G. Vermes, *Jesus the Jew*, London 1973, reissued London and Philadelphia 1994, 160–91; 256–61; cf. *PBJS*, 147–65. For different views, consult C. Colpe, *TDNT* VIII, 40–77; M. Black, 'The Christological Use of the Old Testament in the New Testament', *NTS* 18, 1971, 1–14; R. Leivestad, 'Exit the Apocalyptic Son of Man', *NTS* 18, 1972, 243–67; B. Lindars, 'Re-enter the Apocalyptic Son of Man', *NTS* 22, 1975, 52–72; J. A. Fitzmyer, 'Methodology in the Study of Jesus' Sayings in the New Testament', in *Jesus aux origines de la christologie*, ed. J. Dupont, Gembloux 1975, 73–102; J. Bowker, 'The Son of Man', *JTS* 28, 1977, 19–48. For a later exchange, see G. Vermes, 'The Present State of the "Son of Man" Debate', *JJS* 29, 1978, 123–34, and J. A. Fitzmyer, 'Another View of the Son of Man Debate', *Journal for the Study of the NT* 4/1, 1979, 58–68. Cf. also M. Casey, *The Son of Man – The Interpretation and Influence of Daniel 7*, London 1979; B. Lindars, *Jesus the Son of Man*, London 1983; A. Y. Collins, 'Daniel 7 and the Historical Jesus', in H. W. Attridge et al. (eds). *Of Scribes and Scrolls*, Lanham, Md 1990, 187–93.

13. Among the most important general works on the relationship between the Scrolls and the New Testament are the following: K. Stendahl (ed.), *The Scrolls and the New Testament*, London 1957; J. van der Ploeg (ed.), *La Secte de Qumrân et les origines du christianisme*, Bruges 1959; M. Black, *The Scrolls and Christian Origins*, London 1961; H. Braun, *Qumran und das Neue Testament* I–II, Tübingen 1966; J. Murphy O'Connor (ed.), *Paul and Qumran*, London 1968, 1990; M. Black (ed.), *The Scrolls and Christianity*, London 1969; J. H. Charlesworth, *John and Qumran*, London 1972, 1990; J. A. Fitzmyer, 'The Qumran Scrolls and the New Testament after Forty Years', *RQ* 13, 1988, 609–20; S. Talmon (ed.), *Jewish Civilization in the Hellenistic-Roman Period*, Sheffield 1991, 94–257; J. H. Charlesworth (ed.), *Jesus and the Dead Sea Scrolls*, New York 1992.

14. The controversy about alleged New Testament fragments at Qumran originates in J. O'Callaghan, 'Papiros neotestamentarios en la cueva 7 de Qumran?', *Bib* 53, 1972, 91–100; see further *Los papiros griegos de la cueva 7 de Qumran*, Editorial católica, Madrid, 1974 and C. P. Thiede, *The Earliest Gospel Manuscripts?*, London 1992. Against O'Callaghan see P. Benoit, 'Notes sur les fragments grecs de la grotte 7 de Qumrân', *RB* 79, 1972, 321–4; 80, 1973, 5–12; M. Baillet, 'Les manuscrits de la grotte 7 de Qumrân et le Nouveau Testament', *Bib* 53, 1972, 508–16; 54, 1973, 34–50; C. H. Roberts, 'On Some Presumed Papyrus Fragments of the New Testament from Qumran', *JTS* 23, 1972, 446–7; K. Aland, 'Neue neutestamentliche Papyri III', *NTS* 20, 1973–4, 357–81; H. U. Rosenbaum, 'Cave 7Q5! Gegen die erneute transpruchnature des Qumran-Fragments 7Q5 als Bruckstück der ältesten Evangelien-Handschrift', *Biblische Zeitschrift* 31,1987, 189–205; M. V. Spottorno, 'Una nueva posible identificación de 7Q5', *Sefarad* 52, 1992, 541–3 |7Q5 LXX Zach. 7.4–5|; G. Stanton, *Gospel Truth?*, London 1995, 20–9; E. Puech, 'Des

fragments grecs de la grotte 7 et le Nouveau Testament', *RB* 102, 1995, 570–80; 'Sept fragments grecs de la Lettre d'Enoch dans la grotte 7 de Qumrân', *RQ* 18, 1997, 313–23.

15. *The Essene Writings from Qumran*, 13, 370.
16. Ibid., 372.
17. Ibid., 373.
18. On this subject, see G. Vermes, *The Religion of Jesus the Jew*, London and Minneapolis 1993.
19. On the question of Bible interpretation at Qumran and the New Testament, see J. A. Fitzmyer, *Essays on the Semitic Background of the New Testament*, London 1971, 3–58; C. Vermes, *PBJS*, 37–49; 'Interpretation (History of) at Qumran', *IDBS*, 438–41; D. Hay, 'New Testament Interpretation of the Old Testament', ibid., 443–6; T. H. Lim, *Holy Scripture in the Qumran Commentaries and Pauline Letters*, Oxford 1997.

For a variety of comparisons between the Gospels and the Scrolls, see G. Vermes, *Jesus the Jew*, index. A general survey may be found in Vermes, 'The Impact of the Dead Sea Scrolls on the Study of the New Testament', *JJS* 27, 1976, 107–16.

The first volume of H. Braun's *Qumran und das Neue Testament*, Tübingen 1966, lists suggested parallels from the Scrolls arranged according to book, chapter and verse of the New Testament.

19. Some Qumran passages furnish illuminating parallels to the charismatic-eschatological features of the portrait of Jesus and his teaching in the Synoptic Gospels. See the example given in Chapter 1 on pp. 18–19.

Scrolls Catalogue

1. 'The Unpublished Qumran Texts from Caves 4 and 11', *JJS* 43,1992, 101–36. For a slightly updated version, see *Biblical Archaeologist*, June 1992, 94–104, under the same title. Cf. also J. A. Fitzmyer, *The Dead Sea Scrolls: Major Publications and Tools for Study*, rev. edn., Atlanta 1990. See also F. García Martínez and D. W Parry, *A Bibliography of the Finds in the Desert of Judah 1970–95*, Leiden 1996.
2. The siglum *DJD* designates the series *Discoveries in the Judaean Desert*; for details see bibliography.
3. P. W. Skehan, *CBQ* 26, 1964, 313–22.
4. J. Starcky, *RB* 73, 1966, 353–71.
5. J. T. Milik, *Biblica* 38, 1957, 245–68.
6. P. W. Skehan, 'Gleanings from Psalm Texts from Qumran', in *Cazelles Festschrift*, 1981, 439–52.
7. J. Muilenburg, *BASOR* 135, 1954, 20–28.
8. F. M. Cross, 'Studies in the Structure of Hebrew Verse', *Freedman Festschrift*, 1983, 129–55.
9. E. Ulrich, *BASOR* 268, 1987, 17–37.
10. Id., *BASOR* 274, 1989, 3–26.
11. J. Trebolle Barerra, *RQ* 15, 1992, 523–9.

12. Frgs 19–21 have been identified as belonging to Jubilees by M. Kister, *RQ* 12, 1985–87, 529–36.
13. The numbers 187–195 are vacant.
14. Id., *The Books of Enoch of Qumran, Aramaic Fragments of Cave 4.*
15. Ibid., 256.
16. M. Broshi and E. Eshel, *JJS* 48, 1997, 120–9.
17. J. M. Baumgarten, *JJS* 27, 1976, 36–46.
18. *JJS* 43, 1992, 268–76.
19. *JQR* 85, 1994, 91–101.
20. *JJS* 23, 1972, 130–1.
21. *DSSU*, 207–8.
22. *DSSU*, 211 (only 276–277).
23. G. Vermes, *JJS* 43, 1992, 85–90.
24. In G. J. Brooke, *New Qumran Texts and Studies*, 1995, 53–7.
25. *JQR* 85, 1994, 203–35.
26. *RQ* 16, 1993, 203–23; in Z. Zevit (ed.), *Solving Riddles . . .*, 207–60.
27. B. Nitzan, *RQ* 17, 1996, 151–73.
28. *Enoch*, 68–9.
29. *RQ* 16, 1995, 507–25.
30. *Schriften des Institutum Judaicum Delitzschianum* III, 1995, 125–64.
31. *UDSS* 60–101; Talmon, in Zevit, 327–44.
32. J. Naveh, *IEJ* 36, 1986, 52–5.
33. E. M. Schuller, *RQ* 14, 1990, 349–76.
34. Id., *MQC* II, 1992, 515–30.
35. In D. Dimant and U. Rappaport, *The Dead Sea Scrolls*, 40–52.
36. J. Strugnell and D. Dimant, *RQ* 13, 1988, 45–58; 14, 1990, 331–48.
37. *DSSU*, 55.
38. *Songs of the Sabbath Sacrifice*, 1985.
39. *RQ* 16, 1994, 313–34.
40. *JQR* 80, 1990, 341–7.
41. *DSSU*, 226–8.
42. Ibid., 244–9 (416 and 418 only).
43. T. Elgvin, *RQ* 17, 1996, 205–32.
44. *DSSU*, 166–7. In Fr. 1, line 13 read *ptyym*.
45. Ibid., 238–9 (434 and 436 only).
46. Ibid., 48.
47. Ibid., 268–9 (462 only).
48. M. Broshi, *JJS* 49, 1998, 341–5.
49. E. and H. Eshel, *MQC* II, 1992, 611–20.
50. E. Eshel and M. Kister, *JJS* 43, 1992, 277–81.
51. E. Eshel, *RQ* 17, 1996, 175–203.
52. T. Elgvin, *RQ* 18, 1997, 97–107.
53. E. Eshel, *JJS* 45, 1994, 111–22.
54. *DSSU*, 38.
55. J. T. Milik, *The Books of Enoch of Qumran: Aramaic Fragments of Cave 4*, 304–8.

56. *DSSU*, 95.
57. J. Starcky, in *Mémorial du Cinquantenaire 1914–1964*, Institut Catholique de Paris 1964, 51–66.
58. *DSSU*, 35–36.
59. E. Puech, in *MQC* II,1992, 449–501.
60. J. T. Milik, in M. Delcor (ed.), *Qumrân*, 1978, 91–106.
61. Ibid.
62. E. Puech, cf. n. 59.
63. Id., *RQ* 15, 1991, 23–54.
64. J. T. Milik, *RB* 79, 1972, 77–97.
65. Id., *RQ* 16, 1992, 321–406.
66. Id., *Cazelles Festschrift*, 1981, 337–59.
67. J. Starcky, in *Le monde de la Bible* 1, 1977, 38–40.
68. *DSSU*, 92–3.
69. Ibid., 266.
70. Ibid., 264.
71. Fringe opinion, rejected by leading papyrologists and textual experts, identifies 7Q4–10 and 15 as small portions of the Greek New Testament. Cf. J. O'Callaghan, *Los papiros griegos de la cueva 7 de Qumrân*, 1974; C. P. Thiede, *The Earliest Gospel Manuscripts*, 1992.
72. Ibid.
73. D. N. Freedman and K. A. Matthews, *The Paleo-Hebrew Leviticus Scroll*, 1985.
74. *The Temple Scroll* I–III, 1983.

Index of Modern Authors

General Index

Printed in the United States
48081LVS00005B/31-105